WHILE
THE
MUSIC
LASTS

WHILE THE MUSIC LASTS

A Memoir of Music, Grief & Joy
Emily MacGregor

s
epte
m
b
er

First published in the United Kingdom by September in 2025

September, an imprint of Duckworth Books Ltd
1 Golden Court, Richmond, TW9 1EU, United Kingdom
www.septemberpublishing.org

A catalogue record for this book is available from the British Library

Typeset by PDQ Media

Printed and bound in Great Britain by Clays Ltd, Elcograf S.p.A.

The authorised representative in the EEA is Easy Access System Europe,
Mustamäe tee 50, 10621 Tallinn, Estonia.

Hardback ISBN: 9781914613630
eISBN: 9781914613647

CONTENTS

For my dad –
and for all my other music teachers

PLAYLIST

Some selected recordings:

Narciso Yepes, guitarist, 'Rumores de la caleta', from *Recuerdos de Viaje*, Op. 71 by Isaac Albéniz, track 6 on *Narciso Yepes: The Beginning of a Legend Volume 2*, recorded 1960, Istituto Discografico Italiano IDI6625, 2011.

John Williams, guitarist, 'Sevilla', from Suite Española, Op. 47, by Isaac Albéniz, track 20 on *John Williams – Spanish Guitar Music*, Sony 88697529852, 2009.

Miles Davis, 'Freddie Freeloader', track 2 on *Kind of Blue*, recorded March 1959, Columbia/Legacy 88697271052, 2009.

Igor Stravinsky, 'Infernal Dance of King Kashchei', from *The Firebird*, with the New York Philharmonic, conducted by Leonard Bernstein, track 5 on *Stravinsky: Firebird Suite – Tchaikovsky Romeo and Juliet (Remastered)*, Sony G010003710793V, 2017.

Leonard Bernstein, 'Elegy for Mippy II', with Christian Lindberg (trombone), track 5 on *The Burlesque Trombone*, BIS BISCD318, 2000.

The Jimi Hendrix Experience, 'Castles Made of Sand', track 9 on *Axis: Bold as Love*, recorded 29 October 1967, Sony 88691938922, 2006.

Gustav Mahler, *Kindertotenlieder*, with Janet Baker (mezzo-soprano) and the Hallé Orchestra, conducted by Sir John Barbirolli, recorded May 1967, tracks 1–5 on *Mahler: Song Cycles*, Warner Classics 5669812, 1999.

John Coltrane 'Giant Steps', track 1 on *Giant Steps*, recorded 5 May 1959, Atlantic 8122736102, 2002.

To receive a Spotify playlist of the music mentioned in this book and more, scan this QR code or type the link below it into your web browser.

https://BookHip.com/VRTCSFD

Prelude

IN CÁDIZ

When my dad died suddenly, Isaac Albéniz's 'Rumores de la caleta' was the piece left behind, right at the front of his music stand. It's a guitar arrangement of a piano piece from a set Albéniz composed between 1886 and 1887, *Recuerdos de viaje* ('Memories of a journey'). As he wrote *Recuerdos* he almost certainly didn't mean to leave behind a scavenger hunt around Andalusia for a grieving thirty-five-year-old British woman – but you don't get to choose what your legacy will be.

La Caleta. The main historic beach in Cádiz, flanked by a grand boulevard, palm trees brought back from the Americas and classical university buildings. It looks enough like Cuba that film-makers used this beach for the Havana scenes in *Die Another Day*, the moment when Halle Berry emerged from the water to greet Bond.

It is early morning, July, the skies a gauzy powder blue, and I've been careful not to wake my friends as I set out into the labyrinthine streets from our holiday apartment deep in the walled old town. The tide is quite far out, neither here nor there. I find a place to sit, almost alone, enveloped by elongated first-thing shadows, the sand cool. The beach is already attracting the quietly industrious, pregnant with the knowledge of the crowds with which it will heave in the afternoon. My companions are the squat

1

gulls strutting over the brushed sand and picking at hidden remains of the previous day's spoils, a lone walker throwing a ball for a brown spaniel, here so early that the world has decided the no-dogs rule does not yet apply, a woman doing sun salutations where the ocean meets the sand, two men bringing in a small white boat, two more men reaching down the sea wall to paint it the same ochre that coats the town – *albero*, named for the yellowish rock that, densely packed, covers bullfighting ground. And once I have deferred long enough from what I am here to do, I put in my ear buds and bring up a playlist on my phone. A playlist titled 'Dad guitar music', which belongs right next to another playlist, whose impossible, performatively shocking title is 'Dad funeral'. 'Rumores de la caleta' ('Murmurs from the little beach') by Isaac Albéniz. More specifically, from this very beach. From his selection *Recuerdos de viaje*. And its tones are in my ears, blending with the crashing of the waves. The waves recede behind the music, then briefly overcome it. A strummed gesture, running right through the guitar's register, setting the scene, then tricky triplets and an effortless switch between a feeling of three and of two, bringing flamenco dancers to the stage – to this beach – with the adapted rhythms and modes of Andalusian folk music.

And once, through this recording, I would have heard the echoes, the outline, the ghost of my dad playing it, sitting upright, one knee raised, guitar held at a forty-five-degree angle.

But it's not my dad playing. It's the closest thing I can get: a famous Spanish guitarist called Narciso Yepes, whose virtuosic pace sounds clinical compared with the organic, sometimes stumbling sound of my dad as he was learning the piece. That's the rendering of this music I need. And I almost don't hear my dad in the recording any more. There was a time when I did, but now the alienation has become too great, now the recording has sedimented within my head and obliterated the more fragile, tentative sounds of my father I used to hold in my mind's ear. Sounds that this recording used to allow me to access, to remember. Now they seem to be gone, have dispersed, blown away, too light to secure. They don't stand a chance against the presence and weight in the memory of a recording, ever identical in its repetition. It's a kind of loss there aren't words for.

It's been four years. What else will I lose?

Yet sitting on this beach, La Caleta, looking out to sea, the protective curve of the pier ahead of me, enclosing a sprinkling of boats moored within the bay, the sea washing back and forth, I don't feel particularly sad. Or at least, it isn't the emotion I identify. If I feel anything about this music, it's slightly numb, slightly removed. Affirming once again what I've discovered so far on the pathway of loss: that my relationship with music is not at all what I imagined it would be.

Distance. I sense that Albéniz is wearing a mask writing this piece, that he's feeling something so deep he can't allow himself to go anywhere near it. So he adopts fancy dress, the cladding of Andalusia, *andalucismo*, the south, a lightness whose counterweight is an unspoken heaviness, and he dances high up on top of those feelings, where they can't reach him, defended by his separation from this culture. For Albéniz was a man of the north, of Catalonia, and Andalusian culture was nearly as foreign to him as it is to me.

It's a way of engaging with music that I recognise.

What I mainly notice in the still of the beach is a background thrum of gratitude and safety. Although I've never been to Cádiz before, and I barely speak Spanish, I don't feel alone. Because of my friends here, because of their unfathomable gameness to indulge me in this haphazard tour of Andalusian sites entirely dictated by the whims of my father in the last few months of his life, dictated by the music my father was playing when he died, unexpectedly, outrageously. The music he left behind on his music stand, still in rehearsal.

Chapter 1

A MUSIC STAND

It was all the music's fault.

A barely slept April morning, gallingly beautiful, the day after it had finally turned to spring, and the day after certainty had plummeted away. My mum's computer wedged in the clamour of the dining room table, next to a spine-bent, face-down biography of Angela Merkel, and my father's computer, open, hundreds of tabs crowding the screen for pages he'd never look at again, his sheepskin coat hanging ready on the back of the chair.

He only used one password, and thankfully we all knew it.

There's a thing I could feel myself slipping towards, where we just lose it and cry without control, even though we didn't in the slightest bit mean to. And when it happens, it's not really us, of course; the finger can be pointed squarely at whatever music is playing.

The correct response to that music is resentment.

There are other responses, I'm sure, but they suggest suspicious levels of emotional adjustment.

I was right on the cusp of losing control. That was what I was feeling. I didn't want that. Not now. Not so early. I wasn't ready yet.

Something unlistenable seeped thin and metallic from that computer's internal speakers. YouTube playlists of the classical guitar music my dad had played, a semblance of him. Plucked tones with a half-memory of resonance. And the saddest thing I have ever heard. A weak, sickening semblance of him, which screamed out his unthinkable absence.

Already. Dead barely twenty-four hours, and he'd already been converted into this sad, two-dimensional, technologically mediated sound. And yet the mechanised stand-in tugged at me anyway – fucking YouTube and its fucking algorithms, which had nothing to do with my father, who had been alive and cynical and hilarious and gone barefoot in the Washington, DC National Air and Space Museum when he'd come to visit me because his sandals were rubbing, and wasn't the logical solution to take them off, and isn't it preposterous that the armed guard polices whether or not people are wearing their shoes. I didn't yet recognise the feeling that surfaced, but I came to know it well over the coming days and weeks and months as I drank craft beer selections that had been delivered to my door alone during endless hours in front of the television. Fury. Outrage. And so that morning I sat in the conservatory, away from everyone, learning a new emotion – or maybe it was a way of being – and wordlessly spooned cereal into my mouth, in a semblance of eating, a semblance of living.

'Can we turn that off? It's too much for the morning.' I didn't slam anything. I was measured. Apologetic even. But I'd said something out loud, and in this new light of this new day in which we didn't know how to be with each other any more, in which Dad's death had trapped us alone right next to one another, that was enough.

And the music stopped and I stopped lurching, stilled.

That was the first day of the second part of my life. The first day I woke up without a father and that I stopped believing in the relaxed proximity of yesterday, learned the gut-punch truth that yesterday is irrevocably lost. The first day of my new relationship with music. A relationship that largely involved me having absolutely nothing to do with it, and a brand-new rage.

It's me, music, not you, I would say much later, in my hypothetical conversation with organised sound. *I've changed. I just can't handle you any more.*

But, on that morning in April, I kept spooning the muesli towards my face, and – well, at least then – I didn't cry.

Not many people would feel emboldened to start up a dialogue with organised sound, but being a musicologist by training, I felt I had privileged access. I'd researched and taught the history, theory and sociology of music for more than a decade. I'd always loved music, and now it paid my bills. The day before my father died, I had been marking undergraduate coursework essays on orientalism in Puccini's opera *Madama Butterfly*. (The right answer: there is lots.) I'd recently started a new job as a musicology lecturer and researcher at a university on the London commuter belt. It had felt imperative that I finish my marking on time, even though my father had, out of the blue, been admitted to hospital.

That sense of professional responsibility now seemed to have belonged to a stranger.

And so. This new relationship with music I'd been thrown into, where I couldn't listen to it, didn't want it, it wasn't exactly ideal. But in the months after my father died it barely registered given all the many, many other things that did not feel ideal. Noticing and caring about this particular loss only came later.

It's curious that we don't really understand why music is able to tip us over the edge. If you want to feel totally overpowered by grief, reach for some music. And if people can't access those feelings, they often say they use music to release them. If you want to feel close to the person who's died, there's music that will take you there. But if you're worried about feeling overwhelmed, use music to take you somewhere else. Choose your own adventure; inhabit the music that works. Control your grief. Control yourself. Jump in.

That's because music is a thing we inhabit. It's a place we go to as much as anything. We hear our way past entry barriers: into cathedrals, music festivals, on to smoke-lit jazz stages, concert halls or the fantasy aural spaces of the studio where a sound-world is built to encase our ears; even into the bodies of band members as if we, *we*, are the musicians themselves (more than once I've caught myself drumming as I run to the pace of the Red Hot Chili Peppers); we remember ourselves into familiar company and the school discos, student bars, electric crowds, red-wine tongued late-night sofas, ruched bedsheets where we first learned to love a song. It plays with our sense of time. It allows us to dwell in the past, while pushing us into the future, as we orient our ears towards that note we know is coming, that chord we know is on the verge of happening. The thing we anticipate. It's like a microcosm of living, of being, where you can almost time-travel to a past in which you *live*, anticipating a future. God, it's lovely: what a relief to be back there, like playing at being. It has a presence. You feel it here, in the room with you. People will tell you music is alive. Or it feels like it's alive, somehow.

And for that brief, delicious moment, like that moment when you play with knowing-not-knowing, when you see them in a crowd, in a street, in the distance, just before you have to let knowledge rush into the gap (because you can no longer sustain it), you get to feel them there. You get to be in the same space. Your mind (your brain? your guts? your heart?) says: *Yes. Here we are.*

That's seriously powerful. But it's not always desirable. It starts to feel like you can come apart anywhere. In the months after my dad died, it was phone, wallet, keys, tissues. Without tissues, you couldn't hide what was happening to you. Tissues were the new tampons, effective support for unreliable bodies.

The first time it happened to me was in the Horniman Gardens in Forest Hill, south London. I saw a man in his mid-sixties, angled away from me, a faded baseball cap over his white hair, and I got a toxic double shot of music then false recognition. A youth band was performing in the park that day. An arrangement of Pharrell Williams's 'Happy'. It was the timbre of my childhood, teenage years spent ferried to weekend rehearsals, learning the skills of ensemble playing, then the thrill of drinking alcohol undetected at orchestral residentials. I made-believe that it was him, pretended he could still be someone I could happen to bump into, but the game was already undone, like when I found out about Father Christmas, lay in bed as if asleep, knew it was my mum coming in, pretended so hard it wasn't. And that day in the park I found myself sobbing, tucked away on a bench under a canopy by the raised flower beds, my body language suggesting that passers-by might please politely refrain from noticing, thank you very much. The pleasure and then dissatisfaction, I thought, spotting how surreal it was to cycle through analogies even at the time, was something beyond any point of comparison I knew. All I had to hand was the bone-deep sense that Dad dying was like gravity had stopped working, except worse because gravity hadn't loved me unconditionally.

Dad had taught me all about gravity when I was three, within an unorthodox preschool bedtime curriculum.

It's all about the big forces. Gravity. Time.

But time is the real problem.

The whole fucking problem, in fact.

*

What that laptop wasn't letting me hear:

As so often, my dad is playing his guitar. He's on his boat, a beaten-up 1930s wooden yacht, where every summer it's Dad versus rot, and their grim battlefield is the hull, the stakes: floating or sinking. And every winter, with anti-fouling at his side (and on his trousers, and under his fingernails) he just about does enough to hold out once again against the siege waged by water. The valiant fight against wood's tendency to degrade when wet. Or he's in Berlin, waiting to head out to a jazz club, chasing the 1960s, or he's in Pembrokeshire, a farm cottage in a remote valley he's been visiting since he was a child. They are all places he often goes. Or we are small and he's sitting on the end of my parents' bed, and the music lies flat on the duvet cover, because we are on holiday and there's nowhere else to put it. He's alone.

He's always alone. Focused, studious.

That's how I will always remember him playing music.

At the funeral someone told me he used to play in a band in sixth form at their boys' boarding school in the era of Jimi Hendrix, Dad's talent on the guitar widely admired. I couldn't believe it. My dad was cool in school. He used to play his guitar abilities down to me.

Because my tragic understanding had been that my dad was a mediocre musician. To be fair, he hadn't done a whole lot to disabuse me of this notion.

'I need a hand with this rhythm,' he said. I was twelve, maybe.

My dad was having guitar lessons again, driving forty minutes into winter nights to a teacher in a town on the coast. He tried the rhythm out on the guitar, slowly.

I peered at the music. This was like when Dad had got me to calculate the final marks for his MA in multimedia broadcasting students in the days before that was all automated. You might think handing a bunch of marks for assessments worth varying percentages of a final degree classification to an under-ten among toast crumbs and half-finished glasses of lemon squash was irresponsible, but Dad trusted me with the hard stuff. We were a team. He didn't believe in anything being age specific, although I have to admit that this also meant I knew a lot more than I wanted to about Second World War Japanese torture techniques.

Sometimes, though, I felt like I was a party trick. If you want to know what percentage of the UK manufacturing capacity is now owned by foreigners, it's 25 per cent, and they employ 16 per cent of British workers. Or at least they did when I was eight. Immersed in a sociology study, Dad, on a whim, decided I'd get 50p if I could remember those statistics the following morning. Now, the rhythms I recited to myself overnight are strange poetry etched on my brain.

I concentrated. Reading music was where I excelled; Dad learned more by listening and instinct, I think. There were two lines moving in counterpoint. I tapped on the table, one hand doing one rhythm, one doing the other.

Dad repeated it, pairs of fingers thudding on the edge of the table, like an inversion of the tapping game we'd played when I was a baby.

My godfather, Ol, Dad's best friend (God was only very vaguely involved in our relationship; thanks be to Him for creating the role of back-up parent in His name), told me recently on the phone: 'Your dad was an absolute natural.' He exhaled. 'It was really fucking annoying.'

They'd tried to play jazz together for a time. My godfather on tenor saxophone, which he worked at intensively for ten years, scales and scales, endless scales (the grunt work behind the scenes of jazz improvisation), Dad on the guitar. Ol had been inspired by wanting to play the sax like Joe Henderson on Horace Silver's 'Song for My Father'. Once, they'd even had a fiercely professional jazzer critique a cassette they'd posted him of a recording they'd done in a remote Welsh cottage. (A different one. Wales is full of remote cottages.)

I have the typewritten script. And wow. The man had clearly never heard of a compliment sandwich. In a pedagogically dubious move, he talks about the 'qualitative difference between them'. Whereas Ol was 'in thrall to a mighty self-consciousness, which continues to trammel his free expression', the only danger facing my father was that 'his entry-level performance is so slick that he might be tempted into … polishing the surface (ego) aspects and admiring the view.' That's poison in a friendship that's already basically a sibling rivalry.

'No wonder you gave up. It was meant to be fun,' Dad had said.

And yet Dad used to say he wasn't any good. He complained he couldn't sight-read. As if the two things were linked.

'The guitarist is able to play as if the playalong came from within him … locked onto the beat so securely that it would be difficult to put a foot wrong. A really impressive recording debut.'

Fool I was, I believed him.

Fool I was, I believed so much he told me. I don't mean to suggest he was a liar. I mean that he didn't have a handle on how he was perceived. I was a child; he was my father, and so if he said something it was true. I didn't yet understand how self-belief is something you need to run deep like marrow. Or what it meant if it didn't.

My dad would come back from parties where he'd drunk too much and then analyse in depth his failures to make small talk, how much everyone had been bored by him, how little he had to say.

I still thought he was the best person imaginable.

I think his school really messed him up.

Beside my dad's computer, back in that room, was the thing that was particularly impossible. The thing that would have a hold on me for years. My dad's music stand, layered with all the music he had been playing in those weeks when we didn't know anything was going to happen. He never cleared music away; new music went on top of the old music. The stand was a window on to his inner world, a way into understanding something private: my father's music practice. Next to it was his guitar, awaiting riffs he'd never play again. Their memory, their possibility, was fading away, as those guitars became cold objects too.

'I never told him how beautifully he played,' said Mum, during those early, Rescue Remedy-fuelled days – Rescue Remedy being brandy plus homeopathic dew drops from flowers. So: brandy. 'But I wrote about it in my diary.' Hoping that somehow could have been enough.

It was the wallpaper to our childhood, and no one ever thought to record him. As we grew up, my parents had cast off houses and jobs like coats for new seasons: Scotland, North Yorkshire, South West England. Ours was a childhood of boxes, but the sound of the guitar – jazz, classical – had always blanketed our home, had made it distinctly ours no matter where we lived, when we lived there, how many boxes had been unpacked. Had softened unfamiliar corners of new rooms. Gently cascading classical arpeggios, jazz progressions that felt infinite in the stretching present of how children perceive time. They wrapped around and ran into my make-believe worlds of lava-covered carpets, living shadows and imaginary friends.

And were gone.

A lot of guitar music is designed to be played solo, so much of your time is spent playing alone, just for yourself. It's meditative, that solo labour that makes up a musician's skill. My instrument is the trombone, and I remember hours of working on long notes in a basement practice room in which there was barely space to stretch my slide right out; me, a Thermos of tea and a copy of the *Guardian*, the newspaper with a hefty student discount. I would put on a blue plastic metronome, sixty beats a minute, and it clicked into life, an edge of mechanical thuck to each electronic tick. I played individual notes as quietly as I could, holding them as long as I could, until my breath no longer supported the sound. I held stable for a count of sixteen, strengthening the muscles around my mouth. Dad's clockwork metronome was a forbidding presence in my childhood. It was black and ominous and triangular like a faceless man in a suit, and the moment you released the fastening, the stick was unstoppable. Left to right, left to right, left to right, relentless time you could only stop by catching your finger in the mechanism – risky for small hands. Once you released it from its catch, there was no going back. You could adjust the speed by moving a piece of metal up and down the stick. Engraved on its scale were beats per minute, but also the Italian designations for different speeds: *lento*, *adagio*, *allegretto*, *vivace*. A symbol of the bunkered hours and days and weeks that make up a musician's strength, their technique, their skill.

To play alone is quite a different thing from playing in a group. Trombones are meant for ensembles – orchestras, wind bands, big bands, and at school I was even once asked to play in a ska band by the cool boys in the year above (although I never did); the guitar can conjure its own harmonies alone, its own full and complete musical world. For a trombonist, ensemble playing is often the most lauded skill. Almost always a bit player, you are valued for your sight-reading ability, and your section playing – that is, your ability to play tightly, matching your sound and tuning to others as if you were one instrument. Practice involves endless exercises to improve strength, tone, lip flexibility: you're an athlete doing weights to maintain form. Then studies for technique, and orchestral excerpts to ensure that when you get to that crucial moment when everyone can hear you, you know exactly how to play the Big Tune. But you always knew you were a pawn in another's imagination.

For a guitarist, practising alone, whole worlds could unspool ahead of you. For instance, I never had the easy understanding of chords Dad had. Of how jazz worked. Even if I had no trouble sight-reading my part on a score, I didn't intuitively get the music's inner workings. I'd need to sit down with a pencil and puzzle it out. The complexity of the chords scared me, to be honest, the command it would require. As a guitarist, Dad would know the contours of the surrounding sound. Where my responsibility to the music was small and blinkered, he saw those structures unfold.

And there I'd been, thinking I knew better. I hadn't understood.

I don't think I looked through the music on the stand then – I didn't want to disturb it, to move anything, because then we would be further from the exact state of the world in which he had existed, and therefore further from him. I suppose someone must have looked at that music when we put together the music for the funeral. I don't think it was me. I'm sure I was trying to avoid it, shielding myself. On the day we came back to the house from visiting the hospital where he'd not so much died as already been dead,

I photographed it, part of a sequence I took that day of how Dad's life had been the moment he left. It felt like the only way of holding on. I thought I took a lot of photos and was surprised to learn when I looked back that there were only thirteen. Thirteen photos of the detritus marking out the shape of a life, books by his bed, music on a stand.

What does it mean, to know your father has died?

In the early weeks, when I wrote in my journal in the middle of the night when I could not sleep, I began by stating 'My dad is still dead'. But I didn't know. That was why I wrote it. I was in shock, weightless. All I understood was that I couldn't call him.

There's knowledge, and there's *knowledge*. There's understanding, and there's *understanding*.

Some knowledge protects you. It tucks you away into a space that's intellectual, where feelings can't get you yet. That's where I went first. From the very day he died, I sought out articles online that answered questions like: how likely? How unusual? How tragic? What percentage of people die from pancreatitis? How quickly? Questions that distracted me from the other questions. Could he have been saved? If he'd had a scan sooner? Why wasn't I there? What was it like to die alone, as numbers crashed beyond rescue?

Did he feel abandoned?

I'd texted him saying I was sorry he was in hospital, it sounded a bit rubbish. He never replied.

Some knowledge peels you right open, leaves you face to face with the savage-eyed abyss.

And so this book, my grief, wasn't always felt through music.

It was too much.

It was too little. Utterly inconsequential.

Instead, I wrote. I wrote, and I wrote, and I wrote. Asking a private void for witnesses who couldn't come forward, for acknowledgement of the strangeness and unfairness of this unthinkable world I was in, of what had happened to me, to us.

I wrote because I wanted to understand. But slowly, gradually exfoliating an outer skin hardened against reality, behind which was the rawness. Gently scraping at the strata of my grieving brain. When my dad died, I went into full shutdown. The world was not safe. It did not behave predictably. There was no space for music.

The only inevitable thing left happened. Time passed. In that time, I wrote.

I wrote three versions of this book. All almost entirely different, as I moved away from the terrible epicentre. First I went inwards, and I wrote a manuscript about the skewered reality of this new life, and about a dog. My dog. I got her ten months after my father died. A radical rebellion, given that generally people thought my getting a dog as a single woman with a full-time job who lived alone was an awful idea. She was a symbol of my pledge to the new knowledge that we should do the things we want now, while we are alive. My dad's death and a new dog were the only two things there was room for in my life at that time. I did not want to explore anything bigger than myself. What was in my mind was quite big enough already.

When I emerged from writing that book, it was spring again and the sun was out. My puppy – or the passage of time, or both – had awakened the curiosity I saw in her out of the fury that filled me.

And I remembered music, my music, my dad's music. And I wrote a new version of the book, while my dog slept in her bed right beside me. The version that had appeared in the gaps of my first book, in the absence, the silence, the anger, the complete lack of interest in physical pleasure. The spaces between, where I was still learning to be.

It was around that time, more than two years after his death, that I finally felt able to look at the music on my dad's stand on the day he died. I did it on autopilot: I didn't want to disturb the urge once it came, afraid it would recede. *Do it while it feels possible*, I thought. That photo of the stand on my phone I'd had the foresight to take after we came back from the hospital had been waiting for me to be ready. And now I wanted to know what else had been on the stand, behind the music I could see in the photo. What else he had been playing in those last weeks.

The music had long been carefully closed up and packed away on a shelf.

But it was easy to reconstruct what had been on the stand, because all the photocopies and downloaded printouts he had been working on had been placed in front of a volume of Bach's solo lute works. When Mum eventually put it away she had simply closed the volume, folded it around the loose sheets, preserving everything as it had been.

Mum and I found the Bach volume. It was in the overflowing bookshelf by the dining room table, slotted within a jumble of other music, art books, an atlas. 'The set dressing of our life,' said Mum. The Bach packed in sideways, maximising use of space, above the *Real Book* of jazz standards. Next to the bookshelf leaned four guitar cases. Mum had packed up some of the guitars that had littered the house so they didn't get damaged. Solemn black figures side by side that we didn't yet want to open. But some guitars were still out, still exactly where they were when he died.

And now I was holding it, Albéniz's 'Rumores de la caleta', the passage of music Dad was working on when he died, the page I could see in my photo. I heard snatches of it just from looking at it. I found a recording on my laptop, wanting to make this feeling even more real. I put in my headphones, and he was there. Except. The recording – played by David Russell, a Scottish guitarist – didn't play it like Dad did. Three minutes and twenty seconds long. Russell's version had a frenetic intensity. He never halts, never falters. But Dad would stop abruptly in the middle of a passage when you wanted to say something to him. Or reply while still playing, with an off-kilter artificiality to his voice that betrayed the concentration of multitasking. Dad's style was different to Russell's whirligig confidence. Slower, for one thing. And warmer. He would practise discrete phrases and repeat them. We heard the painstaking mechanics that go into getting a piece fluent under your fingers.

I tried another recording, Narciso Yepes. To my ears, trained on Dad learning the work, the phrasing was clipped, the tone too dry. It was powerfully evocative in a way nothing else could be. Nothing else comes close. But it still only traced the shape of feeling him there.

All these recordings are eternally locked in the same flawless phrasing, the same gestures, telling the same story to a fault every time. The same swirling drama folded around the sudden rose-lit nostalgia of a lyrical major passage at the work's centre.

It was the closest I was going to get. I gritted my mind against reality: it would have to do.

Behind 'Rumores de la caleta' by Albéniz, two tangos: 'Oblivion', by Astor Piazzolla; another titled 'Jealousy'. Handel's Suite, HWV 448: a maritime overture. The Prelude, Fugue and Allegro in E-flat major BWV 998, by Bach, originally for lute or harpsichord. Albéniz's 'Sevilla', no. 3 from the *Suite Española* no. 1. Dad had texted me the Thursday before he died about a potential family holiday in Seville ('I'm halfway to enticing Mum'), and about black holes, and about ideas of truth and the dystopian American administration. Was this music what had sparked Dad's plans for a holiday in Seville – *halfway to enticing Mum*? Or the other way around? I wished desperately for that trip together. My mum, my two brothers – younger, both in their twenties – and I had toyed that summer with going as Dad's legacy holiday; we had gone to a coastal village in Portugal instead, where we'd been before with Dad and could imagine him.

Melancholic flamenco, beaches, murmurs, jealousy, a harbour, the draw and the fear of oblivion. Nihilism, pessimism, all in the need, the hope for something better. It was all there, all Dad.

I played everything there. I didn't know all of it. But with the music I did know, the more I listened to the recordings, the more I found I heard their phrasing in my mind's ear when I thought of the music. If their form was beginning to crowd out my memory of my father playing it, I realised I was staring down another unbearable loss.

I turned the music off. And when I looked at the sheet music, read the notes, somehow what I heard was my father again.

This was a new kind of knowing.

Music, for me, is about self, about vulnerability, about intimacy, about play. About something inside of you that's gentle and amorphous, that moves and flows and doesn't hide. That can also stand still, bravely. Breathing and being. That can't exist in a time of sudden loss, when you pull the drawbridge high.

I was beginning to be able to go near the sort of knowledge that let me live again with my relationship with music. I started asking new questions. Not 'how likely?', 'how young?', or even 'could anything have been done?' but 'how does it feel?' and 'who else?' The knowledge that comes not just from looking at what was special and different and enormous about my experience, but that comes from being. And from being a cosmic speck, from being able to acknowledge that we are all in this together.

The second book I wrote was about music. I understood that it was the thing. But I couldn't put in enough, because I could not absorb myself in it. I could not make it flow. From me. Live. In me. Experience the overwhelm, the closeness, the lack of inhibition. I was still furious with music and with thinking and with learning and with the kind of knowledge to which I'd devoted my life. I hid from myself in intellectual spaces that didn't hurt so much, that insulated me by keeping me angry. It would take yet another version, because I could not yet play, in any sense of the word.

Somewhere in the draft, from when I'd been writing in a pub, I found this sentence: 'Help I'm living in a book, help, I think if I stay here my dad will come back.'

I stopped writing for a month. I filled my days by refinishing the floors in my flat with enormous sanders, 65 kilograms of crude power delivered to my door and up the stairs by a man called Alessandro. Dust mask covering my face, condensation collecting in my plastic goggles, I scraped away at the paint on each individual stair by hand. One by one. Manual labour felt necessary. I needed to be busy. If I stopped, the feelings were too much.

I had written a book about grief both to find my father, and to avoid feeling.

I took a deep breath, and I started again.

I knew that everything had changed back on that arbitrary spring day when I woke up without him. That day was a bright, cold, empty, full, real simulation and newly reckless now, its sky uncompromising blue above me. And so maybe, now gravity had stopped working, now the strings had been released and the roof of generations above blown off the house, maybe now I might learn to fly.

To cross intellectual and emotional boundaries, to be curious about grief and music and method and history and my dad and myself. To burn away the rigidity, the search for comprehensive or academic answers, and follow threads that were as chance as any of the other confluences and coincidences that make up a life. To talk to people, simply to see what happened, and where things took me, and what I might learn.

To return, perhaps, to music, to life, changed.

Maybe, in this new life, I would learn to fly.

But first I would need to learn to play again.

This is the third book.

Chapter 2

TUNES FOR TEN FINGERS

The autumn skies are wide in Boston. Wide, crisp and clear.

But it was dark when I arrived, aeroplane creamed mushroom and rice from a tin dish still uneasy and transitional in my stomach, six months and counting since he'd died. I was standing on the street with my luggage, overheating in my big coat, having just climbed the steps out of the T at Central. I was getting my bearings, eyes on my phone. I was here, back, the place where my life had been three-dimensional and immersive, with regular physio appointments and that hairdresser I had recently switched to and baristas who knew my name dotted along my walk to work, a postdoc research position at Harvard. When I left, we had just rid our apartment of bedbugs, a signature American experience, complete with multiple trips to the laundromat.

I was back, for an academic conference in the city where I'd worked until four months before my father died. Then, the plan was a trip to New York to look at archival materials in the Public Library for a few days. I headed up the street (not the road, the *street*, the words, the code switching easing back) and approaching me was a group of what looked like students, maybe six of them, their mood all tight-wound potential. It took a second, the muscle memory wasn't there any more, before I remembered: veer to the right. Americans think sidewalks are like roads and you should behave like a car. Try this on an American. Ask them if they think there are rules on the sidewalks. Watch their jaw drop when you tell them that British pavements don't have rules. On British pavements, chaos reigns.

One was wheeling a bike. 'Excuse me,' he said, as he knocked my suitcase, the sidewalk just too narrow for both of us. He smiled.

'Excuse me.' Not 'Sorry'. I felt my heart gasp with recognition, belonging. I was home.

As I dragged my bags up the street I lived on for a time, it smelled of incense and faintly of weed and I was disoriented by the sudden totalising immediacy of *everything*. This familiarity was a loss of self and made a mockery of my life in London, a life that was disintegrating fast into the firm red brickwork of the sidewalks, the precise size of the concrete paving, a familiarity and a grounding so unconscious and personal I'd forgotten that I'd forgotten it. It was all in the details: the walking man on the crosswalk, the orange numbers that count down the remaining seconds, remembering the frozen pain in deep winter of waiting in an inadequate coat. These majestic turn-of-the-century Massachusetts houses, three-deckers, they call them, with their wooden outer construction, planks horizontal, pastel colours: sky grey, blue, duck egg, teal, yellow, creosote red. They stood squat, boxy, robotic, nothing like the terraced houses in London. Many were dressed up for Halloween. *Welcome home*, I thought, as I walked past four ghouls haunting a front porch, one a ghastly infant, spectacularly gaunt and scary. There might even be animatronics if you got close and triggered the motion sensor.

Steps up to my friend Caitlin's porch. Pressed the brass button bell, then, inside: more of that bittersweet forgotten familiarity. The shape of the light switches, the proportions of the doors. The lock on the bathroom door was in the middle of the handle and bug screens veiled the windows, careening in the wind.

What was this war on bugs (*insects*)?

'In Britain,' I remembered telling my old room-mate (*housemate*), 'bugs and humans cohabit peacefully.' She was appalled.

Joy swam up through my chest, behind my eyes and buzzed into my forehead.

The words were returning. 'Trash'. 'Dumb'. 'Quite'. 'Rather'. The cadence I added to my voice so people understood me.

When I am in America, when I am in Somerville, near Boston, where I lived, my body believes that my dad is alive.

And me and my dad can do anything. The future is ours.

And so here, back here, is where I first started to find myself truly unmoored.

The summer leading up to this trip, the summer after my dad died, had passed in a blur of stasis. Pale peonies in a vase by my bed when I arrived back in London after the funeral; a copy of *Grieving for Dummies* left on the duvet by my housemate. I knitted a lightweight cardigan in yarn like fine-spun gold, a project that alternated meditative rows of plain and purl. It was a knit-along with Caitlin, left behind in Massachusetts, where you make the same item at the same time, and pretend to yourself that you still live in America.

My cardigan was yellow; hers was a sophisticated grey. You could knit it while you immersed yourself deep in the labyrinth of television streaming, for instance, wrapped up in the new scarf you wore to the funeral, barely moving from the sofa, feeling the rhythm of the stitches moving through your hands. In those months, all I wanted was to be alone. I became an expert on everything Netflix offered, and forgot everything I knew about music history. Or, at least, I told myself I had become a television expert, so afraid was I of losing my sense of mastery as I lost my grip on any sense of significance attached to the professional goals I had worked so hard to achieve.

The reality that summer was simply that I watched a lot of *How to Get Away with Murder*, idolising Viola Davis, drawn into the world of lawyer Annalise Keating: brazen, sharp, flawed, alcoholic. It had been recommended as the perfect grief binge by a friend, someone on the comparatively tiny circuit of people around my age with dead parents. This was a subcategory I'd never noticed before, but who now became elevated, cherished people, the ones 'who got it'. In the immediate aftermath, it had been *Luther*. Immersive, with explosions. I watched it through sleepless nights to prevent thoughts from coming, and I'd like to thank Idris Elba for his services to the grief community. After *HTGAWM*, *Crazy Ex-Girlfriend*. *Brooklyn Nine-Nine*. *Fleabag*, devoured in two afternoons. I was voracious, needed so-called content to keep washing over me to move my mind away from the horror. Reading was impossible. Music was intolerable. Nothing worked except television's unstoppable motion. Forgettable motion.

In my new half-life in London, a city of strangers, I went running daily. On a podcast, I had heard the grief expert Julia Samuel say it was good for the nervous system, and I hoped it would counter the motionless hours using the screen and alcohol to dull the pain. It also meant I could watch the dogs playing on the common, experiencing pure unmediated joy. I slept a lot, and compared notes with my brothers, who were experiencing the same thing. I learned it was normal. And then I went through periods of sleeplessness, and tried to write in the middle of the night to take my mind off it. I dreamed lucidly of my dad, panicking, knowing the time we had was borrowed and finite, that the rug would be pulled away at any moment and it would all be over.

Later, I would dream various versions of a scenario in which he had been dead for a while, but then he had stopped being dead and things were fine again; a misunderstanding, and a sense that my experience had been illegitimate. Except, because dreams let you have it every way, he was also kind-of-still dead. A sense of embarrassment at all the special treatment. Sorry this happened to me. By night, I found all kinds of spaces in which surreal local physical laws meant he could still be located, sometimes just for the duration of a party, or conjured from the sound of a guitar, but invisible to everyone else. Once as a living drawing. Always limited in some way.

Time moves strangely after a death, cloaked and muffled between screaming bare-bright voids. Moments fall away, slow at first, like shale from a cliff, then huge crashing chunks are gone, cleaving you, your mind, your memory into new and vividly exposed shapes. My memories screen-roll past, flicker, jump-cut, and I don't hear anything. A series of emotional snapshots, flash scenes: slippery and hard to place. They blur, they diffract, chasms emerge between them that could be hours or days, there's little sense of chronology: taking off toenail polish in the bathroom deep in the night when sleeping was impossible; unable to eat more than mouthfuls of tomato soup; an urgent need to escape the supermarket, its familiarity – familiarity, *family*, dinners of shop-bought tortellini belonging now to a life we didn't live in – rendered outrageous, its choices overwhelming; Mum rocking on the sofa next to me as I tried to fill out a VAT exemption form for catering at a conference I seemed still to be organising. The salt of tears, cold on Mum's skin. Sitting on Dad's side of the bed, staring at his lovely, messy piles of books that would always now remain unfinished. And sometimes a moment felt so endless and unyielding all I wanted was *out*. To leave. Escape. I was cold and hollow, and when I look back, no sound remains from that time.

I remember thinking *God, I hate the word 'grief'*. It seemed so alien, remote, embarrassingly feelingsy, I could barely say it. Like sparkly dust in my mouth, clogging my throat. Like the Christian Union was turning up at the door to my uni halls and asking me to join them in being earnest and eating pizza together and believing in things. It wasn't for me. More importantly, it wasn't for Dad.

Except it turned out this particular door-to-door wasn't one you could opt out of with a polite smile.

What I remember is a summer of coiling myself into the sofa, of trains out to the South West and back again while googling academic articles that I hoped would reveal the scale of my personal tragedy: 'sudden death in acute pancreatitis', and feeling like a fraud because the articles about sudden death tended to discuss accidents, or natural disasters, or violence (what if someone *just dies*?). I spent a lot of time at Clapham Junction, that purgatory interchange to which Dad and I had always appended 'Place of Dreams'. I took risks. Usually I avoided talking to strangers at all costs, but one afternoon I found myself in a trendy beer shop-cum-day bar, flirting with the barman. He fed me the tap overflow of other people's pints and told me about his career as a session guitarist; I told him about how my dad was newly dead. Brilliant. I was out of sync with the people I loved, disconnected. I hoped to God they'd remember me when I emerged again.

I remember being at the Royal Albert Hall. It was the Proms season, and with choir stall seats behind the orchestra, we were exactly where I loved to sit, where you could believe you were reading along with the back row brass. Today it was Mozart, a piano concerto, live on national radio – and nothing could have seemed more pointless. Strings scurried, then hard black and white keys skipped up and down the dazzling emptiness above, and I felt vertiginous.

People had taken their seats as normal, fidgeted with their belongings at their feet. It was something about the reverence, I think. Or the way people acknowledged you as if you were worthy of respect for coming to this concert, for respecting classical music. Or perhaps it was simply the fact that some people had dressed up nicely. Either way, I was furious, I was detached, everything was suffocating, and I felt disenchanted, foolish, deeply angry with myself for ever having loved this thing, music, which does nothing, which won't protect you.

I was at this concert because my friend Chrissy – like me, a professional musicologist, but unlike me, a part-time DJ with understated tattoos – had received a pair of hand-me-down tickets. And because our identities were complicatedly staked on music, I suspect neither of us felt able to admit to the other that we didn't really want to go.

We were facing the conductor and he looked insufferably smug. He seemed to feel the music in his body, and I started to hate him. *Hate* all of this. As the music continued, my heart began to pick up pace. I didn't have to keep sitting here, taking it. Nothing was holding me down: I realised it would take almost nothing to break this mute stasis.

I was right in the middle of the row. Glare of the lights in my eyes. Perfectly visible from the main auditorium. An intoxicating fantasy started to unfold in a space right between idle speculation and contingency planning, obliterating the music. *I could shout about how futile it all was*, I thought, standing up, spilling my beer, my voice broadcast over Radio 3. My neighbours would recede in horror. Panicked ushers. Waking people from their grand stupor. Surely shouting anything at all would be more meaningful than sitting here listening. And anyway, whatever I did would matter little given that, sooner or later, we were all going to die. It suddenly seemed madness to trust five thousand people to behave themselves. What if those people had been given the powerful insight into the purposelessness of normal codes of behaviour that poorly compensates the newly bereaved, followed up with this wonderful bonus shot of immunity against social discomfort?

I observed with some curiosity that as I considered a spontaneous concert hall intervention, I couldn't summon the usual sense of shame. How interesting. I looked on at this self who lacked remorse or embarrassment. *This is new,* I thought. I suppose I could really do it. Should I? Playing with that option, living on the edge of maybe, soaring on the adrenaline it produced, which put me above it all, away from it all, somehow got me all the way through the first half.

At the interval, I bought a second, or third, beer. At that time, I wasn't counting. It was Chrissy who said it first.

'Do you want to stay for the second half?' She scanned the programme on her phone. I paused, waited to see what she would say next. Surely neither of us was allowed to admit even obliquely that we didn't want to stay and hear all this great music. 'We'd have to sit through what's-his-name, the conductor, performing his own composition, to get to the Stravinsky.'

It was savvy programming, but not savvy enough. In my opinion, not even the promise of Stravinsky (the greatest composer of them all) was going to sweeten enduring something that self-indulgent.

We finished our drinks as the other concertgoers dutifully filed back into the auditorium. And we simply left, went to the pub. It may not have been standing up and shouting 'This. Is. All. Pointless.' mid-Mozart, but it still felt amazing.

Afterwards, I went home alone on the Overground to my flatshare, walked past the café where I'd met Dad for the very last time. We'd caught up there on his way home from London meetings with his journalism students. It was the first and only time I saw him in London since I'd moved back from America. He'd liked the café – it had reminded him of cafés in Berlin. 'Come down and see us soon,' he'd said as we'd parted on the pavement outside. My head spun as I curled into the sofa, and in my Moleskine journal I wrote that another month had passed and my dad was still dead. My handwriting was untidy. I dreamed once again that night what I would dream many nights: that he was playing his guitar, back turned to me sitting on the end of his bed, and that I only had a tiny amount of time to spend with him because we now knew he was about to die, dreaming with a terrible sense of dread, giving myself the moment of possibility. A dream in which he was still available, but in which I was deadly aware that he was about to go. I woke up panicked, my chest tight, stomach filled with rocks, realising the truth once again.

After the sudden death of her son, the philosopher Denise Riley wrote a short book, *Time Lived, Without its Flow* (2018). When someone dies unexpectedly, Riley argues, you inhabit a new kind of time. One that has no flow. It pools, becomes a series of moments, unconnected.

In some ways, you exist outside of time.

Searching for a history of people describing this condition, Riley found very little. But one example is in a poem written by Emily Dickinson around 1864. And tellingly, the metaphor Dickinson reaches for to explain this failure of time is how we experience sound:

I felt a cleaving in my mind
As if my brain had split;

31

I tried to match it, seam by seam,
But could not make them fit.

The thought behind I strove to join
Unto the thought before,
But sequence ravelled out of sound
Like balls upon a floor.

'But sequence ravelled out of sound / Like balls upon a floor.'
A sequence of sounds falls apart, collapsed, meaningless. The
pooling of time Riley describes.

The German philosopher Georg Wilhelm Friedrich Hegel
thought that music is something, as Riley paraphrases 'apt to
grip and secure you [into time] by means of its sequences of
notes'. If music is a thing that holds you into time, I was well
out of it.

Again and again, thinkers come back to sound and music
to explain this loss of self, of meaning, of time. Because music
feels lived. We learn music throughout the brain, including in
the logical bit of the brain that's about processing sequence,
as well as the parts that register movement. We experience
music in, as the memory of, time. It is encoded in our brains
as a memory of duration and – for many people – of motion.
To remember music is to need to replay the whole passage
in our minds. And although hearing an instant of music is
enough to transport us to a very specific place and time in
our memories, we can't recall a passage of music condensed
into an instant, in the same way we can recall a composite
impression of a painting or a photo. If we want to know
whether, say, when singing 'Happy Birthday', the note on
which we sing the word 'birth' in the first line is higher or
lower in pitch than the note on which we sing 'dear' towards
the end, we have to scroll through the whole thing in
sequence in our heads.

After all, what is music, but time heard? Time made manifest?

But for now music would just be pointless balls pointlessly scattered across the floor.

Caitlin and I were drinking tea in my favourite café. It was dark now, and I'd just lost it for the first time on this visit to Boston, in the knitting shop next door where, less than a year previously, I had bought myself red wool – my dad's favourite colour – to knit a cabled jumper with money he gave me for my 31st birthday. Outside the shop, tears fell as I stared at the sidewalk's familiar paving, less bewilderingly marvellous now I'd been here a couple of days. All I could think was: London had all been a mistake. London was new and broken and my dad was dead and I was numb.

I tried to explain to her. The problem was this:

Here, *here*, my dad should be alive, and he wasn't. Here, he had always existed in some place *over there*. The cognitive dissonance was unbearable. Because now that place *over there* was simply nowhere.

She looked at me as if she might understand. She sipped her tea and left a red lipstick stain on the white ceramic. The tables were oddly proportioned, so she was sitting further away than I would have liked. She didn't think I was talking nonsense.

Who was I? That was the question I found myself asking once I'd arrived back in America. Because place makes us who we are. And I belonged here, I was sure. I was here, finally, back with my people, and they understood, even if they'd never been where I was.

We placed our mugs in the plastic crate as we left. No lipstick on mine; make-up in general was still too risky.

The wrong thing. On the morning my father died, we had driven to the hospital, and I had expected to see him. I had come home from London in a rush late the night before: perhaps coming home was our family's ICU protocol. We didn't know. We were forging new norms. His death had not been a realistic or comprehensible possibility when things had happened so quickly. When people first show signs of an illness, they do not suddenly die. That was a principle on which my life had been built. The young doctor who admitted him had mentioned scorpion bites as a possible cause; if scorpions were in the frame, surely we all had permission to relax. This illness was a joke. And instead of going straight in through the double doors to see him, we were taken to a side room. That's when my mum knew. I was still convinced everyone was overreacting. Then they took us into a second, neighbouring room, with pale yellow walls and tissues. *The wrong thing.* Next we processed into the ICU to see his body, only just dead, and I remember saying: 'This is the wrong thing.'

I realised I had been hoping that if I came back here, to Boston, to what felt like my real life and friends, everything would be OK.

The wrong thing.

It had been the wrong thing ever since.

And it wasn't OK. America had been the last hope, and I was broken open by it.

I might have been back in Boston, but I wasn't in a fit state to be at any kind of conference, except the kind where you hide from the presentations in local coffee shops all day, only emerging at 5 p.m. to get drunk with your colleagues. Or one where the point is to just look startled about being out in public, and blurt *My dad died and I've been chain-watching television since April* at all your Important Professional Contacts. Or the kind where you are either supposed to shout earnest things about the meaning of life at kind people who seemed willing to listen, or to shout unfiltered things at your friends you haven't seen in eight months about the fact that you can't help noticing that their sweater is covered in dog hair, their hair is unwashed and are they depressed? I had no bandwidth for filter, for social niceties. Reality looked fresh, new and raw to me, and should be met on its own terms. Say hello, get right up close to the Real.

Luckily the annual conference of the American Musicological Society is large and diverse enough that it did turn out to accommodate some of these unusual requirements. This is an event that offers a special interest group for people who, unfathomably, want to get together and play lutes, an LGBTQ+ disco and a whole cohort of scholars who do music theory, you can recognise them from their bow ties. Our major professional conference is where coveted jobs are won and lost, where clandestine meetings happen over breakfast that make and break international careers. It wasn't entirely clear what showing up at this level of unfiltered shock did for my professional standing, but at least I wasn't wearing a bow tie.

All my academic ambivalences were right on the surface, and I was fragile, and *I don't care*. And *I do care*, all at once. I'd never cared more. I wanted to tell everyone that I thought it was pointless, to monologue wild-eyed about how I'd invested the whole of my twenties in a project – academia – that seemed meaningless when held up against the finality of my dad's death, and therefore the sudden, new, terrible certainty of everyone else's too. All the while desperately self-conscious about how weird I was being. I felt like a recent convert advocating for their new cult while trying to pull off the trick of coming across as balanced. Like my new thing wasn't consuming my every waking moment.

I wanted to show them that I knew I was an imposter, to test the boundaries. To break things.

'I've never read Joseph Conrad's *Heart of Darkness, even though you're all acting like it's a prerequisite for existing.*' (The last bit to myself.)

'Do you think we really, truly care about these questions on cartography and sound and power, or that we're just doing this because we want to write something that's better than anyone else's work and prove to some imaginary external figure how clever we are?'

That second one was at a wine reception. I asked a professor I knew vaguely at Yale this, someone I should really have been trying to impress with my sterling opinions that accorded with The General Smart People Consensus about papers I'd seen that day. However, I hadn't seen any papers because of the aforementioned hiding in the coffee shop a twenty-minute walk away, where I wouldn't bump into anyone, and especially not The Smart People. I had to make do with what I had, and what I had was inappropriately deep conversation.

As I'd presented my own paper, I felt like I was underwater. 'Was it obvious I wasn't engaging with any of the questions?' I asked in the bar afterwards. I'd surfaced with the strong impression that every answer I'd given had been: 'That's interesting, I'd love to think more about that', which is a response you can get away with twice at most.

There was a pause. 'Well, kind of,' a friend told me, not unkindly.

I downed the rest of my Sierra Nevada, and ordered another.

Long before I became an academic, I was a small girl looking for an obsession.

I am nine, and in my grandparents' hallway there is a piano. On top are photos of my teenaged aunts and my dad. It is the kind of piano with candlestick holders, and its keys are not white, like our piano at home, but a dusky, uneven magnolia, like sun-spoiled pages. One year it was Easter while we were visiting, and we followed clues my dad had planted through their house and garden in search of chocolate. Unfurling wrapped-up paper: 'Dead elephant'. A special clue for my youngest brother: I'm not allowed to answer it, although *I know, I know*. I had asked once about the mottled colour of the piano keys. 'They're ivory,' Dad told me. 'It's what elephants' tusks are made from.' It was faintly grotesque news. Was I touching something dead? Yuck. I couldn't bring myself to ask what had happened to the elephants. If I didn't know for sure, perhaps they weren't dead.

Greedy for new music, I am hunting through the neighbouring drawers, finding things my aunts and my father had played as children. Scale books. Yellowing pamphlets of pieces for post-war 1950s and 1960s grade exams long past. Here I first internalise that sense of the discipline of progress through music, and I like what I find. This is how you get to be a proper person, I reason, scent of old paper, print of the notes. Grade 4, grade 7 (very difficult). I wonder if I will ever be good enough to play them, marvel at the possibility, the strict sense of progression, the future I can see ahead of me that is also someone in my family's past.

The grandfather clock chimes 10 a.m. further down the hall. My grandparents' hallway floor is wooden and polished by someone else. You can slide on it in your socks. I often visit the piano in that dead time right after breakfast. We get to have a Kellogg's Variety Pack, because being at my grandparents' is basically the same thing as being on holiday. My favourite is Honey Nut Loops and we eat them from Johnson Brothers Blue Denmark chinaware, sitting on orange-painted wood and wicker chairs while the dogs lick our ankles. I love the dogs, a cairn terrier and a cavalier King Charles spaniel, who is secretly my favourite, although

I wouldn't want the cairn terrier to know. Sometimes in the afternoons, I go into the kitchen and sit next to their baskets. In the corner of the kitchen, on the dirty cream wall by the Aga, is a chart of all our heights. Ours increasing bit by bit (everyone thinks I'll be tall like my mum); my grandmother's mark, my dad's mother, substantially lower than it had once been now she is in her seventies. She laughs this off. Shrinking isn't going to get in the way. She is someone who breaks walnuts with the force of her thumb joint and a well-placed bash with the other fist. Who, in younger years, captured errant scorpions with saucepans. When she takes shotguns to be serviced in her local village, she doesn't think twice of open-carrying; she speeds down country lanes, my Italian cousins crying 'You're a whizzing granny!'

I find Beethoven's Bagatelle no. 25 in A minor, better known as 'Für Elise', and also find that I can play it, or at least I can play the beginning, and that is all that matters, because that is the part that everyone knows. It is amazing. I immerse myself in its melancholy as, delicately, I execute the octave reach in the left hand, then first finger crossing over. This is a tricky new skill, a hand shape made by a real pianist. I make liberal use of the pedal – press, release, press, release – another thing real pianists do, which I dream of mastering. My hands cross, I play with rubato, that is, I use artistic licence with the timing, try to shape the pathos of the repeated semitone into a story. Probably much too expressively, but who cares: I'm nine and I'm playing real music, alone, by the front door, discovering something about myself and the world and taking off the stabilisers. I hadn't known I could play the music that people know. So far I've mainly played things from beginner methods with cheery covers: *Tunes for Ten Fingers, More Tunes for Ten Fingers*. But here I am, let loose for the first time on

Proper Repertoire, which reaches out infinitely, made of exhilarating possibility and potential and things I might one day be able to do.

I also discover there that if you press down the sustain pedal and hit every note from top to bottom of the keyboard one after the other as quickly as you can, you are left with a roar like a glorious thunderstorm. I show my brothers. We do it all week, and it doesn't delight the grown-ups as much as it delights us.

In Boston I wandered through cut-and-paste corridors in the conference hotel, disoriented myself in identical-looking stairwells, found myself at a paper on cactuses and burlesque and sex-positive sex work (so striking were all these elements, I completely forget how music fit into the argument). I felt empty, and I mostly wanted to drink alcohol. I escaped the conference and I went running, through familiar streets in Cambridge and Somerville. Running through a life I'd let go, running up the disused railway line towards Alewife, autumn colours, oranges, browns, scorching my eyes. I used to send photos of these trees, these awesome, unique colours, to my dad.

I alternated movement and complete inertia.

A friend and I then travelled together to New York and I missed my dad some more. New York was a city where we once went together, where there had seemed like so many possibilities for future visits, where on an impulse we had been to the Lincoln Center to hear a jazz mandolin gig and eaten rosemary-salted fries that cost more than Mum could tolerate. New York, where I secretly hoped one day to live, and where I thought Dad would visit me. Stone lions guard the entrance to the New York Public Library. In the reading room for special collections, where the young archivist wore a jacket with actual elbow patches, I vacantly opened archival boxes, removed beige folders, photographed hundred-year-old letters and newspaper clippings.

We went to a pizzeria in Little Italy, and learned too late it had one significant drawback: no drinks licence. We made do with blood orange San Pellegrino and planned the wine we would take from the liquor store to our hotel room later. We played 'guess the relationships of the people at the other tables'. A Grindr date at 2 o'clock, we speculated, on the long red seating? We didn't think they'd hit it off. Leaning over us, cutting into our speculations, a middle-aged stranger dropped by our table on her way out.

'Cheer up, it might never happen.' I froze. I immediately saw myself from the outside. My friend and I were both small, slim, white women with dark hair in our early thirties. The pressure of relative youth hung oppressive over the table: its covetedness, its supposed superficiality, the obligation to perform happiness so as not to incur others' disapproval. What could we possibly be unhappy about? We had our whole lives ahead of us, I felt her wondering. Only something trivial like our love lives.

What if it happened already? I wished I'd had the presence of mind to spit. To catch her off guard, take away her self-satisfied righteousness. Being young does not inoculate you against the sudden death of your favourite person, the person you can always call, because he is always interested.

But instead I just smiled at her.

My fury leaked from day into night. Back in the hotel room near Penn Station, we slept in single beds, lined up like matches in a box. Usually I sleep quiet and still and I wake up in exactly the same position I closed my eyes. Not that night. My friend told me in the morning that in my sleep, I said suddenly loud as daylight, 'I don't give a fuck.' Well, quite. Being unconscious was evidently no respite from the anger that coursed through my being.

I went back to the Lincoln Center on an impulse, not for jazz this time; instead, we saw *La Bohème* at the Metropolitan Opera, turning up in the same clothes we'd been wearing to the library, our rucksacks lumpen against the shimmering drift of ball gowns. It's one of the most emotional operas in the canon, a love story that ends mercilessly with Mimì's consumptive death in the poverty of Parisian poets. My friend cried. I felt nothing at all.

In New York, and in Boston, as I retraced the steps of my old life in America, music still wasn't doing it for me. Or if it could have done anything, I'd turned off the switch that let it, wanting to be invulnerable at least sometimes, somewhere, at a time when jigsaw puzzles (we wouldn't do a jigsaw puzzle this Christmas) and wool shops were enough to send me to a place of public vulnerability I'd never been before.

I knew I hadn't always felt like this.

Because I wasn't kidding when I said Stravinsky is the greatest composer of them all. And that is because nothing could possibly be quite as much fun as playing the trombone in a performance of his *The Firebird* Suite, and that in turn is because of the 'Infernal Dance of King Kashchei'. It's ballet music. Terse physicality leaping from the orchestra. Playing it is up there with feasting and skiing and a good date you think you already know is leading to sex. (Skiing is a recent addition to the tight nexus of 'best things', and I now know why people spend all their money on it: you fly, you actually fly over the snow.) The thrill. The energy. This is runaway music, and it will take all your concentration to stay ahead of the orchestra's dangerous metrical shifts. Because to stay ahead is the only way to stay in time. The sheer volume, crispness of the attack, edge of your seat, straight back, timing the fizzing syncopations, locked in tight with sixty or so other musicians. Flooded with adrenaline, waiting for the risky high glissando, like walking the tightrope – will you fall this time?

This is what trombones were made for. This is excitement of the highest order.

Rehearsing the suite from Stravinsky's *The Firebird*, however, is another matter. Of the five movements in the 1911 arrangement, there are three in which you don't play anything at all. Nothing. Not a single note. And if you play the bass trombone, the lowest of our trio, make that four movements. You get your part and you find that this epochal modernist work that changed the twentieth century fits on exactly two sheets of A4 (and just one sheet for the bass trombone), and that most of it is summarised as follows: 'II. III. IV. Tacet.' On closer inspection you realise that of the opening movement, I, you only have to pay attention for the very first twenty-seven bars. The rest of it is also marked, you guessed it, 'Tacet', which in common parlance means: permission awarded to switch off and – historically – get your book out, or – latterly – read the news on your phone. Brass players tend to be very up to date on current affairs and active on social media. I prefer the 1919 arrangement, in part, self-interestedly, because we have more to do, and in part because the 1911 arrangement made the spectacular error of missing out the 'Finale', which begins with a horn solo of unrivalled beauty.

The history of playing the trombone in an orchestra might most accurately be told as a cultural history of what people were reading during all the rests. Or as a history of counting. Or as a history of not counting and praying your neighbour is taking care of paying attention to where you are in the music – or how will you know when to come in? The embarrassment of missing your cue is to be avoided. The whole orchestra has to stop and it is abundantly clear at whose feet the blame rests. The conductor might even rap their music stand with their baton.

Sometimes you can dance with danger and read your book in movements where you will be playing, too, so long as you know the cues well, that is, the music to listen out for immediately before you will be expected to enter and play. Sometimes those cues become bodily things, memories of particular fears. I recently put the kitchen radio on part way through the 'Dies Irae' of Mozart's Requiem, which precedes a huge trombone solo movement, the 'Tuba Mirum', a sonorous dialogue between the second trombone and a solo bass voice, one of the most majestic moments in the instrument's repertoire. Out of context, it took a beat or so to place it. What I did know, though, was that an eerie and unmistakable sense of dread came over me, its provenance confirmed when the trombone began the iconic solo I've spent hours that amount to days in practice rooms perfecting, the movements of the slide second nature in my wrist.

But all the waiting is worth it for those moments when you and you alone can be heard, when you cut through the orchestra's texture, growling, angry, unleashing the drama and volumes of which you are capable, when you are unmistakably there. When you ride with the orchestra at its most exhilarating, and you stay on. For the music like the 'Infernal Dance' in Stravinsky's *The Firebird* Suite.

Or, at least, it had been worth it. I didn't know what I thought any more. I often wondered about how I had become a music academic. Perhaps it was inevitable, given my love of knowledge – a childhood nourished on the physics of gravity and how angles worked and Kafka and raw cynicism – my love of music and a guitarist father in academia; perhaps it wasn't, but rather a random path, the confluence of circumstances, a story I put together later. Yet here I was, back in the US after my father's death, and I realised it was a long time since I'd felt like that little girl playing 'Für Elise' at the piano in her grandparents' hallway. Something had changed, and it had happened long before my father died. Despite years of music being at the centre of my professional life, somehow, so slowly I hadn't even noticed it happen, music had become something arid, engulfed within a sandstorm cloud of concepts and theories. A means to an end. For reasons I didn't want to probe too hard, it had been a long time since music had been the mesmerising, experiential thing for which I once would have done anything, into which I had poured countless teenage evenings and weekends, which had taken me, dry-mouthed, on to the stage in the school musical. Which had once pulled me away, after a term of study, from the sensible Oxford degree in maths and philosophy in which I was enrolled. Because even worse, behind that sandstorm lay something close to terror, the fear of expectation, the high-chested breathlessness of living up to how much other people expected me to know about it, and what I was expected to like and dislike, the internalised norms that kept me in the in-crowd. It took my father being gone, a soul-jarring shock, for me to realise it.

Chapter 3

KINDS OF BLUE

'Freddie Freeloader' is the second number on Miles Davis's album *Kind of Blue*, although the first Davis recorded in the iconic *Kind of Blue* sessions in 1959 with his all-star sextet of jazz giants such as John Coltrane and Cannonball Adderley. Sitting right on the back of the beat, the track is the very definition of cool restraint – 'cool', after all, was what they named the whole jazz style of which Davis was at the vanguard – and it's also the very definition of what we always referred to as 'Dad music' when I was a child, when it was the only music I knew. This was music that for me was barely music; more something that cloaked the air, unfurled through the smoke of my father's occasional evening cigars, unravelling up into the lamplight and pooling at the ceiling, part of the haze through which I tried to decipher the world.

Now, though, if I hear 'Freddie Freeloader', it only ever takes me, with a precipice lurch, to one place. To one image.

It takes me inside a beautiful roundhouse, a modern chapel, its design inspired by the ancient burial mounds common in South West England. Purbeck stone walls, banks of grass covering the sloped outside, encircled by a narrow moat. The owners planned that one day the building would be surrounded by flora, but everything was recently planted, so there was an eco-spaceship bareness about the place. We chose it because it looked out over the sea – well, just about. You could make out the sea in the far distance, especially if you already knew it was there. We also chose it because apparently it had once been the subject of a two-line exchange between Mum and Dad as they drove past its signage from the main road. Without anything else to hold on to, without any other plans, details that in another life would have no significance at all had to become lifeboats. It was tasteful, upmarket and I'm sure Dad would have been really grumpy about it. *Pretentious*, I heard him say. *But Dad*, I replied silently, batting for Mum, who was making the decisions, *we have to have your funeral somewhere*. Even if it would have been more fitting to have something small on the back of a boat, drink a few beers, pour our drinks in the sea as a half-symbolic gesture, recreate the life he had lived on his weather-beaten wooden yacht off the west coast of Scotland when he was in his twenties and early thirties. He would have hated the chapel's earnestness, and the formality, the neat rows of solid chairs, and the idea that these spruced-up, middle-class spaces made feelings real.

No matter where I am, if I hear 'Freddie Freeloader' I'm transported to that day, to the moment the service officially began, when people were invited in, and we were strapped in on the rollercoaster of ceremony, a performance you can't get off, and we were met with the shock of his coffin, sprayed with wildflowers. Everything felt hastily put together, out of step, out of order. Mum dressed up to star in the biggest of all events, not as mother of the bride, but instead publicly becoming a widow. The feeling was of entering a really sad jazz club, a Dad space. It's not so easy for me to describe 'Freddie Freeloader' now, because it's become hard for me to listen to it. I haven't put it on to help me write about it, but I know it so well it lives in my sternum. And it sounds like this: breathy horns over the chugging of a shuffle-feel rhythm section, a sprinkling of keys, a standard twelve-bar blues, in no hurry – we can do this for ever. Because we get to the end of the phrase, the twelve bars, and – you guessed it – we're going around again. Right-in-the-moment immediacy, timings impeccable. Laying down a sturdy groove, made up of a call (the horns) and a response (those keys dusting texture and movement on the remainder of the line). The horns never stray beyond the range of six notes – or what you could comfortably fit under your hand on the piano, even if you had quite a small hand. Like I said, restrained.

They call this modal jazz. Broadly speaking, this means jazz that's based on fluid scales and the possibilities of melody, rather than improvisation rooted back to a pattern of fast-changing chords. More like soloing on one chord for an extended period.

This is music that means many things to many different people. This is the sound that defined a generation; for the jazz community, it's a landmark that stylistically shifted the whole idea of jazz. Chick Corea described *Kind of Blue* as having 'practically create[d] a new language of music'. When I said it was the definition of cool: well, I'm in good company – I'm pleased to report Miles Davis was Bob Dylan's 'definition of cool', too. What appealed to some was how it suggested the romance of counterculture, drugs, outsiders. For others, it suggested actual romance: this is make-out music, the music of seduction of the sixties, seventies and beyond.

To be honest, I would have been happy never to have learned that last part – how many people associated the music with sex. It was an association that sat annoyingly at odds with the innocence of how I felt about it. Because for me, it was none of those things. It was simply the music from before I learned what music was. When categories of self, other, environment were hard to parse, and this was the music that lived between them. It was a feeling of safety and Sunday and a feeling, deep in all my father's actions, that reality was something to be seen laterally, or some version of laterally that even people who see the world laterally don't really understand. I could cocoon myself in my dad's belief that the world's rules and social norms were completely mad, even if I couldn't wholly bring myself to believe I didn't need to subscribe to those external conventions myself, and was left straddling the threshold, one foot outside.

So much meaning entangled in a groove that lives right in the moment and has its ears pinned towards infinity. And in my impossible memory of that impossible day, as we took our seats in front of the coffin, it sounded subversive, underground, undoing the chapel's expectations and careful formality, like Dad would want. It sounded like sitting at the top of the stairs in the dark in my pyjamas, and watching Dad's cigar smoke curl around the lampshade above the kitchen table through a doorway below; it sounded like the coolness that I hoped everyone attending would see in my father. I looked around and wondered which of my remaining family members I should be sitting next to, now four not five, and whether it mattered. The iron emptiness in my abdomen was back. I tried to perform normality when everything was anything but by flipping through the order of service, and then as Coltrane's tenor solo faded out, what came were nerves alongside resignation as the celebrant welcomed everyone. I gave a talk which I couldn't bear to think of as a eulogy, and it was funny, but also: I don't think I'll ever get an audience more predisposed to laugh at my jokes than on that day when I played the role of bereaved daughter at her father's unexpected funeral. Adrenaline mainly blotted out the reality of the situation, which only surfaced in terrible glimpses.

*

My mum read from T.S. Eliot's *Four Quartets,* which is a poem deeply preoccupied with the question of time, and named after a musical genre, the quartet. With his *Four Quartets,* Eliot hoped to make poetry become the most ideal version of itself, in a parallel way to how Beethoven had sought in his late string quartets, written when he was deaf, to attain an idealised form of music reaching beyond its own limits. Although any number of combinations of four instruments could technically come together to form a quartet (and some standard iterations include jazz quartets, consisting of bass, drums, keys and a single horn; or, for instance, I've played in trombone quartets, for which there is a surprisingly large repertoire), the string quartet is the most traditional ensemble. When someone says 'quartet' in the classical music world without any other context, the assumption is that this is what they're referring to. Beethoven wrote six late string quartets; Eliot wrote four. Music was following us everywhere as we tried to pull filigree threads of my father's essential Dad-ness out of the dense fabric of our lives.

Mum read from the first quartet in the cycle, 'Burnt Norton'.

Words move, music moves
Only in time; but that which is only living
Can only die.

My mum was standing behind a multi-faith altar made of a polished stump of wood, there, out of step, out of order, dressed up, dress loose, holding it together into the safe constraints of Eliot's words. She wore the pink scarf she'd bought for the funeral. I had one too, except mine was green, white, black, pink. Mum had returned from our local Georgian market town with a selection of scarves in that period between death and funeral, living instant to instant where all you get to do is feel sick all the time. 'Don't worry about paying now, just bring back the ones you don't want,' the shopkeeper had said. She knew what had happened. So we had new scarves. Mum was upright, assured, her words clear. Not her own words. I sensed that would have been too much. Another's words. Easier that way.

And the words half-swum around again as I struggled to make them make sense, and then left them to be for now, part sounds, part knowledge of sadness, performed beautifully by my mother –

... music moves
Only in time; but that which is only living
Can only die.

The words repeated over and over, as I heard contained in Mum's reading echoes of her rehearsing them at home. Endings and limits and music and lives, all striving towards an infinity, a beautiful, perfect existence outside time none could reach.

One of my favourite bedtime stories, invented by my dad, was titled 'The Parallel Lines'. Its unlikely protagonists were two lines, one male, one female, travelling infinitely in parallel through space, their exploits unfolding night by night only after I'd brushed my teeth, or on especially long car journeys. They longed to meet, and the story hinged on the mathematical axiom that parallel lines meet at infinity; naturally, off to the infinite edge of the universe they were therefore heading. Reaching the infinite being a necessarily unattainable goal, it was thus a parable for the modern condition. For the story to work, I simultaneously held all sorts of conflicting ideas to be true: that they were travelling through space, and that they already existed as infinite lengths. It seemed fine. It was part of Dad-ness. I imagined them whizzing through the universe, past the planets and solar systems I had learned about from my *Children's Illustrated Science Encyclopedia*.

'The Parallel Lines' was the best story anyone's ever imagined and a clear crowd pleaser, if your crowd is a particular kind of four-year-old girl.

The eponymous heroes of 'The Parallel Lines' ate carrots stored on nets stretched out between them, and they were accompanied on their exploits by a troupe of personified numbers, positive and negative. (Hello, concept of negative numbers. You can add positive numbers to negative ones? Amazing. Negative ones to positive ones? Even better. Storytelling possibilities abound.) Minus one hundred kept getting lost, due to his negatively small size. This was a story populated entirely by abstract concepts, to whom Dad managed to give rich, often fraught, interior lives. Sometimes the parallel lines visited unknown planets, with strange kings and queens.

Once, on a particularly far-flung planet, the parallel lines entered a vast swimming pool, where, in an epic twist of plot and physics, the laws of light refraction and a bit of narrative massaging meant they crossed for the very first time. I suspect this episode is lodged in my consciousness thirty years later because it so clearly disrupted everything I thought I knew from Dad about parallel lines. In that fantastical swimming pool, which may also have been filled with suspended blobs of purple, or floating triangles – entrance points to further worlds – reality swerved away from me.

'Your dad was a one-off,' said our friend Jan at the funeral.

One thing they don't tell you about your father's funeral is that you will be the star of the awful show. You're the centre of attention. People you've never met queue up to talk to you. And one after another, well-meaning neighbours said to me 'We wish we'd got to know him better', as they offered their condolences. As if it had only been a matter of time.

This sentiment was incomprehensible. 'They'd never have got to know him. All Dad's relationships were full,' said one of my brothers.

Burnt Norton is the name of an abandoned Cotswolds manor house whose gardens Eliot visited with the woman he loved but never married, Emily Hale, and the poem – as has only emerged very recently with the release of the Eliot–Hale letters – was Eliot's love poem to her. Eliot named all the *Quartets* for places, some in England, some in the United States, mapping out his autobiography. One of the points being made is that time is bound by place. This is one of those dizzying ideas which is both very obvious and very deep, the kind where you're sure it's completely facile until something cracks open and you see a flash of depths and unrecognisable colours, and maybe a chalk-wielding physics professor in front of a mid-century blackboard, but then your brain blinks and they've all gone again and yes, of course, time simply needs to have a place in which it can happen.

I didn't return to these poems for a number of years. It wasn't because of the sadness. More a lack of ownership – that was Mum's portion of the funeral. Also because Eliot's meaning is far from intuitive (don't quote me, quote Eliot himself, who wrote in 1921 that 'poets in our civilization ... must be *difficult*'). And we didn't even have those letters to help us out until 2020, which by the way wasn't enormously helpful, them being at Princeton University, and it being a pandemic. All of which is to say that as Mum picked it out around the time of the funeral, and as I listened to her practise it, in what, in fairness to me, was a suboptimal state for incisive literary criticism, I didn't really have a clue what the poem was about. A passage from a Great Literary Work.

As the words washed around me, I sensed feelings of waste, of loss, of aching, and of music as time passes; but I could not have explained the first thing about what the poem was 'doing'. I simply understood that it evoked a futility that I think my dad would have liked.

What Eliot deals with are the big questions, though. As I learned much later, it's an investigation of a particular sensibility about time, and a search to make meaning of time. I suspect this might be a serious mid-century scholarly way of dressing up another question: the search to make meaning of love; time is that bit more abstract, rational, macho. The question of loss, love, music and memory, and how those things, so core to our experience, are intertwined. That is the subject of the quartet. Those are the questions he sidles up to, even if they remain there, still unanswerable at the end.

That T.S. Eliot, he is not messing around.

Oh, and it's also about God – how God's eternal present makes meaning from the futility of human time – but I didn't work that part out until much, *much* later. Maybe not the best choice for Dad, in retrospect.

I suppose you can't get everything right. Complicating things further, I would later learn that Eliot also had some hard-to-stomach attitudes about race.

I was at a seminar in a poetry library a handful of years later when the *Four Quartets* came back into my consciousness. My eye caught a slim green volume on the shelf with 'T.S. Eliot' picked out along the spine, and as the seminar leader spoke, my gaze kept alighting there, my mind on the tutor's words; Eliot and the funeral in my subconscious. I thought: *Well, maybe now.* Peeling away from post-seminar socialising, I snuck back to the room and I found what I'd been eyeing up from afar wasn't actually a book of his poetry, but instead, a companion book of analysis, an explainer of T.S. Eliot's work, which made the whole thing feel much more approachable – but it was a Very Serious one from the 1950s, so I could still feel clever about it all, while hoping its analysis wasn't too dated. Elsewhere, on another shelf on the opposite wall, I located the *Four Quartets* themselves. A painfully spare, elegant, small paperback. Standing by the shelf, I read 'Burnt Norton' again, curious, and remembered the patterning of the words. This long after the fact, I wasn't sure I would be certain which portion my mum read, but I was. The rhythms were furrows in my memory.

George Williamson, my academic guide in the green companion volume, told me that 'Burnt Norton' apparently begins by 'collapsing time into the present, a semblance of eternity'. Eliot writes: 'Time present and time past / Are both perhaps present in time future, / And time future contained in time past.' Like each of his quartets, 'Burnt Norton' is split into five parts; Mum read the final section. The structure mirrors the movements of a string quartet. Typically a string quartet has four, but Beethoven played with the form for his late works; for instance, op. 132, String Quartet no. 15 in A minor has five movements. I learned later that Eliot scholars are also generally very confused on this point. Why five segments? I wondered how far the musical parallels might run, what music might tell us about the workings of these poems, or indeed, the questions Eliot is trying to answer. I wondered about whether the four string voices – first violin, second violin, viola and cello – could be traced contrapuntally within the quartets. Perhaps not. More fundamentally, I wondered whether Eliot was suggesting that in music we might find, if not the answers, then the experience that illuminates his questions the most fully.

Through music and through words, we seek 'to know the timeless in time', Williamson tells me, unlocking the meaning of Eliot's poem. Both music and words, arts for whom time is the medium, are condemned to exist within time, not outside of it. In the realm of Becoming, rather than the realm of Being. They can only come to approach Being with use of pattern, of repetition, the features that could allow them to stand still, suspended in eternity. Eliot compares them to the stillness of a Chinese jar, its patterning nonetheless in perpetual motion.

We humans are trapped in the realm of time, the realm of Becoming. For Eliot, love exists in the realm of Being, unmoving in the realm of the timeless. Love *is* timeless. But desire is movement, it's perpetual change.

There, that wasn't so hard, was it? Once you've got a trusty 1950s academic at your side, understanding Eliot on time is child's play.

The loud lament of the disconsolate chimera.

When Mum first tried the poem out, there was a lot of familial uncertainty around how to pronounce 'chimera'. Kim-e-ra? Chim-e-ra? Also: 'disconsolate chimera' is quite hard to say out loud, especially when you're really sad. Just a small note for the poet.

I skipped to the end. The poem, and the passage my mum read, concludes like this.

Quick now, here, now, always—
Ridiculous the waste sad time
Stretching before and after.

But through music, through its patterning that brings us ever nearer to infinity, we seek to catch the aspect of timelessness in which love resides.

And we get closer to those we've lost.

For quite understandable reasons, it never occurred to me to question why we were choosing the music we were for the funeral. Why the impossible task seemed to be: *Summarise Dad in music, in a way he'd be happy with.*

It's lucky there were so many impossible tasks that week; it took the edge off them all.

But there's scholarship about it. Journal articles you can download about how and why people choose the music they do for a funeral. It's about investing the funeral with personalised meaning. Apparently, in contemporary secular funerals, we use music to try to convey the identity of the person who's died. The academic scholarship historicises it, too: in our late modern, individualised culture, so much of our appeal to memories of the person who's died in our funerals supposedly steels us against our intolerable existential fears – 'against the terror of the forgettable self'. *Screw you, journal articles,* I thought. It made it sound so impersonal, so mundane, despite being the most consumingly personal and extraordinary thing I had ever attempted.

Since Dad wasn't going to die, we hadn't been left with any instructions, so to put together the music for the funeral we spent a week trying to pull something that might seem Dad-like out of the ocean of Dad music. The idea that a single piece of music, or even a selection, would encapsulate him was beyond conceiving. All we could do was recreate him collectively and play music that was really more about us than him. That had been the tone of the whole funeral: we don't know what he wants; perhaps this will do. It makes us think of him. Despite being the people closest to him, we weren't remotely qualified to go into the recesses of his mind and try to work out what he would want.

Mainly, I thought, furious, *he would want not to be dead yet.*

There was plenty of music I didn't even know he liked, and I worried that we'd created a superficial version of him. We huddled around a laptop and listened to music together as we tried to select what to play and I fought to keep it together. I don't know exactly why it felt important to seem in control then, but it did. I didn't want to break down and so in my mind I erected makeshift architecture. New pillars to support myself and behind which to hide feelings, emergency partitions to put memories into and under, boxing and protecting and walling the self that needed to be a certain way around my family, that needed to be able to string together a series of photos into something like a PowerPoint for the funeral display and end it with a photo of their – my – dad heading out to sea on his boat, all while holding it together, while barely crying, only feeling it when I pressed send on the material, submitting it to Obitus funeral services, registering the finality of the strange, strange, alienating, undignified upload process.

Obitus. What a name. But no one registered its strangeness at the time, or the lunacy of attempting to invest in an online funeral management platform with the heft and seriousness befitting bereavement. Perhaps this was because the bottom had collapsed out of the notion of meaning: it could have been called anything; everyone was beyond caring. Unfortunately, at the funeral a tech error meant our slideshow ended not on the intended photo of my dad heading out to sea, but on a grainy phone photo of my dad and the family Jack Russell mongrel that we thought we'd cut. 'Wow, he must have really loved that dog.'

It served us right for trying to be poignant.

That was the week I created the Spotify playlist 'Dad funeral'. Those two words did not, could not, belong together. For the longest time after the funeral, I didn't go anywhere near it, nested between yoga playlists, 'Florence Price' (African American classical composer and pianist; research and pleasure), 'This is Vulfpeck' (American white bro funk; pleasure) and one I made for teaching.

I wish I'd known to ask him what music he'd like at his funeral, and not because it would have saved us trying to work it out without him. Nor because these studies I was now reading suggested it's healthy for the grieving process: that relatives who plan music for the ceremony together with the dying person find it helpful for their grief. But simply because he would have said something unexpected; because I would have learned something about him that now I'd never know. He'd recently admired the music for *Killing Eve,* for instance. Pati Amor, in 'Killer Shangri-Lah', husky, a velvet shuffle, with the reverb smudginess of kohl-lidded eyes. Her sentiment: the necessity of having killed someone, sung in the second person, as if over their shot-up body, any regret tongue-in-cheek. Irritating her may have been their only crime.

I wished a lot of things.

And one thing I wished in particular was that our devastation was as unique as it felt. Maybe that explained why the journal articles made me feel so furious. It was clear from reading them that our funeral had been like everyone else's. For instance, people use music to manage the flow of the ceremony, and to manage the emotions of the people assembled. Explaining how they designed the music, people often said they wanted to create a sense of uplift at the end, an emotional arc towards hope. Apparently, a lighter closing piece of music also helps with the transition from the funeral back to normal life, functioning similarly to the wake that follows – tea, wine, nibbles, chit-chat. I couldn't appreciate the comfort that comes in shared experience, because the only thing I had to hold on to at that time was the outrageousness of what had happened.

So we played some more music. Villa-Lobos, Prelude no. 1 in E minor. With the slideshow of photos of my dad.

Just a standard-issue atheist funeral. Other people choose

God; we chose malfunctioning PowerPoint and bleak meditations on aesthetics and time.

I liked how 'Burnt Norton' had the intellectualising, the separation, the problem solving around existence I so closely associated with my dad.

Other people choose God. Or, at least, they choose ritual.

And some of those rituals involve not listening to music.

It's like they can see inside my head.

When someone dies in the Jewish community, the intention is to bury the person as soon as possible. After the funeral, the family sits shiva, where it is customary to stay at home for seven days so that extended family and friends can visit. Some leave the door unlocked; some visitors bring food. Many men don't shave. And it's traditional not to listen to music.

I have a severe case of funeral envy.

'I was really fascinated when I learned about the music thing,' Matty told me. I was chatting to him after a dinner I'd been to with a number of people I didn't know very well, Matty included. We sat opposite one another on a long table. Matty is an advertising executive, has spent his whole life in London. He's Jewish: his grandfather, a judge, escaped Berlin for London in 1933. Post-Brexit, he's planning on making use of his Holocaust-survivor descendant entitlement to German citizenship.

Not listening to music continues after the week of shiva, Matty told me. You're not meant to listen to music for the whole first month after someone dies, and some people don't listen to live music during their first year of mourning. It's to do with avoiding enjoyment; keeping everything low-key for a bit. You also continue not to shave for a month, and don't go to celebrations like weddings. In fact, you're allowed to avoid weddings for the rest of the year, if you like.

I was drinking a glass of red wine. He wasn't. 'I drank a lot when I was younger. I had to stop for a bit. Now I only ever drink Guinness. That's if I drink at all – it has to be worth it.' He said, 'There are still mates of mine who can do all-nighters, up till four then back at work the next day, get totally wasted, with enhancers, if you know what I mean. I envy them. I do miss that.' He shrugged. As is clear from all the focus on alcohol, we were having the kind of conversation you only really have with people you barely know. So I decided to shift to the depths. I wanted to talk about death. I was great fun to be around.

I was pursuing this because I'd recently learned about Orthodox Jewish grief rituals. I had immediately been envious of how structured and sensible they seemed, but I wanted to know the degree to which those traditions were taken up by people whose relationship to Judaism was similar to what mine is to Christianity – i.e. they grew up with it around, but they didn't consider themselves religious. I wanted to understand the extent to which these rituals get transferred over into secular Jewish life.

And the answer was: actually rather a lot.

'I think the Jewish faith does death really well,' he told me. He insisted that he wasn't at all religious, and then qualified sheepishly that his family had been at the synagogue on Friday nights a fair bit in recent months to get his daughter into their preferred school – and anyway, the Friday night service was 'really chill' with lots of music. 'But even people who have absolutely nothing to do with religion the rest of the time, mates of mine who are scientists or whatever, when someone dies, suddenly a rabbi appears out of nowhere, and they're doing the whole thing.'

I mentioned the Kaddish, the mourning prayer, and hoped I was pronouncing it right. I told him I'd heard that Orthodox Jews, mainly the men, have to attend prayer services at sunrise, lunchtime and sunset in the first year after a death, and that I loved the idea of a built-in mechanism for getting you out of bed, at a time when getting out of bed seemed pointless and impossible. You were expected somewhere. The only thing that had succeeded in getting me out of bed at that time was the knowledge that, if I didn't, my puppy would wee on the floor.

'Well, Orthodox Jews go to the synagogue all the fucking time,' he laughed.

I wondered if I had it right that people say Kaddish during the service for a year. 'Almost right. Eleven months.' He told me that friends had found real comfort in it. 'In the sounds, I suppose. In the rhythms.'

It's not music, the Kaddish, but the way he described it, it sounds as if it might be.

The Kaddish had been explained to me by the writer Sally Berkovic, who is a member of the Chevra Kadisha, those who ritually prepare bodies for Jewish funerals. The Kaddish is a call-and-response prayer between the grieving person and the rest of the praying community. She showed me the text in Aramaic and its transliteration, and she guided me through the verses, showing me who says which part. Although most of the service is in Hebrew, the Kaddish is spoken in Aramaic. She told me about the pop-up lunchtime office 'synagogues' for London professionals, improvising a space to make sure that the people who needed to recite Kaddish could still do so even if they worked in corporate city jobs. In the Orthodox tradition, you need a minimum of ten men present for Kaddish, so people pull together.

The Kaddish is the soundscape of grief. It marks that strange lost time after a death, over and over again.

'That's so funny,' Sally said to me when I told her about the experience of choosing the music for my dad's funeral. 'I never thought about planning the music for a funeral, or even planning a funeral, because there's a structure. You just do it. Well, I guess the family could decide who's going to read each prayer. But that's it.'

Matty continued: 'At the service, you can see who's saying Kaddish, and you can just tell from their body language who's just lost someone, and who's coming to the end of that year of mourning. It's totally beautiful.'

'How much of the language in the service generally do you actually understand?' I had a vague memory Hebrew gets taught for the bat mitzvah and bar mitzvah.

'Not a fucking word,' he said expansively, and grinned. 'Obviously. And it's like, biblical Hebrew.' Serious again, he said, 'It's not about that, though. It's just rooted so deep, knowing these sounds have been repeated for centuries. Knowing how many people have said them, what it ties you to. It's really moving. In fact, I took a friend of mine to the synagogue a couple of weeks back – the Friday service, the one we're doing for the school thing – he'd never been before, and that was the thing he talked about. He was so moved by the music, by the sounds. It's that sense of history and depth and connection.'

'We'll nail that call and response today,' said the rabbi. 'I don't know *what* happened last week.' He shook his head in mock dismay.

I was in a bright, airy hall. In a synagogue for the very first time, being addressed by a tall rabbi who wore black jeans, an untucked pinstripe shirt and a black cardigan with oversized buttons. It was a few months after my conversation with Matty, and this particular synagogue had come with his seal of approval. 'I've worked with them before.' This was not the kind of synagogue where they do the Kaddish three times a day. This was a Liberal Synagogue, affiliated with Liberal Judaism.

A clear blue day, 10.45 a.m. and I'd parked my bike outside a red brick building tucked behind the main road. I'd never noticed the synagogue before, even though I pass by all the time. Another dimension of life, belief, experience, right in plain sight.

The first person I had encountered after I was buzzed into the lobby with its anonymous Dettol-dry scent was a child dressed as Spiderman – 'Spider*girl*,' she corrected me – putting paid to my concern that I wasn't dressed smartly enough for Shabbat.

In this service, the line between speaking and singing seemed fine. Spidergirl's mother – denim dungarees, Breton shirt – had shown me where to get a copy of the Siddur, the prayer book, from a bookshelf outside the sanctuary, where the service was held. She'd had the good sense to pass me on to the steward, who had a nose ring and told me not to worry, everything was pretty self-explanatory, but he'd be on hand to help if I got stuck or lost. I took a seat near the back and discovered that mostly it was just about turning to the right page when the rabbi told us to, although I fell at the first hurdle by opening the book from what I thought was the front, and discovering all the numbers ran backwards. Hebrew is read from right to left. Two columns, Hebrew on the right, English translation on the left, and I noticed a little musical note symbol on the pages that indicated the sung passages.

A lot of the service was sung, beautiful ancient melodies, modal scales, stepwise motion, unaccompanied. Some melodies were sung solo by the rabbi, in Hebrew. The rabbi's voice was an open baritone; his singing always the most prominent. Other melodies were sung all together, in unison. But we'd hit a moment where something more complicated was going to happen: a call and response between the rabbi and the congregation. The rabbi held a note while the congregation responded below it. 'Hallelujah', 'Hallelujah'. Once I got the hang, I hummed along a little with the Hebrew, joined quietly on the 'Hallelujah's, the only Hebrew word I recognised.

'You're the musicologist!' the rabbi had beamed, coming over to greet me before the service started. When I'd first come in and scanned the room, I hadn't been able to pick him out as the man in charge. Only when the service began did he put on his tallit, a shawl that he folded and refolded into different arrangements as the service progressed. He explained to me that sometimes they have a choir, but not today; maybe I'd like to come back on a day when the choir was in.

Safe to say, it was not at all like I'd imagined it, in so far as I'd been able to imagine it at all: a service perhaps all in Hebrew, in a dark hall that I'd be anonymous within, something alienating and hard to follow. Maybe there'd be incense? I realised I had been imagining a High Anglican church service. Instead, everything was bright, painted white, royal blue carpets and pew cushions, with the cool morning light from arched windows on each side of the pews infusing the space. Flowers – white and pink roses, holly, red berries – flanked the bimah, which I learned later was the name for the raised platform from which the rabbi gives a sermon, and everyone was doing their best to make sure I knew what was going on. Some parts of the service – those where members of the congregation were involved – felt somewhat under-rehearsed, and the result was just this side of shambolic. 'Well, that went perfectly!' the rabbi announced dryly after the semi-chaos of several members of the congregation helping to take the Torah out of the ark to be read was over.

The Kaddish came at the very end of the service. At this particular synagogue, the rabbi explained, the whole congregation stands for and participates in the prayer, and they name the people they are remembering before they start. In contrast, at more Orthodox synagogues he'd attended, only those in mourning – in the first year, or marking the Yahrzeit, the anniversary of the death – stand and say the Kaddish. He said that he had felt rather exposed when he'd had to do that. This way, no one feels exposed, and they do it together.

The rabbi asked everyone who they were remembering, and then he checked in with the online attendees. Someone mentioned three people, their over-amplified voice jolting the hall.

And then the congregation stood together, and spoke the Kaddish. Movement as one, the motions that make a community. I turned the pages of my Siddur, and felt a nudge, and an open book appeared from behind me: I'd misheard the page number. First, there was a brief reading from George Eliot's *Middlemarch*, about how we are inspired to live better by those who have died, and honouring the unremembered who came before us. This was one of five meditations printed in the Siddur to set the tone before the Kaddish.

I listened as the congregation spoke the Aramaic of the Kaddish. As with the other prayers, a few more confident people were speaking it along with the rabbi. It was clear that this was a text familiar to the congregation in its repetitions, its rhythms. Spoken in this old tongue, letting us fall, circling round and round, through the ages.

I could hear birdsong outside, and the mewing of a tiny baby at the back of the pews.

Immediately afterwards, the rabbi announced that – unusually – we were going to read it again in English. I had the sense that this was for my benefit.

This time, I read along.

It was then that I realised it was the Yahrzeit. How hadn't I noticed? By complete coincidence. Murmuring those words, not quite sure what it meant that I was joining in. It didn't matter to me at all that it was about the glory of God; it could have been about anything. I was just glad of the chance to mark the day, together with others, to be a part of a long, long history of remembering the dead, saying these words, reminding ourselves that they matter. My dad died this very week. I didn't raise my voice to give his name, given my unusual position as participant/observer. But I knew that it mattered that I was here, and that if I had said his name, people would have cared. People might have asked me about it afterwards, as the rabbi suggested. Check in with the people who name someone. He even suggested some opening lines to use on the grieving. 'How are you doing?' or the more traditional: 'Wishing you a long life.'

I've been brought up non-religious. I don't believe in God. And yet, this touched me all the same. I felt it somewhere unconscious, this speaking and repetition. The knowledge that these same words have been said to honour those who have left us, over and over again through the centuries. It's the connection to deep history, generations lost, forgotten, that is comforting. A connection that happens in your body, as you stand together, speak together.

But as I read the Kaddish in English, I didn't know if I was allowed to feel like I belonged. And then the service was over and we were encouraged to go downstairs to mingle, and enjoy wine and bread together. This, I learned, is called Kiddush, and happens on Shabbat and on Jewish holidays.

As it happened, downstairs was a community hall-type room. The wine was served in shot glasses, already poured and waiting for us on a side table. We drank it down in one swig. I chatted with people, mostly about music. A tall man who'd been involved in bringing out the Torah dug in his bag to show me a book he was reading about George Harrison. 'I wanted to play you something,' said another man with a shock of curly hair. He got out his phone, and he introduced me to Israeli singer Lior Elmaleh, and played me a track from the Orchestre Andalou d'Israel. He was enthusiastic about how Middle Eastern scales use micro tones – the notes sounding between the semitones that construct a Western scale. We both leaned in, trying to catch the sound of Elmaleh's voice over the chatter of the congregation, the chatter of Kiddush.

And now the gathering was transitioning, tables were being folded away, turned on their backs, legs in the air. Several members were gearing up for a Hebrew class. I said my goodbyes. When I left, I unlocked my bike, and I felt like I could do anything in this bright early spring day. I got a rhubarb and custard brioche from the café across the road, and as buses blared past, I ate it in the calm of the sunshine.

Of course, we didn't have a Jewish funeral.

We didn't sit shiva, and we didn't get to say the Kaddish for a year, our community knowing to treat us gently in that year of shock. We didn't have a fixed date to lay a headstone, the anniversary of the death, as the Jewish faith provides. So Dad's ashes sit in the stiff green box from the crematorium, on top of the piano in Mum's hallway, and we don't talk about it. No one organised our time, organised our sound in that first year of grief.

Instead, we had a poem about aesthetics, and time, and love, which I'd had no interest at all in getting to the bottom of. A different soundscape of grief. One that was only accidentally religious.

We ended our funeral on the metronomic sunshine of Albéniz's 'Sevilla', flamenco ornamented with citrus arpeggios as we placed white roses on his coffin. At the time, I didn't notice the connection between the piece and the trip Dad had mentioned the week before he died, but it was right there.

We all got giddy, sad, nothing-matters drunk in a pub garden afterwards while a Scottish photographer, an old, old, friend from a time in my dad's life I didn't know, told stories I'd never heard of journalistic assignments in Ayrshire with my dad in their twenties. He did excellent impressions of my dad's English accent. 'Eauw, helleaw Stewart!'

I was very sick in the bathroom in the night.

Chapter 4

OBLIVION, WITH NADIA BOULANGER

The Parisian musician Nadia Boulanger was a composer, a conductor and a world-class pianist and organist – as well as being probably the most famous music teacher of the twentieth century. For her, music was a way to take yourself out of the linear experience of time. This was part of why it was so profoundly important to those who grieve. 'Nothing is better than music' she wrote in 1919, shortly after both the First World War and the untimely death of not only her twenty-four-year-old younger sister Lili, a precocious compositional talent, in 1918, but also the sudden death of her lover Raoul Pugno in 1914, '– when it takes us out of time, it does more for us than we have any right to expect: it has expanded the limits of our sorrowful lives ... bringing us pure and new towards what was, towards what will be, towards what it has created for us.'

Music, Boulanger believed, allows us to step outside of time, but this isn't Denise Riley's sense of breaking from time. For Boulanger, it's something else, something restorative. Something reparative. Something almost religious. *It does more for us than we have any right to expect.* In the way that it gives us a moment in which all moments are contained, in which a sense of a present moment is prolonged; an extended present in which we mess with time, depart from the deadly and inflexible rules of loss. I thought again of those vertiginous opening lines from Eliot's 'Burnt Norton', where past, present and future are collapsed together like the sort of Russian doll Escher might have made if he'd turned his hand to Russian dolls, and I thought I knew what Nadia was talking about. And – just maybe – the bloody T.S. Eliot was starting to make sense too.

Boulanger's meditations on what music does to our sense of time are echoed in current academic thinking. Music is understood to create an extended present that can disorient your feeling of time passing; some describe it as a time-within-time that we experience within music. Psychological and cognitive research, some of which involves examining which parts of the brain are active when we are timing durations or events, and some of which is based on reported perceptions (such as the impact of factors like tempo or tonality on listeners' perceptions of time), suggests that perception of time while listening to music is complex, and may be different to time perception in other parts of our lives. My musicologist friend Lola, who we'll meet later (she has her own reasons for researching music and loss), has written, 'music is the experience of the present moment. Truly immersive and concentrated listening/performance is one in which the subject loses track of extra-musical time: the pace of a musical piece momentarily replaces the time-space continuum of everyday life.' She adds: 'Music can refer to the past, but unlike linguistic syntax, it cannot create a past tense.'

Boulanger was born to very musical parents. Her father was a composer and conductor; her mother, a Russian singer, as well as being a princess. Both Nadia and her younger sister Lili became stellar composers, studying at the Conservatoire de Paris. In 1913, at the age of just 19, Lili was the first woman to win the hugely prestigious Prix de Rome composition prize – nearly a unanimous judges' choice, facing much older, male competitors; Nadia had claimed second place for one of her works a few years previously, in 1908. Winning the Prix de Rome ran in the family: their father had won it in 1835. He died when the girls were still little. But while Lili was brilliant, she was also sickly, in chronically ill health and often in pain since a childhood bout of pneumonia. She died aged twenty-four of intestinal tuberculosis.

After Lili's death, Nadia gradually gave up her composing ambitions, focusing on conducting and teaching, and going on to outlive Lili by more than sixty years. She became a one-woman finishing school for composers of all stripes, who came to study with her in Paris at the Fontainebleau School of Music. She was the generator powering the music industry with talent from Quincy Jones to Philip Glass, Aaron Copland, Elliott Carter, George Antheil, Daniel Barenboim, Marion Bauer, Leonard Bernstein, Thea Musgrave, and even Astor Piazzolla, the Argentinian composer and virtuosic bandoneon player (a kind of button accordion) who wrote 'Oblivion', one of the tangos left on my dad's music stand. Some say that in so doing, she changed the face of twentieth-century tango, encouraging Piazzolla to regenerate a musical form that had fallen out of favour in the 1950s and 1960s, rather than emulating the neoclassical style favoured by modernist art music composers. She told him to write what he loved. To stay true to himself. She taught so many of the twentieth and twenty-first century's notable composers and conductors, it's almost easier to draw up a who's who of people she didn't teach, especially if we're talking about Americans. Everyone wanted lessons with her; everyone wanted to see what impact her mind could have on their music.

It's impossible to untangle Nadia's own musical creativity, her musical life force, from her relationship with the death of her sister, the rising star composer, so tightly were the two braided together. A dual tale of talent promised and left unfulfilled. Especially after her death, Lili was often idolised, approaching sainthood. A contemporary wrote of Lili's life having two stories: 'there is the story of a child of 24 years who has died without having hardly ever ceased to suffer, and the story of a genius that, in order to reveal itself, chose this fragile and charming body.' Within five years of Lili's death, Nadia had given up composing. She told her contemporaries 'the music I have written is useless. Not even badly done, useless!', while teaching virtually everyone you've ever heard of to exceed their own expectations, to write better music. It's hard to know what the music of the last century would be without her hand on the tiller.

'The thing is, Nadia really *idealised* her sister Lili,' Jill Rogers told me from her home in Bloomington, Indiana. Jill is a musicologist who has written a book about music and trauma in France just after the First World War, in many ways an obvious time to explore music as a way of processing mass grief, given the sheer volume of loss people were experiencing. She is especially interested in the emotional experience of music. She's been to many archives and studied a lot of letters and notebooks, as well as the music of both Boulanger sisters. Her voice has the quality of focused sunbeams, and I could see her mind overtaking the speed with which she could get her words out.

Jill explained that Nadia had a particular conception of her sister. 'It doesn't matter whether or not this was actually true to Lili.' In part, it had to do with the idea of the *femme fragile*, which people have argued worked to Lili's advantage as a composer in a thoroughly male domain; such fragility made her talent seem less threatening to male competitors and critics; if she'd had a tougher image, she mightn't have managed to have the success she did. (Which may explain her older sister Nadia's comparative lack of success in winning prizes: was she too challenging to gender expectations?) 'And one of the things I think Nadia really idealised about her sister was Lili's selflessness.'

After Lili died, Jill explained, Nadia started not only taking on all of Lili's projects, but doing so specifically in the ways that Lili had done. Nadia started to adopt the way that Lili had talked about things, or the way that Lili wrote, right down to how Nadia started to write things down in her date book, in a style quite different to Nadia's writing prior to Lili's death.

'What I argue she was trying to do was to resemble her sister.'

This brought me up short. *She wanted to embody that selflessness she saw in Lili*, I thought. She took on all of Lili's priorities. I'd been distantly aware of the possibility that after my father's death I'd been embodying his values, his preferences, but I'd been avoiding thinking about it. Do we start to mimic them, take on their characteristics and values as a way of staying close to them? I had read somewhere that daughters tend to drink more after fathers die for exactly this reason. I certainly did. My favourite café got a well-timed alcohol licence so I could segue seamlessly, come 3 p.m., from flat white to white wine. The time that the edge badly needed to come off the day, to come off the feeling of existing. It was a fuck you to the professional responsibilities that still seemed to be piling insurmountable and alien around me, after the unimaginable had happened. A couple of weeks after the funeral, for several consecutive days I had dragged myself on to the university campus to mark undergraduate exams, still wrapped up in my funeral scarf, and was so angry that this was required that I went to the student bar at lunchtimes. I only had a half-pint, but it was a gesture towards how utterly unfathomable it was that I still had to do these things. I wasn't in a fit state to be marking anything.

I was my father's anger. I drank two cans of Stella Artois on the train home to south London from the university. Life was unbearable. I wanted nothing to do with it. I rejected it. I came home one day and inexplicably I wanted to smash all my housemate's ordered spotty mugs, hanging from their neat hooks in the kitchen. The world was unbearable. I was my father's anger at the world. I was my own anger. I didn't know where, if there was, a distinction.

I was angry with my dad for dying and making me this way, and I was angry with everything for being like this. No one had told me. No one had told me this was an option. No one had told me it could happen to me. By which I mean, I hadn't believed things like this happened, apart from to unlucky, tragic families who somehow belonged to a parallel universe. It wasn't the normal order of things.

Is it possible to want to be your father and bitterly rebel against the system and its structures, against male authority, all at the same time?

Jill's voice brought me back from these thoughts, telling me how invested Nadia was in music. 'I think her understanding of music was that it kept people who had died alive and present.'

Jill had a compelling theory about why Nadia really gave up composing within five years of her sister's death, one she hadn't published because she didn't have quite enough primary evidence to support it. She leaned towards her laptop. 'For Nadia, in order to truly embody what she understood as Lili's spirit, she had to give up composition. That's what I really think is happening.'

This was fascinating. I had known that Nadia gave up composition after her sister's death, but hadn't had a good sense of why. It had just seemed like a waste to me. Nadia had

had huge compositional success; why would she stop? Why didn't she go on to become one of the leading composers of the twentieth century in her own right? Why, instead, dedicate her life to teaching and to nurturing talent? I wondered what the loss of Lili had done to her.

Jill explained that she thought Nadia felt too guilty that Lili had died. She asked me whether I knew the songs that Nadia wrote after Lili's death. I admitted that I didn't. Nadia wrote six songs after 1918, all of which dealt with topics such as unrequited love, solitude and emotional pain, for instance 'Le Couteau' and 'J'ai frappé'. 'They are *dark*. With loneliness and *despair*.' Jill's voice landed hard on 'despair'. 'They don't have that narrative of darkness to uplifting victory that was so popular during the First World War.' By contrast, Lili had been deploying that same darkness-to-uplift narrative right up to her very last composition, the 'Pie Jesu', which she dictated to Nadia from her deathbed. Lili seemed to stay positive even as she knew it was the end. The contrast with Nadia's songs, all written in the 1920s, right after Lili died, is strong. 'I also think music composition became so difficult for Nadia because it was something that showed Nadia her own limitations in embodying Lili's spirit. She couldn't be as hopeful as Lili, so she felt she was failing.' Nadia struggled with accepting death peacefully, as she thought Lili had. 'So she gave up composition in order to twofold more resemble Lili.' To be more selfless, to self-sacrifice, in the idealised way she thought Lili had, devoting herself to things that served other people, like teaching – and because she found that she couldn't emulate Lili's optimism in her music, anyway.

At thirty-one, I supposed I was too old for my dad dying to officially be really tragic, and at sixty-eight, so was he. Equally, though, few people close to me had been through it before. While I was the guinea pig with whom some of my friends learned to respond to other people's grief, I was also old enough that my peers were reasonably mature, had seen something of the world and of human emotion. Even if few had lived it first-hand, many had by now at least one experience of another's grief, so I wasn't getting too many of the hurtful it's-too-sad-I-don't-know-what-to-say-or-do errors that my younger friend told me she experienced when her mum died. For several months her twenty-two-year-old peers, still nervy and coltish, gave her a wide berth.

Sometimes people's words were unhelpful. Over Brazilian food, noisy restaurant, candlelight studding the tables, someone told me about her grandfather's death, and how her own mother had later been grateful it was swift. I had to stop her. This was making it worse. I was livid at the suggestion that I relate to her mother, and I was in no place to look for any positives in the suddenness with which my father had died because it was still too fundamentally outrageous. He was fine and then he was dead. She didn't understand what I felt as the acid of her normality. In trying to connect, she became further away, receding behind the sliding door of my pain and anger. Such interactions solidified the borders between where I was and where they were; between what they understood, could communicate – so often rooted in the deaths of grandparents – and the hugeness, the hereness of what I was experiencing. Abstractly, they knew the idea, but so little of the terrain. And I knew they'd be joining me one day: I just needed to wait. For now, though, I was here without them, nursing a drink, wondering when to get out the canapés.

I visited friends in Oxford and I insisted on sleeping alone, on having the single bedroom if there was one going or, if that wasn't possible, then certainly not sharing a bed in some laissez-faire communal sleepover fashion, because I didn't want anyone near me, let alone to touch me. In the end, when after a wedding five of us camped for a night in my friend's bedroom, two in the bed, I slept under the desk in a sleeping bag in an effort to be as far away from everyone else as possible. We went to a narrow pub garden together the next day. A jazz quartet was playing under a gazebo, *Real Book* jazz standards. Duke Ellington's 'Caravan'. A middle-aged white man was on the guitar. His hands moving, familiar patterns on the fretboard. I asked if we could leave, drink somewhere else, afraid I would break.

Unfortunately for both parties involved, when my dad died I had a new boyfriend. Let's call him Ramin. I'd been seeing him for just under three months. In this new reality, Ramin's presence had become largely intolerable, punctuated by encouraging-feeling blips of wanting him around, but I couldn't predict when they would come, and this became a new source of stress. He was still on the planet where our relationship was a green shoot, where we had responsibilities to one another; I was now far away, my planet remote and barren. I gravitated towards people with dead parents. In so far as it was a decision, it was semi-conscious. Some things only played well with this new crowd. For instance, if you heard of the sad death of the mother of a colleague in her sixties, in my new pack, you could say: 'How dare she still have two parents at her age?' and people would think it was hilarious. Quite a different reception awaits if you try it with the wrong audience, as I did over pizza one night. A startled hush, my implied pain and the question of whether they would be so lucky blanketing the table like new snow no one knew how to disturb.

The relationship with Ramin came to its inevitable end. Three months could not withstand the force of what had happened. I was furious he needed anything from me at a time when I had nothing to give.

Like a new weather front, a kind of radical sanity that might have been madness had arrived, and who knew for how long it would settle. Helpfully, for all sorts of things, everything now felt utterly meaningless. My job. Organising a conference. Going to events I didn't want to go to. Staying at events I didn't want to be at. The fact that making a certain kind of small talk with taxi drivers felt prohibited. I wanted to know people's deepest fears and whether they loved their dogs.

Or maybe I just wanted to be my dad.

In her book, Jill explains that for Boulanger, musical performance was a means 'to recall the presences of those that exist only in our pasts, and to imagine, with them, a better future beyond the pain of the present.' These feelings I was having, these ideas are not new. Boulanger was writing at a time of profound and senseless loss, at a time when she and her friends and colleagues were dealing with many griefs, many traumas, and turning to music to help them. Playing music – quartets, trios – that let them believe their loved one was still in the room. Playing alone, even, and imagining, remembering those people who once filled in the other parts, in sync, in time together to make a harmonious whole. Lines that could never sound quite the same played by anyone else. Musician soldiers wrote of using music to recreate their friends: 'I have my flute with me – I enjoy practising a little and recreating [my former] roommates.' These were people who had seen the war close up, on the battlefield, or working in hospitals. A buttoned-up culture, unable to say much about grief, for fear of undoing their wartime heroism. But music could still be therapy. Respite for minds frayed and scattered by the sounds of constant bombardment.

Boulanger thought that 'a person's music is inseparable from his or her soul', and this was why it had such a profound effect on the grieving. Music reanimated the feeling of being in someone's presence. It was impossible to extricate it, its existence, from the musician who created it, whether musician, composer, or both. 'There's this letter Nadia writes to Stravinsky,' Jill said. 'I forget what piece it was, but she tells him, "Whenever I hear this piece, you were there with me."' Jill didn't think that for Nadia this was metaphorical; instead music really did take on this ability to allow her to truly feel that people were there. Religion mattered here: Nadia was a devout Catholic, and Jill mentioned the significance of physical objects within Catholic grief and its practices. 'I'm thinking about relics, but also prayer cards – these were things that people kept as a material memento of the person.'

It seemed like music was a sort of immaterial-material memento.

But the picture of Nadia's ideas about music and grief got stranger still. Occult beliefs about where people's spirits went after their death were a normal part of early twentieth-century French life. Spiritism, the practice of attempting to continue contact with the dead through mediums and seances, had been hugely prevalent in France in the nineteenth century, and it was enjoying a resurgence after the First World War.

'I think from a contemporary perspective we look at it like, "it's just goofy seances: whatever. Charlatanism." But people really believed it. And so that tendency to think that spirits lived on after someone died was being scientifically—'

'—researched.' I finished her sentence.

'Real research into afterlives,' she continued. 'And then I loved finding in the archives these guides on how to recall a spirit. They're these little pamphlet-sized booklets—'

'Like those ones during the war called things like "How to Put on Your Gas Mask"?'

'Yes, exactly,' Jill laughed. 'But more "How to Raise the Spirit of a Loved One". "How to Speak with the Dead". Step by step. I love how much it was about sensory experience. You were supposed to use objects from the person to try to recall them. If the pamphlet writer had talked about music, he would probably have suggested something like putting on a record.'

This understanding that sensory experience was the key to manifesting a dead loved one is vital. 'I do think all this comes from all the discourse these folks were living in – like Marcel Proust and Henri Bergson,' – Bergson was a very famous French philosopher who wrote a lot about time, memory and perception – 'that is to say, contemporary ideas of how memory worked and how music, and sensory experience more broadly, was something that could really allow you to embody the past.' Nadia probably went to Bergson's lectures – her friends certainly did – and she included Bergson's ideas in her own lectures.

In Bergson's concept of *la durée* – time not as it appears on the clock, but the eddies and flows in the speed of how we live and experience it – he theorised moments in time as made up of, influenced by, everything that we have experienced before that moment, and everything that we know or don't know that will happen after.

'And like everyone else around then, she would have been reading Proust's *In Search of Lost Time*. Bergson and Proust were real cultural touchpoints for a lot of people.'

The French author Marcel Proust comes up a lot when people talk about sensory memory, and about how music can instantly bring to mind specific moments from our pasts. Leaf through the opening of his *In Search of Lost Time*, and you'll find his famous motif of the taste of the madeleine dipped in orange-blossom tea that not only immediately recalls his childhood, and specific memories of spending time with his aunt Léonie, but whose status as metonym for this mammoth work of literature also reveals how little people quoting from it have generally read, myself included.

Both Jill and I would have been hard-pressed to find a madeleine, or indeed orange-blossom tea, in our childhoods. But Jill mentioned she had an equivalent: a particular pear-scented body lotion. 'Whenever I smell it, I know exactly where I was. I think music is something that does this too. In fact, Proust talks about this – there's a particular melody that gets associated with his love interest in the book. Whenever he hears the melody, it conjures her for him.'

She thinks that in this way, music is a subset of the capacities of broader sensory experience, including sound, taste and smell. 'And that's where we get the idea that the experience of remembering a loved one is deeply embodied.'

I could see where Nadia was coming from, and it was clear that Nadia was a person of her time, shaping her understanding of music, time and grief from all the ideas and the theory around her. Was I, were we, really so different? Because all this discussion of spiritism and turn-of-the-century seances was a stark reminder that my own relationship with music is conditioned by the time and place I grew up in. I don't believe music *really* connects us to the spirit of the dead, in the way Nadia did, but then again, in early twenty-first century London, with its secularism and post-Enlightenment rationality, you'd have to venture quite far off the beaten track to find circles in which spiritist ideas were accepted (although London being London, there's no doubt that you would find them, and probably quite quickly if you knew where to look). Today, we're more likely to think of 'using' music to control our grief, within a world-view where we tend to think of everything as something we exploit for individual gain, as we shape ourselves in this era in which the illusion of our uniqueness is paramount. But there are other ways of thinking.

Later that day, as I chopped an onion for a pasta sauce, my watering eyes reminding me not of a childhood aunt, but of my mother first teaching me to fry onions on holiday in Pembrokeshire, I came back to the idea of wanting to re-enact the person you'd lost. My mind went to my rejection of music. Had I taken on my father's opinions about music? When I thought I was being authentically myself, seeing through all the bullshit to the hard, bright core of reality? My father's relationship not necessarily with classical music, but its bourgeois spaces, concert hall culture, had been troubled at best. I never once went with him to a classical concert, unless he was there because I was playing in it. Jazz, yes, but classical music: no.

Chapter 5

THE RIGHT INSTRUMENT FOR YOUR CHILD

If he wasn't there, who was I? It was the question I couldn't escape, as I allowed my sense of self to be absorbed into the television maze, where it didn't matter who I was anyway.

I had been to Boston, to that academic conference, to New York. I had returned, and had put the television back on, and it stayed on, I think, until around the nine-month anniversary of his death, when an opportunity to decide who I was came about. I was shortlisted for a permanent job at the kind of university where the walls are made of old stone, as an assistant professor of music theory. (Those are the people who wear the bow ties.) This meant I was going to interview. Permanent jobs are the holy grail in academia. Friends joked that my job seemed mainly to involve applying for other jobs. It was a frighteningly accurate characterisation of the amount of redundant labour in the system. In academic musicology there's only the faintest possible chance of permanent employment, and many well-qualified people are running on hamster wheels. It makes a lot of people pretty sad.

I was going to have to think about music again. It was unavoidable.

I crawled from the sofa and went through the motions, because what else was there energy to do? I dutifully got out my folders of notes stored under the bed and made myself a temporary expert on a miniature by Chopin whose name I can't even bring to mind any more, let alone sing the melody, because grief hides your memories from you. All I have is a blurry image of sparsity on a single page of piano music, and a sense of acute sadness, and falling. Did I want this? Who knew? I'd have to work it out later. Follow the path, one step, then the next. Like sight-reading live for performance. With that same, sudden, manic adrenaline.

I made myself understand that piece's construction inside out. What Chopin was doing, and what subsequent theorists have suggested Chopin was doing with his unexpected harmonies: the course that harmonic river runs and why. How he was manipulating your expectations. So I could teach a fake lecture on it to other music academics. And so when they pushed me, tested the edges at the job interview – just another exam to pass – I would succeed. No one would know, no one would learn my secret. That this music intimidated me, because I was always afraid going near it would be the beginning of someone realising I didn't belong. Or that I wasn't quite smart enough to be someone I recognised as myself, someone other people recognised as me. To fill the shape that had been made for me. Or that I'd somehow made for myself.

I worked ten days' straight, papers strewn over my bedroom, the only space I had to myself in my flatshare. And after it was over, after I travelled home, I lay broken on the carpet, numb and slightly hot with the clammy beginnings of a sickness that was pure exhaustion.

I hadn't realised when my dad was alive that none of this, my life, my academic ambitions, would make any sense when he wasn't.

There's a joke – or maybe it's a parable – attributed to David Foster Wallace I heard recently about two young fish happily swimming along. They pass a senior fish, who says: 'Morning boys, water's nice today,' and the pair keep swimming, until eventually one turns to the other and says, 'What the hell is water?' Well, water was my dad. Gravity was my dad. He was a prerequisite for existence, so much so that I didn't, couldn't know that the point of doing all this was him, because he was always there. I genuinely had no idea he was the lynchpin that held this particular dream, academia, together.

And then one terrible morning, the water dried up, and I was gasping on the shore, seeing, suddenly, all the same things that had always been there with a deadly clarity.

No one got that job. They later pulled it, citing financial rethinking and insecurity as a pandemic dawned.

I put all my notes and the scores back under the bed.

I still did not want anything to do with music.

*

Did you know?
Nine children out of ten could succeed in learning a musical instrument!
The Right Instrument for Your Child (1985), back cover

Around that time, someone sent me a black and white photograph they had found of my dad playing the violin as a child, sepia-toned, from around 1960. In the photo he is in profile, his hair combed into a severe side parting that echoes the line of his arm holding the bow; the creases in the shoulder of his tweed jacket – too adult on his frame – show the discomfort of this position. His glasses have black frames. He is dressed like a history professor, but he looks about twelve, or younger. I suspect the photo is staged as it's formal in subject and construction, but I can't be sure. Nor can I be sure if it was taken at home or at school. It's the only photo I'd ever seen of him with a violin. I'd almost forgotten he'd ever played it. I don't imagine he had a lot of choice in the matter.

This isn't an image that's about the pleasures of music-making. It's about mid-century discipline and mid-century discomfort. Stiff line of the jacket, around his elbow, reaching towards the bow. When I look at the photo, I feel sad.

Children like my dad had to learn the self-reliance of adults quickly. In all the childhood photos I've seen of him, he's staring fixedly away from the camera, as if he's been told to, or as if in his mind he's not really there.

My dad went away to boarding school at the age of seven, part of a class and generation of children removed from their families too young. Living the spartan, loveless ideology of post-war England. This was the 1950s, that era of wasted pain and institutions and duty and austerity. It was thought to be the right thing to do. Boys were expected to be robust, unbreakable; if they weren't, they would be. It was simply a matter of time.

Your parents were not coming back for you. From now on, you would receive your parents in doses, mandated by someone else. A fate in which your parents conspired.

You learned quickly that crying wouldn't make them come back.

I don't really know anything about my dad's time at boarding school. He never talked about it, other than to indicate how much he hated it. I learned, without knowing what I was learning, not to ask about it. He was derisive, as if it were utterly irrelevant. So that's how I thought of it, if I ever thought of it at all. Irrelevant.

Occasionally, though, I saw glints of the sadness underneath. When he visited me at university he would remark on the moment of saying goodbye to your parents and it all being over, always too brief. I could feel a memory of the awful stiltedness of goodbye, of once again not being rescued. I didn't feel it as severance, though. I was in my twenties; I had an independent life, and so I didn't want to be given that knowledge of my father as vulnerable. The pain of recalling it now is fierce.

I cannot square this photo of my father and the violin with my memories of him playing the guitar, where he looked relaxed and focused.

Not long ago, I had lunch with Ol in the Waterstones café on Trafalgar Square.

'I was taken to a country house in the Cotswolds recently,' he told me, strongly implying that given the choice, he wouldn't have gone, 'and it took me right back to Warwickshire – it smelled exactly like your dad's parents' house,' he said. 'The carpets, the bookcases, the dust, the smell of polish, the iron boot remover.' I was right there, too. My grandparents' house. The entrance hallway, where they kept the piano. The heavy floral curtains and bowls of potpourri. 'I had this visceral reaction to it. I'm not sure your dad would have even crossed the threshold.'

I murmured assent, knowing this truth, both wanting to reject that world, all of it, out of loyalty to my dad, and feeling sadness at my dad's deep anger.

'Your dad hated anything that was "high culture". He was much happier taking your brothers to the cinema to see the latest *Iron Man*.'

I knew what Ol was getting at.

Ol told me that except for what Dad played on the guitar, he hated classical music.

I'm not sure this is true. I'm not sure the issue was high culture, classical music per se, but more attitudes surrounding it: the way he thought that the people who listened to it thought they were better than you. He was allergic to a certain strain of British intellectual snobbery: it made my dad furious. I know this because I can also summon these feelings, after a lifetime of absorbing them from him.

By the same token, though, my dad was furious about British strains of anti-intellectualism. This was a contradiction that, for him, ran right through the middle of his conflicted attitude to British culture. I don't know whether my dad understood that sometimes, people genuinely love classical music. They don't just love it because it makes them feel superior.

The same went for literature. Bourgeois spaces and institutions.

'Your dad came to my confirmation,' said Ol. 'Even though he was an atheist. I was really touched.' He divided the chocolate brownie we were sharing with a fork. 'He was into early Eliot, though. Like "The Love Song of J. Alfred Prufrock".

'"In the room the women come and go / Talking of Michelangelo",' Ol recited. 'Things that got that sense of being on the outside. Not feeling part of that world of drawing rooms and point-scoring intellectual small talk. A sense of inadequacy. An absolute lack of self-worth.'

'Feeling alienated,' I said.

Like my dad, I also learned the violin as a child, but quite differently. In the late nineties, in groups of six children crammed around three music stands in a room that doubled as musical instrument storage, near the assembly hall. I can smell the hard pine solvent edge of the rosin now, see how it would break up into shards in your case, puff into the air as you rubbed it on the horsehair of the bow, then creating more friction when the bow moved across the strings. The simple joy of *having* a violin case, something that was just yours, with its faux-velvet interior, closing the Velcro over the violin's neck, all that tactility. I want to go back there, pick one up, for a violin to be *mine* again, with my rosin and my neck rest in the storage compartment. All these things of my own.

The cool touch of the chin rest under your jaw, shoulder rest cushioning your collarbone, head tilted to the side. I haven't played the violin in over twenty-five years, but I am craving it. That hungry feeling of wanting an instrument, to possess it.

Rote-teaching violin is not actually a great way of getting children hooked on music, even if they do come in smaller sizes for smaller bodies. It's not a gateway instrument. The violin is physically uncomfortable, whether or not you are wearing a starched shirt and tweed jacket. This is something I first learned in a bible-like book my mum brought home from a charity shop when I was about ten titled *The Right Instrument for Your Child*.

The violin is a hollow box, made of thin, resonant wood, which amplifies the vibration of one or more of the four tensed strings. The player has to make the string vibrate by scraping sticky horsehair across them.

If that sounds to you like a difficult way of making music, then you are one step along the path to understanding why learning the violin is immensely hard and demands years of dedicated work.

The Right Instrument for Your Child was a book I *loved*. Being a musician seemed to be one of the greatest things you could be, and here was a book that demonstrated the value parents and teachers put on choosing a musical instrument. A whole book. It was in monochrome with just a touch of red, and I inhaled it. Practically slept with it under my pillow. It was filled with photos of children learning instruments in the early 1980s, and it taught readers – presumably parents, occasionally ten-year-olds – which personality types best fitted which instruments.

Unless your child is exceptionally conscientious and patient, it is unlikely that he or she will continue studying a stringed instrument to the point of any real achievement, which takes not months but several years.

Violins contort the child, gripped between the player's chin and collarbone.

suits the light and wiry gymnast or dancer ... particularly satisfying to girls who adore ballet.

The Right Instrument for Your Child illustrated the Ben-Tovim/Boyd System, named after the authors, which would help parents to establish The Right Instrument for Their Child. Or, in my case, help children to form unconscious and gendered beliefs about the sort of person they were. The thesis was that many children begin a new musical instrument with gusto, but quickly lose interest because they have chosen The Wrong Instrument. The Ben-Tovim/Boyd System, however, was here to help avoid such mistakes. It was alluring. It featured a flow chart. A mixture of music and a pop-psychology personality test, and thus addictive for those, like me, raised on 'Which Spice Girl Are You?' *Sugar* magazine questionnaires where you add up all your a's, b's, and c's, and learn important new knowledge about yourself as a unique individual: you are Sporty Spice! All through the process of a few simple questions. You did a series of tests on the 'Physical Suitability', 'Mental Suitability' and 'Personality Suitability' of your child, created what Ben-Tovim/Boyd called 'The Three Way Profile', finalised a 'Short List' and eventually, the test yielded the holy grail: 'The Right Instrument'.

Chapter One. How Musical is Your Child?

I remember doing musicality tests in school. You had to say whether a given note was higher or lower in pitch than the previous note, and make a small line in pencil on a multiple choice form that was then marked by a computer. Those tests I took were part of a long history of psychological testing for musicality, not all of it glorious. In fact, there's a significant historical association with eugenics. Eugenicists tried to measure musical talent as a means of showing that different populations, particularly racial groups, had different levels of innate ability. Once they'd supposedly proved this, it wasn't much of a leap to the conclusion that some groups were better than others, and most chillingly, that they therefore had different relative levels of humanity. Because what's especially interesting here is how easy it was to elide musical ability with a person's perceived humanity, and how little people noticed that this was a sleight of hand.

Alex Cowan is a friend of mine who researches how music and musicality were used to support eugenic ideologies in the United States, and he explained to me that this all stems back to the initial testing of hearing in the mid-to-late nineteenth century. At that time, scientists and psychologists hypothesised that a weak link existed between the ability to hear differences in pitch or durations or note intensity and the musical talent of their test subjects. By the early twentieth century, when these musicality tests were developed for mass dissemination in schools and even people's own homes, although the underlying science hadn't changed, that weak link had hardened in people's minds, now going unquestioned. Abilities to recognise differences in pitch, duration or the intensity of a note, for instance, became seen as innate qualities. But the testing was flawed: for one thing, this overlooked people's clear capacity to improve their performance on such tests with practice. Not only that, the tests were closely associated with the norms and standards of Western art music – classical music – giving a big advantage to children with existing training, or greater exposure to this kind of music. Hardly surprising, then, that when these tests were used to determine which children should be singled out and nurtured as musicians, the same inequalities of opportunity linked to race and economic background that existed across the population tended to be reproduced. And perpetuated.

After the Second World War, and in the wake of Nazi atrocities, scientists and psychologists largely, and rightly, took a careful step back from exploring human difference within a framework that suggested different groups had different levels of value.

Everything I read in *The Right Instrument for Your Child* solidified into unconscious doctrine, and one of those doctrines is that although all instruments might be different, and they might suit different sorts of musical ability, they were also all equal.

All except for one, that is. The oboe is, according to the authors, a poor choice for virtually everyone.

In the hands of an outstanding professional musician playing chamber or orchestral music, the oboe can sound exquisite. Played by most children who are learning, the sound is unpleasing and rasping, which offers limited encouragement to the player or to other members of the family within earshot. If your child is vaguely thinking about the oboe, or the school is trying to persuade her to take it up and play in the orchestra, there is only one word of advice: Don't!

It seemed either Ben-Tovim or Boyd (or both) had been seriously wronged by an oboist, and had never got over it.

Dubious personality profiling aside, it's quite a radical book, proposing that people should account for the fact that different instruments place different physical, mental and emotional demands on players, and yield different physical, mental and emotional rewards. Making music should be fluid. You need an instrument that provides as few obstacles between you and musical expression as possible.

And so, as a child of only medium levels of grace and patience, the violin was not to be The Right Instrument for me.

It was in that practice room where I learned the violin that I first discovered the beauty of the cello, because there were spare ones stored there you could loan from the school, promisingly enormous under their canvas shells, the bows a different size to the finer violin bow, a different kind of rosin needed for the bow hairs. *The Right Instrument for Your Child* sanctioned the switch.

If there is such a thing as a stringed instrument which is fun for beginners, this is it ... The initial sound is not discouraging, as it is on the violin.

I upgraded. I was in heaven.

In that room, I also learned the more utilitarian beauty of the trombone. Less tactile, but also less kit was required, which suited me better. Less faff. Getting it out, I didn't need to tune each string before I started. To rosin the bow. Just slot in the mouthpiece, and off you go.

You may not have thought about a brass instrument, yet the brass are the instruments of tomorrow for the vast majority of children.

Boys especially are drawn to these shiny powerful instruments, but increasingly girls, too, play the less aggressive, middle-sounding brass.

Looking back, it's hard to say exactly why I chose the trombone. If I got asked now, I'd say: because it was a bit different. Because it was surprising. Because I already had a sophisticated, if unconscious, grasp of gender, and gender subversion. Because I grew up in a household of boys. Any of the above, all of the above or none of the above: honestly, it was quite random, like so many of the contingent choices that steer your life. All I can say is I must have felt drawn to it somehow.

It had all begun when I had found a pamphlet on our kitchen table. It was about the instruments for which the Yorkshire music service offered lessons, and it was so exciting.

Percussion? 'But wouldn't it be nice to be able to play the tune?' Mum said, piloting me away from several years of parental torture. I wasn't letting them off the hook that easily: I instead set my heart on the harp (expensive). Luckily for them, within a matter of weeks we had left Yorkshire, moving right across the country to the south coast, and the harp problem evaporated, because my new school only offered group violin lessons.

Then we moved again, and I started another new school.

We were summoned single file to the hall one day to hear older children demonstrate some of the different instruments we might play, as we sat on a floor with black rubber plimsole marks you could rub off and that faint smell of washed-up peas and polish.

I left that session wanting to play the oboe. The child who had played the oboe had performed Scott Joplin's ragtime classic 'The Entertainer', and I knew 'The Entertainer', ergo I wanted to play the oboe.

Disaster loomed, according to the wisdom of *The Right Instrument for Your Child*.

When I later learned 'The Entertainer' on the piano, I couldn't stop playing it. I was an addict. Even now, writing about it, my hand maps out the motion on the computer keyboard, and I'm sure I haven't played it in twenty years. Thumb on the D, first finger up on the black note next to it, thumb crossing underneath, then reach, reach, reach for the C six notes above. Ping, ping, ping.

Once my parents learned how much oboes cost, I was gently dissuaded from that too, even though I don't think they yet knew the unequivocal position on the oboe maintained by *The Right Instrument for Your Child*. So it was to be my second choice from the demonstration day: the trombone.

Trombones were not expensive.

On the trombone, as on the violin, the player has to form each note, adjusting the position of the slide microscopically to give exactly the 'shape' of the note he wants.

This is very satisfying to an artistic or creative child.

Mum got me an ex-Salvation Army trombone through the free ads for £30. It was silver. People described it as a pea-shooter because it had an unusually narrow bore. Its slide was gunked up.

'Someone would have just put it on their wall,' said the man who sold it to us. 'Much rather it was being played.' The case was broken; my mum fashioned a circular lid out of industrial cardboard and gaffa tape. My mum is enterprising.

So: the trombone. Hello, wildcard second choice.

I couldn't quite believe I was allowed to play it. Such a strange and unfamiliar object, from a world I didn't know a thing about (what even was the Salvation Army?). Mine, though. I was allowed to play this, to be a part of whatever this was. I didn't know what it was. I pulled the silver instrument out of the case and put it together. All I knew was that you buzz on the mouthpiece to make a sound. Roughly how to hold it. And I knew a couple of notes, in first position, with the slide right in close by your face.

the brass instrument on which you come nearest to singing.

A sense of possibility, and a direction I hadn't anticipated at all. Where would this lead?

I had liked that the trombone was enormous. I liked the idea of something that big being mine. The expansiveness it implied. The fact it would take up so much of my bedroom. The novelty, the weirdness. Mine. This enormous thing: mine. Really.

This is the only wind instrument (that term embraces both woodwind and brass) which is possible for children with very poor finger control. The fingers do nothing except support the instrument and move the slide in and out.

I wondered who I would be.

It did feel like stepping into an identity. One of men, mainly. I had a vague sense that the kinds of men who played the trombone hung out in pubs; beery smoky men. People I wasn't.

I was picking up on the knowledge that I would be a novelty, but I was being encouraged. It wasn't usually an instrument for people like me, and yet I was being welcomed in with open arms. I felt cool and wanted.

It took a while for us to fall in love. I remember self-consciously carrying the instrument around, taking it to school. This is mine, this is what I'm learning. Somehow, this trombone is something to do with me. So it wasn't final; it was a shape I was trying on for myself. Did I like who I was? Did I like the school brass band, or did I want to be in the string ensemble? Did I like the people I sat next to?

Playing the trombone gives no outlet for the angry energy which makes a good trumpeter.

Most children who succeed on the trombone are quietly sociable, sensitive and artistic.

What does it mean if, ultimately, the right instrument for your child is the one that means you can hang out with the boys? Be one of them?

Almost, but not quite.

Before I was born, before he met my mum, Dad lived off the west coast of Scotland on his boat.

It is May 1980 and Dad, Stewart and – the man who does not yet know he will become my godfather – Ol are off around the Mull of Kintyre on Dad's 27-foot wooden yacht. Novices attempting the Scottish equivalent of the Cape of Good Hope. Fearless, young, overconfident. Taming tidal races. Stewart is a photographer, impish, he wears a Fair Isle jumper; he works with Dad on the paper, a regional Scottish one. Dad's glasses are hexagonal, with thin gold rims. I know these details because I have seen the photographs.

The weather is bad.

They moor overnight off Craighouse, Isle of Jura. A trawler ties up next to them, filled with the biggest, toughest Scots. Ol and Dad hate their public-school backgrounds and everything those backgrounds stand for. And in England those backgrounds are inescapable; you can be judged, no matter how much you resent what and where you've come from. But these Scots don't care: you're just English, and if you are OK, you are OK.

The fishermen invite them on board. A bottle of whisky emerges.

Several hours later, pissed, 'Go and get your guitar, Phil.'

Alone on deck, the wind hits Dad all at once, steely rattle of the stays, leg over the railings, one then the other, lurches into the cockpit, pulls open the cabin door a little too forcefully, hears the roar of the men on the other boat, mood ebullient like the sea. He collects the instrument, the floor gently churning from side to side, and he's back on deck, wind spreading sea into the darkness, the two bound boats an improbably tiny island, sky impenetrable, light spilling from the trawler's cabin.

On the trawler again, Dad starts up, playing the blues, and what comes out of his mouth is the unvarnished truth:

I work for Keith N. Jeffreys
and it makes me feel so lonely

It's a hit. 2 a.m. singalong, a boat full of drunk men chorusing 'I work for Keith N. Jeffreys', Dad's boss at the newspaper, over and over. Isolated, in the middle of the anchorage, the twentieth-century condition captured in two lines. The 'Keith N. Jeffreys Blues' is born.

Four hours' sleep, vast motors are shuddering. Bleary, Dad emerges on deck.

The weather is worse.

The fishing trawler is off; the men are going home.

'Where are you heading?' one shouts over the engines.

'We're off round the mull,' says Dad.

'Weather like this? You must be fucking mad.'

Dad, at the helm; Stewart, comatose in his bunk until midday; Ol, feeling violently sick. That's the under-slept but resolute crew, undeterred by this greatest of all Scottish nautical challenges. The plan: leave at dawn, circumnavigate the mull, reach Campbeltown before dusk. The reality: twelve hours at sea, the wind and tides against them, yellow rain macs done up tight and high as they will go. Perilous conditions. Visibility is terrible, fog plasters hair to foreheads, seeps into pores. They think they've done it, they're round, but then a car ferry crosses their path. There are no car ferries at the Mull of Kintyre. They are hopelessly lost. Ol gets out a road map. They are nowhere near; they are at the Isle of Gigha. They have made about a quarter of the distance they planned. They turn around.

'You're so fucking talented,' Ol would say.

Dad never saw the benefit of being good at the guitar. 'It doesn't solve anything. I don't have what you have, the only skill that counts. Being able to talk to people.'

As you may have guessed by now, my dad mostly lived in his head. It's not that he didn't see the world around him. He did. But it was all filtered through a watchful layer of cynicism.

His feelings were deep, and I felt closest to them when we talked about ideas.

My head is also where I feel safest, but I don't know whether this was the best place for me to set up home.

Perhaps he didn't spend so much time in his head when he was at sea.

But even then. It can be quite solitary. Maybe at sea he retreated there even further.

If you'd asked me how much impact my dad had on my life choices before he'd died, I would have said: *Obviously very little.* My dad was a rebel; I conformed. And yet. There was a current, everywhere at once, propelling my course. It was him who had once said, 'You might quite like academia, if you did it properly.' Implying that he, turning to it in his forties, sidestepping the need for a doctorate, hadn't.

He had no idea what he was letting me in for.

When small children tell you what they want to be when they grow up, they say 'firefighter'. Or 'doctor'. Or 'fairy-scientist-witch'. (That last one was actually a proposed Halloween costume, and a strong one at that, but I think the point stands. After all, my youngest brother was once keen to train professionally as a lion.) What they do not say is: 'musicologist'. So little-known is this profession that I didn't know what a musicologist was *even when I was doing an undergraduate degree in music,* that is, taking the first step in training to become a musicologist, in a building where your exposure to them is far, far higher than average: they are the people teaching you. And yet after I finished my undergraduate degree, this is what I found myself studying to become. Initially I had applied for a postgraduate degree intending to focus on trombone performance, but I changed my mind after I'd been accepted: after all, I was going to Oxford, an institution known for its academic strengths, rather than for developing skills on a musical instrument (and this time, returning to Oxford having left an undergraduate degree there, I knew better what I was getting myself into). My main focus became a dissertation, and learning my way around the discipline called musicology. Then, I went all in with musicology: I signed up for a doctorate.

Musicologist. I've always bristled at the word, worried that it will make people suspicious about the seriousness of what we do before we even get started. It puts me in mind of a four-year-old wearing a lab coat and daring people to laugh. It can't help but sound a bit made up. And sure, it is a science, like 'biologist', or 'psychologist', but only in the German sense of the word: *Wissenschaft*. Knowledge creation. Musicology sounds considerably less made up in German, where the discipline is called *Musikwissenschaft*, music science, science in the sense of knowledge creation, and the profession is 'music-knowledger'. But the English word 'science' just doesn't carry those connotations of knowledge and understanding. It takes you somewhere rather more clinical.

In a matter of a couple of years, musicology went from 'profession I had never heard of' to 'basis for entire sense of self and self-worth'. We call these worlds disciplines for a reason: they discipline knowledge, but they also discipline you.

I didn't exactly mean to, but with these new priorities, I stopped practising my trombone.

One evening, midway through my PhD, I found myself out with the boys. Again. It's not that there weren't any other genders in postgraduate musicology – there were plenty of options; rather it was that I craved male company, craved the sort of cool I mistakenly believed increased in proportion with how close I could get to being seen as one of them. I now understand that I held a subconscious belief that if I hung out with them, I too could still grow up to be able to have that easy James Bond authority men get when they walk into a room wearing a suit.

Beware your subconscious beliefs.

We'd just been to the Oxford music faculty colloquium, where an invited speaker, usually an academic, was hosted by the department to talk about their work, followed by crap wine served from a trestle table in the faculty building.

After the colloquium we mingled in the lecture hall, and I stood in a circle with some of these boys as they discussed how convincingly the speaker had or had not used Gilles Deleuze's theories within the argument in his paper.

Let me explain. It wasn't long after arriving in Oxford for postgraduate study that I learned that being good at musicology wasn't the same thing as being good at music. Instead, there were new ideas to get your head around, new ways of impressing people. And vast swathes of the discipline, especially – but not exclusively – at Oxford and at trendier London universities, were involved with knowing a lot about what's known as critical theory. Continental philosophy.

There's this topos, 'sexy France', to which younger male academics throughout the humanities were drawn in the early-to-mid 2010s, and possibly also before and since. People sitting around on floor cushions, smoking, wearing black roll-necks, discussing intellectual things. Maybe drinking, too – if so, a heavy red wine, or something chic and very alcoholic, but in a sexy French way. Absinthe, for instance. Women are an important element of this picture: they either wear no make-up, hair loose, or they wear black eyeliner and red lipstick, and they are sexy and French.

These men were, needless to say, a type: serious and erudite, with good cheekbones, often slightly underweight, and occasionally German. You could recognise them because they would name-drop people like Gilles Deleuze or his equally excellently named companion Félix Guattari, saying things like 'rhizomatic', and you would scramble on to the internet to speed-learn Deleuze's theories to some kind of passable conversational level. A tall order given that even the *Stanford Encyclopedia of Philosophy* admits that to explain Deleuze's work 'removes much of the performative effect of reading the original'.

All this in the name of impressing the kind of man who wore plaid shirts and interrupted you to tell you what you didn't know about feminism.

But to fit in, I needed to at least be able to nod in the right places in good conscience. I needed to seem like I, too, could belong in sexy France.

Recently, I had been regularly waking up in the bedroom of just one of these men, to the view of a volume of Rainer Maria Rilke conspicuously laid on his bedside table. A consequence of this entanglement was that I had become able to convincingly disguise myself as someone who cared about these obscure, but fashionable and important ideas, even though I hadn't yet worked out whether I actually did care about them. Another consequence was that in adapting myself to the ways of sexy France, I placed myself in someone else's fantasy. I now found myself fighting with these men who thought the world was infinitely categorisable, and that my use was in reflecting back at them their own brilliance, a dynamic with which, by learning about Deleuze, I complied. Annoyingly for my sense of self.

When we left the faculty building, inevitably the next stop was the pub. This one was down an alley off the high street and had dark wood tables and a beamed ceiling.

It was late. All the others had now dropped off, and I was the last woman standing. Straight men, a couple of more senior doctoral students, the speaker and a faculty member (they'd studied together in their youth), everyone older than me. I couldn't match the whisky they were drinking, which was Johnnie Walker Red Label, a penchant of the invited speaker, so I was on real ale, the slightly incongruous drink *du jour* (not everything we associated with knowing critical theory was strictly speaking French), and because no one was at the stage of sobriety where they could still convincingly posture about advanced continental philosophy, the conversation had regressed to somewhere these straight men found common ground. Not sport, but The Great Composers.

Specifically, one of them had kicked off an argument about which of The Great Composers, if our ship were sinking, we would be happy to throw off the metaphorical boat. The composers we'd do away with and never listen to again.

This could not be more stressful. In this kind of conversation, I was screwed. I could feel them all rolling up their metaphorical sleeves, ready to spar, to show off their already-developed big opinions like shiny medals and perform a kind of comprehensive knowledge for which my own doctoral topic, a deep-dive study of the sources around a set of six little-known symphonies in a particular year in the early 1930s, left me somewhat disadvantaged. Their kind of knowledge favoured the more trainspotting, collector-type of mind.

There was no way I could participate as myself. What was I doing here? I prayed this conversation would be brief, so I could go back to my identikit college room and the safety of the newest episode of *The Apprentice* on my laptop. Or possibly text Rilke-man and see if he was still up. But for now, time to walk the high wire.

Donizetti went early, ditched by our ringleader, the hosting academic. The subtext was arcane, but made sense to us: he was ribbing one of the current custodian quasi-godparents of the discipline, for whom Donizetti was a favourite.

'All orchestral music from Beethoven to Brahms.' A bold statement to get the ball rolling.

'You mean Liszt?'

'Yeah, Liszt, Mendelssohn, Schumann, Schubert. Could live without all of them.'

'What about Berlioz?'

'Well. Generally more trash, moments that make no sense, but much more imaginative than the rest. Could do without all Schumann's symphonies. Things only pick up again with Brahms.'

There was a pause as everyone processed this.

'Controversial, I know,' ventured someone else, 'but Shostakovich.'

This was actual heresy, going against every received musical opinion around greatness. 'Interesting,' another said. 'Someone once taught us that symphonies one to four are great, and then they got much worse around five, when Soviet control came in.' He shrugged. 'But actually, one to four aren't that great either.'

'Always Prokofiev over Shostakovich, surely?'

'Yes. Prokofiev one and five. Both fantastic.'

'Four is always weird, isn't it? No one writes a normal fourth symphony.'

My mind had gone blank. I badly needed to think of a composer I wouldn't have to work hard to justify never listening to again. I dared to make a suggestion. 'I could live without Elgar.'

'Well that goes without saying...' the ringleader said, loquacious now, eyes beginning to glass over. I worried that mine looked the same. 'We could *all* live without Elgar.'

I felt hot. I was a beat behind. I'd said something too obvious.

But I was afraid of saying something more controversial (Richard Strauss!). Because what if they pushed me? – *Why? Strauss is great!* – and my mind went blank, the facts were gone, they discovered I didn't have the information at my fingertips with which to justify my opinion.

This kind of conversation doesn't give points for linking ideas up in an interesting conceptual way. Or empathy.

'Well, all English music—' said another

'Do away with it all—'

'But save Holst's Suite in E-flat,' I tried.

'Yes, a formative musical experience for so many!'

Appreciative nods.

Thank fuck that landed, I was back in the game. I took a sip of my Hopping Hare to hide my relief.

'Maybe we change the rules so we're allowed to save one work before we throw them off the boat,' I said. 'And for Holst, it's the Suite in E-flat, the wind-band work beloved of fifteen-year-olds.'

'I don't think Holst would mind that, to be honest.'

'And save Vaughan Williams four,' said one.

'That's the symphony with all the brass at the beginning, right?' I wanted to prove I knew what I was talking about. This, worryingly, was precisely the area in which I was supposedly an expert.

He looked at me, his expression inscrutable. Was he making a performance of humouring me, or couldn't he read what I meant? Or had he already forgotten? '...Sure.'

'Haydn?' someone threw out.

This was something I could genuinely get on board with. 'Oh well,' I said, now emboldened. 'In that case, all music pre-1800.'

'What about Mozart, though?'

'He had his sights set on 1800.'

'He was dead by 1800.'

'Still, he was a very 1800 kind of composer,' I countered. I would have to style this out. 'Even if' – and this was only to make sure no one doubted whether I knew exactly when he'd died – 'he wasn't very productive after 1791.'

I finished my Hopping Hare and left not long after that. I didn't like ale all that much, either.

It wasn't long after the job interview that I sought therapy for grief. I spent afternoons in a room filled with patchwork throws and brass trinkets, where a tortoise (of course there would be a tortoise) hid in a darkened corner, and I quickly discovered I wasn't yet ready to talk properly about my dad.

When my therapist suggested I might think about writing a letter to him and reading it out in our session, I felt concrete close around my insides.

'Yeah, that might be a good thing to do at some point,' I said, while thinking, *Hard no, absolutely not*. I hoped she wouldn't mention it again.

It's obvious that you will feel awful when someone dies. What people don't tell you, though, is that what's coming might not be the expected emotion, that is, sadness. Perhaps it was no surprise that I got saddled with the emotion I was most uncomfortable with: anger. I was angry all the time. Having never been angry before, this was quite exciting. Everything was more colourful, more rage-filled, more exhausting. Everything felt in higher definition, even when things felt sleepy and low, bruised and empty.

My therapist was really into the idea that I might find my voice and strengthen my ability to set boundaries through music. 'But you used to sing,' she said. 'You could sing again.' *Why do people always hear I'm a musician and assume I want to play music?* I thought, angrily. *It's so lazy*. What I heard was that she wanted me to join an amateur choir or something. Why did no one understand? I was done with choirs. Music felt like work. Music, I thought, was something non-specialists like my therapist romanticised. But I had intellectually overcome the need to sing. In the last few years, when people asked what I did, I'd started describing myself as a historian, to avoid the hateful question: *What do you play?* To avoid being dragged into a conversation with someone well-meaning who wanted to enthuse about the jazz of the 1930s, who made me feel ashamed that I no longer felt those feelings too, but didn't know why, and couldn't admit it to myself.

Sure, something isn't working, but music isn't going to help me, I thought, resolute. I'd already tried music, and it had failed me.

Chapter 6

'ELEGY FOR MIPPY II' AND OTHER DOGS (MINE)

A piece of music that's punctuated my life as a trombone player is about a mongrel dog. 'Elegy for Mippy II, for trombone alone'. Specifically, it's about the mongrel belonging to Leonard Bernstein's younger brother Burton, part of a quintet of pieces for brass dedicated to specific dogs written in the late 1940s, and published in 1950. Burton had three successive dogs all, perhaps unimaginatively, named Mippy, hence 'Mippy II'. In 'Elegy for Mippy II', the musician takes the trombone for a walk, the instrument both perfectly in sync with the trombonist, and delightfully unruly.

I've always loved taking dogs for walks. Most opportunities came when I was at my grandparents'. I loved the intense connection between us (an intense connection I believed in wholeheartedly, even though these dogs were not mine) and I loved taking that into the outside world. Performing it. *Look at me, I'm walking a dog!* I loved all the responsibilities. The sense that there was important work to be done, and that you could organise your life around it, and that the information would all come neatly packaged in a 'how-to' book. *How to Care for Your Hamster* was my first foray into that genre (and I still remember the depth of feeling I had for the pictures, pictures I studied day after day, until the beloved hamster arrived). After that, I raided the books on looking after dogs at my grandparents' and at my local library. I had a hardback book with a torn dust jacket that had belonged to my great-great aunt about caring for poodles, perhaps from the 1940s, and I meticulously created pencil studies of the black and white photo inserts.

I sang a refrain familiar to many parents, my offensive carefully timed.

'*Please* can we have a dog?'

Mum deflected skilfully. 'When I was your age, I used to save up my pocket money for a Westie. But back then, you needed a dog licence.'

I figured it wasn't exactly a no. Mum related to my desire for a dog. I kept hoping.

We did not get a Westie, though, or any dog. Until. After. I. Left. Home.

Throughout 'Mippy', the musician taps their foot on the beat, rhythmically, marking time as the trombone bends those rules, skits up and down the register, glissandos all over the place; somewhere, I read someone describe the trombone as 'kept on a tight leash'. It's whimsical, soulful, sort of jazzy. It's a rare piece for solo trombone, just you and the instrument, together, alone, meandering, and the trombone plays with the beat. It croons, it sails, you hear a dog lolloping around. A good player gives it attitude. It ends with four solo foot taps from the player, answered by one of the lowest notes on the instrument, and then it's gone.

It's a piece about play. A piece that's curious about what the trombone can do, that reaches for its extremes. Extremes of register, skipping from high to low, extremes of dynamics. Sometimes it whines, sometimes it barks.

As a child, my main knowledge of dog breeds came from being an avid collector of Puppy in My Pocket, sturdy plastic models that gave me an unusually comprehensive grounding in dog breeds (wire-haired fox terrier, Dobermann pinscher, corgi, St Bernard – complete with miniature barrel of whisky on its collar). There was a magazine, whose fortnightly release at the local newsagent I anticipated eagerly. The magazine made excessive use of pink. The model dogs came with Top Trumps-style fact cards rating categories like their obedience, and their 'hug-ability'. On a metric of paw prints. I knew this was embarrassing, but it was a small price for information about dogs.

I first played 'Mippy' when I was sixteen, and I didn't get it. It's hard. I sight-read it with my trombone teacher Nigel in my lesson, in a low-ceilinged upstairs room with a Persian carpet at the music school. We kept it on the roster for a couple of weeks, Nigel noting it down in my 'to practise' book, me packing it away in my rainbow nylon charity shop shoulder bag, before probably he forgot about it.

Three years later, it was back on the stand, this time introduced by my trombone teacher at university, who was a professional trombonist with a permanent seat in a leading orchestra. And this was when I really wrestled with it, and learned *just* how hard it is, and just how very, deeply wrong I'd been in thinking I was about as good as you could be. When I was sixteen, I thought the challenge was reading the clever rhythms, and there are some technical moments that involve jumping immediately from very high to very low, which are difficult to execute, requiring big changes in airflow (if you're playing with perfect technique), and big changes in the tightness with which you're holding your lips (if you're not, and – spoiler – I hadn't been). Nail that, and in my teenage overconfidence, coupled with a rural West Country lack of exposure to much better trombone players, I thought you more or less had it. But I was miles off. Sure, you might be able to play the notes, but it's so much more than the notes. There's so much to capture, to get it sounding relaxed, to allow the trombone that freedom from the meter, from the tapping foot. You need complete control. You need to feel carefree with the instrument. Playing needs to come as easily to you as speaking. And only then can you have it, this lilting, laid-back song.

In the end, it's all about the sound you make. Sound, sound, sound. That's all elite brass players think about. The core of what you're doing, your individual voice, making it as big and round and sweet and open and powerful as you can. Yellow and mellow and sonorous. Mastering the technique is one thing, but the sound is what separates out the giants.

And now there were so many hours to be spent working on sound, just sound. Breathing. Inhaling. Dropping my shoulders, releasing tension. Taking lessons in Alexander technique with a man at the music college across the road. Lying flat on my back on the floor, preparing to stand and play while maintaining that same flat back, that relaxation into the floor, all in the hope of infinitesimal improvements in sound through releases in musculature, resonant cavities in the body, the chest, the head. Playing with a practice mute to develop the breadth of your sound – a practice mute being a mute that greatly muffles the noise you make, so you can practise without bothering your neighbours. Playing with a practice mute was a bit like resistance training.

You'd hear cautionary tales about people whose sound 'got too big' after they played with a practice mute too often. People who never recovered. That said, my trombone teacher would also tell cautionary tales about your inevitable death if you ate more than eight bananas in a day, so you had to take all these stories with a pinch of salt. There's a heady blend of hard science and fervently held superstition in the high-wire world of music-making. Because making music combines belief, confidence and something close to magic.

That life was beguiling. Play every day, focus on your sound, this ephemeral milestone pulling ever further away from you as you approached, as you sought the sublime goal of relaxation while under tension, relaxation while holding something heavy, relaxation while under pressure.

Because another thing you might not know is that the pressure to play perfectly is enormous. The most frightening thing I have ever experienced. Everyone will know if you don't. And everyone will know if you are nervous. You have to play perfectly without showing any signs of stress.

To do that, it helps if you truly aren't feeling any signs of stress because you just know beyond doubt that you'll play it perfectly no matter what. And for that, the options are: insane brilliance, insane confidence that comes from insane brilliance plus endless practice, or mind-altering substances.

That last one is not a joke.

Back when I was studying, alcohol was a popular choice of drug among seasoned brass professionals: for instance, operas are so long, and have so many lengthy periods where brass players aren't needed that the trumpeters and trombonists might be found in the nearest pub *midway through a performance*. Beta blockers were another option – although more typically the choice of amateurs. It's easier for many to learn to maintain enough precision of technique when their motor skills are inhibited, than to learn the other thing: to control the nerves and the doubt. For the cockier, there's a macho element to nailing everything even after multiple pints.

Perfection is a bloody difficult feat to achieve when you're pressing a heavy hunk of metal to your face. If you're going to play 'Mippy' with style, you and the trombone have to bridge the distinction between human and metal to become a single flowing thing. To create a sense of ventriloquism, to have the control that then allows the trombone to play the part of a separate animal. You can never look up to a note, as a professional once told me: never be afraid of it, always know you'll hit it. Always know your technique is there, that your muscles – in your face, in your core – are strong enough. Always know your breathing is relaxed and expansive enough. You have to play all the time, and your training is one in meditation, free-diving: remaining totally relaxed when the adrenaline flows.

The discipline required to play with that total freedom was something that, after three years at university of focused practice, two hours a day, I nearly achieved.

But not quite.

I never quite got there.

An autumn of sporadic therapy sessions found its way to winter, somehow, then winter felt the first hints of spring, and in that year after he died, I felt like I'd never felt before. Lost. Blank. Incapacitated. *Bereft*. Amid the dried-out kerbside Christmas trees, I had moved flat, leaving my housemate behind, and setting up in a new area of south London where my new therapist was no longer convenient, so I stopped going. Moving barely registered as upheaval given everything else; more as relief. Easier to spend time alone now I lived alone, and I could have my space exactly as I wanted it.

Ever since I'd moved back from America, ever since my dad had died, my trombone had been sullen in the cupboard of my bedroom, protected from dust but not from guilt. Now I'd moved, it had upgraded to being sullen in the corner of my living room. And because there was no way that music was going to help me, I wasn't going to be playing it any time soon. No, I'd come up with a different idea. I was off to visit a puppy. A puppy I'd found on a well-known private pet sales website, and who, inexplicably placed in a ribboned wicker bowl, peered out of the ad alongside her two black and white siblings. I was recklessly going to meet her even though I knew about the physical law dictating that once you've met a dog-for-adoption, you'll be taking that dog home.

I took Chrissy with me – Chrissy, who I'd skived half a Prom with. We brainstormed the pros and cons on the train to a village outside Slough. I was fixated on how I would be able to maintain my travel-heavy lifestyle as a single woman with a dog. Chrissy had previously told me about how her friend, a magazine photographer, had a lurcher and still managed to do loads of travel for international shoots. On the train from Clapham Junction (Place of Dreams) towards Slough, I got her to repeat the story about this friend like a mantra. *Tell me that it's possible. Tell me I haven't gone temporarily mad.* Because old me had cared a lot about being able to go anywhere at a moment's notice; new me cared a lot about having a dog. She texted her friend again, another voice to add to the dog lobby. The reply was a windswept voice message: she was walking said lurcher. Chrissy held the phone up between us and we leaned towards it to catch her voice. 'It's not always easy,' she said. 'But the thing is, you get to have a dog, and having a dog is the best thing ever.'

If she could do it, why couldn't I?

As Berkshire flashed by the windows, I looked around the train at the quietness of people's lives, the backs of their heads, travelling alongside me. It fostered my resolve. Who knew what they were coping with. Who knew how long any of us had. It was as simple as this: if I didn't know when I would die, I didn't want to die not having had a dog.

Fuck everything sensible.

I imagined sashaying through the card-entry gates at my workplace, nodding at the security guards, the puppy in a bag with her head obscured by a trailing scarf. Before, I had been the sort of person who assiduously met deadlines, who'd been mortified to discover that I hadn't been observing the proper lane rules on American pavements; now, in a world lit bright by the nihilism of loss, rules only seemed an issue if you got caught; and even then, what was the worst that would happen? You'd be arrested, but no one would be dead. Deadlines raced by with barely a glimmer of relevance. *We're all just wandering around this virtual reality we call life,* I thought, *and everything is up for negotiation, and anything can change at a moment's notice.*

Chrissy and I agreed that a robust network of dog sitters would be needed.

We went through a very ordinary-looking front door to a very ordinary-looking detached house, and there was my dog. The last puppy left in the litter. A designer breed you've never heard of, and that seemed more than a little made up: the 'Coton-doodle'. I'd had to google the non-poodle half, the Coton de Tuléar; 'clownish' was a word used in the description. That sounded good, right? I sat on the vinyl floor, coaxing her to play with a tuggy toy, and she squeaked at me, and I marvelled at how possible this all felt. All I had to do was give this woman money and this puppy would be mine. Conceivably, for ever. Stranger still, this was what everyone here expected would happen.

And now those basket-puppies' least desirable sibling was a black nugget curled up on my lap and making reaching my laptop tricky. Hard to determine which end was her head and which her tail. Obviously she was the greatest dog on earth. I don't think many people would describe me as spontaneous, but I have always had something of an impulsive, nihilist side (I present my sudden late-PhD nose piercing as evidence), making it not all that unlikely that I will one day get a tattoo, even though I don't especially like them. Chrissy once described her tattoos as staring at infinity. Making your peace with death and decay, but also a reminder that nothing's that important actually, so treat life lightly. I liked that. I resolved to make it work. I wondered about this reckless feeling. People tell you to beware it, but I felt like it was something I wanted to hold on to for as long as I could.

I called her Datch, short for Datchet, the village I collected her from. I think I thought that if I didn't over-labour the name, it might shield me from the consequences of this leap, and that if I didn't think about it too much, I maybe wouldn't ever have to notice the truth of this horrifyingly permanent responsibility.

The first week I had her, I lost weight. Checking what she was up to was incessant. What she was or wasn't chewing (socks, carpet, laptop case, my hair). Where she was or wasn't peeing. There was no time to eat. Positioning her right by my bed, like they say in the books, she howled in her crate through the first night. And the second. And the third. I wrapped a hot-water bottle in the blanket scented with her mother I'd been given by the breeder, in the hope that this poor simulation of her mother's warmth would be enough to soothe her. So driven to distraction was I, I even began wondering about adding a ticking clock for the heartbeat, as one 1970s puppy book advised, but this tip was so patently based on some kind of Edwardian ideal of nurturing that would probably also involve never showing your puppy any physical warmth, and then sending your puppy to boarding school as early as possible, that even in my abject desperation I couldn't quite believe it would be effective. When I closed my eyes, I saw cruel images of the 1960s baby monkeys subjected to the 'wire mother' experiment, snuggled wide-eyed into the fleecy model 'mother' covered in cloth, looking for comfort, even when the cloth mother didn't provide any milk: milk only came from the one made exclusively of wire.

I was exhausted. Shut in her crate, Datch wailed when I showered. Heartbreaking keening. I read all the books, googled constantly. She weed on the carpet. Multiple times a day. Before she arrived, I had optimistically covered the area around her crate in a camping groundsheet to preserve the lovely aesthetics of the rest of my new home. I fast discovered that this was nowhere near enough of an intervention to save the carpet, a pale cream, chosen by people who had clearly had no intention of getting a grief-inspired puppy. I improvised with flattened boxes from my recent move, covering the entire floor of the flat. When she urinated on them I cut out the soggy patches with scissors, and covered the gap with Amazon packaging. It was unorthodox, but, well, barely anyone, and certainly no one who would care, came round in my year of isolated television watching.

From the second morning, Datch had imprinted on me. She was convinced I represented absolute safety. A close friend came over for dinner and I stood in the hallway and she curled up in a ball, fitting on top of my socked feet, taking up no more space than my feet did. *This is permanence*, I thought, dizzy and slightly sick. Someone had told me it took just one night sleeping in a room together for a dog to trust you. *What is this instant trust made of?* I wondered. I'd thought it was what I'd wanted but actually it was off-putting; I joked to friends that she was coming on a bit strong. I'd need time to reciprocate her feelings.

We played 'chase the hedgehog' up and down my hallway. She grabbed bin liners I had put down – more vain efforts at carpet preservation – and raced around like a tiny superhero with a cape.

I wondered to myself what I had done.

I slept when Datch slept, mostly. Pleasant when she took a nap in the afternoon; less pleasant when she woke in the night needing to be taken outside, resulting in two flights of stairs followed by twenty cold minutes in the shared yard by the bins just off a busy main road. But it felt good to sleep when a puppy sleeps, to live on puppy time for a while.

I'd ordered up a major Bernstein biography, the most comprehensive one there is, according to my Bernstein-expert colleague. I hoped to find out more about this piece I'd known for so long. No sign of 'Mippy II' in the index. After scouring the pages, I finally found a mention. I felt surprising elation, like seeing an old friend's name in a newspaper, but I soon realised there was little there. Scarcely any more detail than I already knew: I learned that the other pieces in the suite were 'Fanfare for Bima', written for the cocker spaniel belonging to one of the most powerful musicians internationally at the time, the conductor of the Boston Symphony Orchestra, Serge Koussevitzky; the three 'Mippy' pieces, named for each of Bernstein's brother's three successive dogs of the same name; and 'Rondo for Lifey', Lifey being a Skye terrier owned by Academy Award-winning Hollywood actor and singer Judy Holliday, star of films like *Born Yesterday* (1950) and *The Solid Gold Cadillac* (1956), neither of which I had seen. And that was all. Pieces about dogs, I supposed, belonged to the category: whimsy, musical trivia. And so, a hole. What I wanted was pictures of those dogs with their people. I wanted to see Koussevitzky throwing a ball for his spaniel, Koussevitzky brushing dirt off his trousers with a cry of despair after an exuberant muddy paw was misplaced. Bernstein feeding scraps from his plate under the table to his brother's dog. I wanted to know about their home lives. But instead all I learned was that *Brass Music*, the title of the suite, had been a commission for the Julliard music school in New York. Nothing here about Bernstein's relationship with his brother. Nothing about the intimacies or rivalries that led to these pieces, to Bernstein's choice to make these pieces gifts.

Dog music is not the sort of music to which multiple pages are dedicated. Dogs are not wolves; nor are they foxes, both of which are wild, and therefore respectable subjects for the nineteenth-century transcendent romanticism of men and mountains. Dogs, not so much. Nor do dogs belong within the abstractions and agendas of twentieth-century art music: machine-music modernism, Dada, minimalism, for instance. Wolves and foxes, they belong to the beyond, to the sublime of the unknowable. They slink, they hide, they hold wary mystery deep in the woods. They are fantastic metaphors for the unknown.

There are traces of wolf in dogs' desire to disembowel teddy bears of their stuffing, though. Dogs are deviant wolves that humans have tried over thousands of years to make into their own children.

Not long ago, I went to an exhibition of dog portraiture at the Wallace Collection in central London, an exhibition that represented a brilliant move on the part of the gallery's marketing team. Heavily advertised on the Tube with paintings of David Hockney's dachshunds in bold blue, mahogany and sand, I fully understood that it was going to be a bit silly and gimmicky; predictably, I went anyway. I was very much the target audience. 'From Gainsborough to Hockney' was the exhibition's tagline, which disguised the fact that the bulk of the collection was by nineteenth-century English painter Edwin Landseer. 'The Hounds of Edwin Landseer, and a Handful of Other Artists Doing Dog Commissions' would have been a more accurate, if less marketable, description. Wandering around, admiring a spotlit portrait of a terrier so alert and finely rendered I felt I could see what it was thinking, I confronted all sorts of feelings. First, the knowledge that I was having a downright fantastic time. But I also knew it was kitsch, and felt a complicated sense of shame around my enjoyment of the gallery. The *Guardian*'s critic had given the exhibition a damning, and I think unwarrantedly harsh, one star. I balanced competing needs as I sought to make the whole thing both a real and an ironic experience. The idea of kitsch art, kitsch music, was something I remembered writing an undergraduate essay about, drawing on arguments from philosophy.

Dogs are mostly transparent. There's discomfort in that transparency. In how it lays bare the needs of our human selves. We don't want to be seen as doting, devoted; after childhood, we are ashamed when we show others how much we need them. Dogs are an uncomfortable mirror, reflecting back the sort of image of ourselves, our deepest longings, that we rarely want others to know about. Mostly we even hide these feelings from ourselves. We pretend we are above them.

What struck me most in that exhibition, when I wasn't escaping my unease into the abstractions of contemplating kitsch, was a tiny element of the Royal Collection. Royal dogs; the epitome of the British love of dogs in our top-down stratified social hierarchy. I couldn't tear my eyes away from a handful of tiny drawings taken from the Royal Archives: portraits done by Queen Victoria and Prince Albert of their own dogs while they were taking drawing lessons, pencil, pen, watercolour. Material that tells you about who people were behind closed doors. The animals they cared for, their names scratched in tiny, loopy handwriting below the images. Waldina and Waldmann, a pair of long-bodied dogs, facing one another. A terrier called Podge. A greyhound called Swan. A basket of puppies, labelled 'puppies'. It wasn't the insight into the monarchy that drew me to those drawings; it was something important about the honesty of love. Dogs giving us a glimpse of the home, of real lives beyond a public persona or portrait, the hours and actions that make up their day and make up who they are. These amateur drawings told me more than any of the technically accomplished professional paintings, with their political statements conveyed through animal allegory. Something personal and private and beautiful.

I don't know the full story of Bernstein's music. It was a commission, and it fulfilled some of his obligations to his publisher. But it strikes me as important that he chose to write for friends, for family. It was also a gift. The kind of music that demonstrates how well we know someone. Some gifts are handmade, a material intimacy. People doing what they do best, and in so doing, giving a piece of themselves. But they don't lose that piece of themselves; it makes them bigger. And, reading past the edges into the fuzzy hinterland of that Bernstein biography, noticing what was not said, I realised how music and this sense of intimacy, of home, of knowing someone and all their foibles behind closed doors are so entwined. Because this music is about the safety and comfort of home. Of domestic spaces. About people's playfulness. How they care for another being. And there's something about the trombone, soulful, baleful, slightly clumsy, that suits a doggy piece. Melancholic like a dog looking up, awoken from their sofa nap.

Music-making comes from the home. It's where it starts. Small children reaching upward for piano keys, young adults cradling guitars like lovers in bedrooms and houseshares. We ready ourselves somewhere private; one day, we will play with and for other people, we will rehearse outside the home. By convention, biographies of musicians begin with their parents, with their influence, with how they supported their offspring, gave them music lessons.

A love of music passes through the home, can be passed through generations.

And I think the question I didn't know how to answer, and probably wasn't ready to articulate then was: how do I play music now? If I wouldn't be on those stages, blinding lights and the ghost-shape of an audience beyond the thickened dark, what was it for? Who was it for?

'No, she's actually a Coton de Tuléar crossed with a toy poodle. No, you've not heard of the Coton de Tuléar. Neither had I. Long white fluffy coats. Lovely temperaments. Look them up on Google.'

Getting a dog spectacularly broke the hermetic seal I had constructed around myself in public, a seamless collaboration between British social norms and my personality. It came with many things I hadn't expected. The first: how often people ask you your puppy's name. The second was how often people hazard a guess at the breed. The frequency of both, multiple times a day. Every day.

And in my new life, I had unwittingly become an advocate for Madagascar's national dog.

In my new life I also spent my time correcting strangers. This felt like a good thing – an advance both personal and also broadly feminist. Usually I acquiesced and agreed. Now I told people they were wrong. Apologetically.

Walking through south London with a puppy was a completely different experience to walking alone. You could make eye contact with people. A young woman on a train, buzzing, sour-tongued but vulnerable, the sort who everyone hopes isn't going to start on them because they won't be allowed to pretend they haven't heard, asked if we'd been for a walk and melted when I asked if she liked dogs.

'Yeah, I love 'em,' she said wistfully, before returning to haranguing her partner about their dinner plans. Datch brought out the best in people and made me feel invincible walking the streets, dispelling the muted grey of south London mistrust.

Whenever we travelled, Datch and I, we attracted shy glances, grins, children and parents pointing as I tried to gauge people's willingness to have a puppy lick them – Datch insisted on trying to lick the exposed skin of strangers and friends alike, ankles being a particular risk area. I held her close and practised getting her to lie down. It was a shock the first time I went on the London Underground again without her, the passengers back to their indifferent old selves.

I'd got used to this newly mellow, open London.

And then things changed.

Chapter 7

SILENCE

We were all told to stay at home. Mirroring my mood, the world as we knew it turned upside down, in on itself, as it went into what they, and then we, called lockdown. Concentrated introversion, space, a magnification of the gaps between us. We all hibernated. For months: months that skirted the kind of time you measure in years.

And I loved it. You weren't meant to love it. Nonetheless, I wanted it to go on for ever. No one wanted me to go anywhere with them, meet them, anything. I had nationally mandated permission to stay at home and keep watching the television shows that continued to provide the solace, the distraction I craved. The pressure was off. It was perfect. Designed for me in all but one way: Datch. She'd come to live with me in my second-floor flat without a garden six weeks' prior to lockdown's announcement. And now, holed up in a one-bed together by law, she and I were learning intense lessons about proximity and dependence. Building a strong foundation for acute separation anxiety, the kind where she howled primally and constantly when, later, I even thought about leaving the house alone, and it wouldn't be clear whether it was her grief or mine embedded in those howls.

The world was curiously silent for a lot of this time. Live music-making was forbidden. Gatherings in the park: forbidden.

All the places and ways in which people might make music in public spaces went hand in hand with meeting people. And all forbidden. Music never just happened around me, as it did normally, in cafés, bars, shops, concerts. In the day-to-day of living. Instead, noise only existed in my flat. Radio 4. Silent parks without even the rumble of trains broken by a summer of protest, political energy spilling from the heat boxes of our homes.

As lockdown progressed, I listened to audiobooks. I discovered Jane Austen, as many people did, immersing myself in a historical world of isolation and distance dictated by social norms. It felt fitting. I listened to podcasts. I had Radio 4 on all day long, to keep a sense of community in my flat as I lived there alone with my puppy.

In lockdown we had to seek music out. Listening to it involved active, conscious choice, and it transpired that I didn't want to. I didn't choose not to listen; I just never made a positive choice to do so. I'm not sure I ever really thought about it. And so, insofar as music went, lockdown was a strangely silent time, but I didn't really notice. I was glad concerts were cancelled. If I couldn't go to them, I didn't have to confront how music made me feel.

The first time we saw a band, three musicians on a park bench, legal status uncertain, it was a cold day and a smattering of people danced in parkas and wellies.

I wonder if this is anything like how it feels to visit a psychic or a guru, I thought. Sitting at my computer, I was experiencing the self-conscious jolt of hope and ego and doubt that comes when an expert might be about to reveal profound explanatory knowledge about you specifically: your neuroses, your past, your brain. In this case, why I had such trouble with music after my father's death.

'I have a very complicated relationship with the music from the funeral,' I said. 'And I don't understand it yet.

Some days it's one thing, some days it's another, and there are also periods in which I don't think about it at all. But I would never actively seek it out.'

It was a cool fine day in October, and I was on a video call to Dr Janieke Bruin-Mollenhorst, warm, angular and animated. A leading academic researcher on the topic of ritual, specifically music for funerals, she was talking to me from her home office in a place called Nieuwerbrug aan den Rijn in the Netherlands. I'd come across her via Twitter, when, using my credentials as a music academic, I'd sought the help of a specialist who studies the intersection of ritual, music and grief. Rituals and rites of passage fascinate Janieke, because of how deeply they reveal things about ourselves. 'You get so close to the identity of people,' she told me. 'Who they want to be, how they want to be.' When she told me that she had just finished writing a chapter about how people related to the music played at a funeral in the months and years afterwards – whether people still listen to it, whether there are any changes in how people experience it – I felt a clench in my stomach. This was what I wanted to understand. I wanted to know why my relationship with music had become so complicated.

'Well, the good news is your reactions are completely normal; you remind me of some of my interviewees. The bad: there aren't any concrete answers. What we understand about music and grief is still very blurry.'

Damn.

Given the kind of research that has been done so far, Janieke wasn't able to tell me much that wasn't, well, basically something that we know intuitively. 'It's very diverse,' Janieke said. 'It differs from one person to another.' She explained that how people relate to music after a death depends on myriad factors: not only on how connected they were to music generally, as well as to the specific music for the funeral, but also the person who died's relationship to music. It was reassuring to hear there wasn't some magic knowledge I didn't have that would explain everything, but it was still hard not to feel disappointed.

At the start of our conversation, she briefed me on the list of relevant reading materials she had sent me in advance. And that, being a diligent scholar, I had mostly read. Even if some of it had made me angry. I didn't mention the anger.

The research into how people relate to funeral music isn't extensive – there's only a small handful of studies. I'd printed out a stack of paper, found a highlighter and braced myself. I was in brand-new academic terrain. The studies were from journals like *Death Studies* and *OMEGA – Journal of Death and Dying*. Written by people who work in social work departments, cultural studies, palliative care, clinical neuroscience, centres for cancer research – and a centre for music, pedagogy and society. I felt as far away as could be from home turf like *Twentieth-Century Music* or the *Journal of the American Musicological Society*. Which was good, because that home turf still enraged me. What I wanted from Janieke's literature was very different to my usual academic aims. I wanted to find myself in the research.

But as I read, I felt a growing sense of irritation, intensified by the bracketed citations that punctured the text's flow. My experience of grief was being contained within these structured sentences. I felt fragile as a moth, but here my experience was pinned down, a specimen, alongside many others. And distanced further with professional-sounding vocabulary, like the Latin names used by butterfly collectors (lepidopterists). Ordered and structured. It wasn't comforting; it made me angry. And it made me angry about the whole academic project and its manner: to flatten, to desiccate, to inform. Where were the people? Where were the unruly feelings?

I started to hate the word 'bereaved' and the careful, detached expression 'deceased person'.

Here are some things we know. Or we think we know.

We know that some people seek out specific music after a death, and others can't listen to it at all. Music becomes what's known in grief theory as a transitional object, allowing people to 'feel close' to the deceased person at times when they could 'tolerate and integrate the harsh reality of the loss.'

We also know that a lot of people avoid music because they don't want to be confronted with difficult emotions.

We know that music can provoke us to recall specific memories in our lives.

We know something about how music elicits different emotions. There is a set of different psychological mechanisms which interact with one another, and their origins are in different evolutionary stages in the development of brain function: ancient ones like our perception, in our ability to respond empathically, and in the later development of our inner imagination, the thing that allows for an understanding of time.

We know music can trigger tears, and something about the mechanism for this.

We know a lot of what, and a bit of how, but we don't know much by way of why.

We still don't understand how music is entwined in the process of grieving, how music is entangled in our love for those we've lost. How or why music is so fundamentally, so profoundly human.

I abandoned the articles. The answers I wanted simply weren't there.

I didn't fully trust this research. It's worth noting that, in so far as my disciplinary training goes, talking to Janieke was a significant rebellion. For someone intellectually raised in the world of historical musicology, communing with a religious studies scholar with the sorts of research methods she uses was not entirely unlike going to see a homeopathist. I've been trained to view such methods, similar to those used by music psychologists and music therapy researchers, with deep suspicion. But I had felt compelled to know what these other approaches might yield.

When I flipped through research relating to music therapy, for instance, uncritical chapter titles like 'the power of music' made me squirm: what do you mean, 'power'? If there's one thing my training has taught me, it's that it is intellectually unserious to suggest that music is just magical! Has everyone taken leave of their senses? My hackles were raised: there's masses of critical literature in the sphere of cultural history that historicises music's effects on people. It would be impossible to write those words – 'the power of music' – unironically in the discipline of historical musicology. Because we think we need to be able to view it with a clear head, not bow down to it reverentially. We want to understand it from all angles: how it works, how it affects us, how people have thought about music throughout history, how it's embroiled in social hierarchies and ideologies that we might not want – think of how the Nazis mobilised Wagner's music. Or think about the fallacy that listening to classical music makes you a more moral person, think about the role of national anthems or football chants in building identity. And remember that not everyone can hear music, and not everyone responds emotionally to music at all.

And yet. I write all this uneasily. Because for all our intellectualising and historicising and critical approaches, we always seem to return to the core problem of music. The problem of how there's some quality within it that resists every attempt we make to understand how it works, how it emotionally affects those of us who can hear it, simply what it *is* to us, some excess that eludes every angle we approach it from. We always fall short.

So: what makes music so special? For musicologists, whose approach is essentially a cross between literary criticism, history and interpretative analysis, the question is a bit embarrassing. *Nothing!* We want to shout. *It's just like everything else!* I think the embarrassment comes partly because we don't want to seem like we're professionally engaged with something indefinable when we share university campuses with chemists and computer scientists, people with concrete concerns and the kind of importance you can see on a metric. And then among ourselves we circulate the most up-to-date philosophical thinking on the concept of the ineffable.

For psychologists, therapists, sociologists of music – those with empirical methodologies – by contrast, the question is generative. What makes music so special? Why can music move us to tears? Why's it embedded deep in our sense of self and our personal histories? *Let's find out!* I think this is because they fundamentally believe in the robustness of their methods, and therefore that those methods will one day provide, if not a complete answer, then at least significantly better insight into the human condition.

Historians think their optimism is misplaced. That there are too many variables. Hence the theories of the ineffable.

But it's not like we haven't been looking for an answer. There is centuries' worth of literature and philosophy grappling with the specialness of music, at least in the Western tradition, which likes a solvable problem. While Kant thought that music was a mere decorative art, background noise, within the space of a generation or two, under the German Romantics, music was elevated to something that transcended reality and connected us with aspects of our inner soul that we couldn't otherwise know. I mean – really hefty stuff. Music was invested with abilities that exceeded those of the plastic arts, like poetry or sculpture. Music had some seriously special powers.

Today, researchers put musicians and listeners in fMRI scanners to try to work out the precise effect of funk grooves on the brain. Or, to help escape the artificial world of the lab, they use imaging skull caps – EEG caps (EEG is shorthand for electroencephalography) – that monitor electrical activity in the brain during real-life experiences of music. We can only work with the tools we have, and although the tools are amazing, they produce descriptive work: we learn which parts of our brains light up when we hear music that we want to dance to. That's fascinating, of course, but it can only take us so far. No matter how hard we stare at those scans, we still don't know why we want to dance. Is the cause revealed by our brains, or in the music, or the time and place we hear it, or in the relationship between all these things, or in some other place we haven't thought of yet, and how can that be measured? What's really going on in our minds, when we know from studies of dementia patients that we remember music long after we've lost the ability to use language, forgotten the names of our children?

Identifying music's power is quite different from explaining it.

'And I think that's really beautiful,' I remembered Michelle Phillips, a music psychologist who works on time, once telling me. 'People have tried to explain, and to capture, and to model these experiences, but we may never be able to do it completely. We can chip away, and we can find things that are interesting, but perhaps you can never fully capture music empirically, with survey data, or brain data, or with interview data. You may never capture everything, and perhaps at least part of the essence of an individual musical experience will always elude our research methods.'

And maybe, beneath it all, 'we can't really say', or 'we don't know how to know', or 'we may never understand the thing that actually matters', was the answer I wanted. I didn't want such a profound experience to be explained away. I didn't want to lose the inexplicable magic that music might hold. The excess. The thing beyond. Because magic was all that might bring me closer to him being alive.

So much of thinking about music is about coming up against the limits of what it's possible to know. When you get right down to it, Janieke told me, all most researchers can say with much confidence is that many people try to use music to control their grief. This intentional relationship with music people have in their grief is well described by a contemporary grief theory: the Stroebe and Schut Dual-Process Model. When I had looked into the scholarship before we met, I had found that it's one of the few things of which researchers are convinced about how people use music in bereavement. The Dual-Process Model says you shouldn't be confronting the loss all the time. It describes a process in which you get to look at the loss for a bit, feel really good and terrible, then go away and do something else, switch off, repress a bit, live a little, because constantly going through photos – or listening to music – is exhausting. To grieve is a process of oscillation, Stroebe and Schut claim, shuttling back and forth from one mode to the other: from loss-oriented to restoration-oriented tasks.

Current thinking is that your relationship with someone doesn't end when they die: the relationship changes and grows over time. People use music to continue bonds with the deceased, as part of a process in which the relationship with someone who's died is still considered an important active relationship in someone's life, but one whose nature gradually changes.

And then Janieke said something that really caught my attention. About how people responded to being asked about the role music from the funeral plays in their lives months or even years after they've lost someone significant.

'A lot of people say, "I do not listen to it *yet*. Because I think it's going to be too emotional."' She thought people often subconsciously think the funeral music works as some kind of test: *Am I already out of my bereavement process?* 'It's very interesting, but also... very problematic.' She suspected a lot of people have fixed ideas about bereavement and grieving: that grief can be overcome, that it's a process that can be worked through. The idea then is that when they can listen to music again, it's a signal that they've reached the end of the grieving process. 'But it doesn't work like that.'

At my computer in London, I sipped my tea. *Something to be careful of,* I thought. I wondered if I'd been thinking about music in this way. Not necessarily thinking my ability to listen to music will signal I'm over it, but something similar: when I can confront the music, I'll be grieving *properly*, doing proper self-realisation of some kind. Which I supposed might be just as dangerous a misconception.

She had to go, had to cycle to the station, confirming my two main stereotypes about Dutch people. But there was still one more surprise. 'Before I go,' she said, 'may I introduce you to my mates in my home office?'

A cheery set of Lego coffin bearers suddenly filled my screen, yellow and blocky with hip joints bent at jaunty angles. 'Lego funeral people!' I cried. And with that, she was away to catch her train.

After she left the online meeting, I tidied up my notes and deliberated whether to bother finishing my cold tea. Something was trying to surface, to tug at my attention. What was it? What Janieke had said about music tracking the grieving process, and about the intentional nature of the relationship, reminded me of something I'd read in the studies she had sent over. Something that had resonated with how I perceived the dangers of particular music. I rifled through my printouts, and finally I found the passage highlighted: it was in a study based on a set of interviews with people bereaved through cancer:

> A particular piece of music, precisely by being so intimately linked to the lost object, can be too searing and too real a reminder of the loss ... Rather than consoling the music will pierce the protective mechanism on which the bereaved rely. In these instances, a work of music may be pointedly shunned or proscribed, treated like a hallowed mausoleum.

The writer went on:

> Such a suppressive response, perhaps paradoxically, actually serves as a sacred conservatory, preserving through silence a displaced embodiment of the beloved.

The music sitting there, on Dad's stand, untouched since he died. I hated the overblown language, but this nonetheless felt right to me. I thought it captured why I couldn't go near it. My feelings of fear. Through forbidding yourself certain music, leaving it well alone, you keep the person who's died alive.

Chapter 8

RUMORES DE LA CALETA

Eventually, we all began to emerge stilted from that hibernation, exhausted by short interactions, tentatively enjoying a new, but changed, light. As we emerged, I was able to go to our family home again, the one we used to refer to as 'my parents'', now, the words still clumsy, 'my mum's'.

I was finally back. Alone in the dining room, I was surprised to find that I now wanted to return to the music that was on the stand when we came back to the house that day, the music Dad was playing, that he left unfinished.

Of course, it wasn't untouched, as it existed in my mind. Mum had been alone in the house for more than two years. It was unreasonable to expect that nothing would have changed. The stand was empty. I went and got Mum, and together we located the music she'd carefully packed away, folded inside a volume of Bach, and I reconstructed the contents with that photo I'd taken on the day he'd died, and I held the middle pages of 'Rumores de la caleta' in my hands, the page that he had left open, and although I didn't know, really, that this was what I was doing yet, I was beginning to be ready to put music (his? mine?) back on the stand.

When Dad practised, one of his method books was *The Advancing Guitarist: Applying Guitar Concepts and*

Technique by Mick Goodrick. *The Advancing Guitarist* was surprisingly philosophical. Nothing like any other music method book I'd ever come across. 'Probably one of the most terrible feelings a human being can experience is regret,' leads the concluding chapter. There's a section titled 'On Being Self-Critical'. Dad didn't need any encouragement in that regard, said Mum. 'Students tend to think that eventually, after they learn whatever it is that they think they need to know ... they won't feel insecure anymore,' it declared. 'This thinking amounts to wishing that you didn't dislike your playing so much. It's fantasizing that things will gradually change for the better.'

'Well, as good as it sounds on paper, it seldom (if ever) happens. In fact, it tends to get worse. If you start off being critical, you tend to remain that way.' I thought of another story Dad told me when I was very small: not 'The Parallel Lines', but one of his darker contributions to the children's canon: the tale of 'The Giraffe and the Crocodile'. The narrative began with the titular crocodile biting the giraffe's leg; what followed was a blow-by-blow account of the giraffe fading in and out of consciousness as it slowly bled to death. Dad had insulated me against the hope that things would change for the better early.

Here was Goodrick's twist: 'Being self-critical actually has a lot to be said for it. People who are self-critical tend to improve in music because they always seem to see so many things to work on. They tend not to get involved in overly developed egos ... Often they are compassionate.' Dad was a great listener and he always had time for us. You could call him up any time for a lengthy chat about anything you wanted.

I turned the stapled sheets of Albéniz's music back to the page Dad had been working on when he died, the major-key middle section. Albéniz would have been newly living in Madrid when he wrote *Recuerdos de viaje* ('Memories of a journey'), the collection containing 'Rumores', having grown up a prodigious musical talent in Barcelona. By 1887, when he was twenty-seven, *Recuerdos* was one of an opus of fifty works he had amassed to his name, mainly for piano. He composed quickly; he was a fluent improviser. Come 1890, three years later, his success had snowballed, and after repeat concerts in Paris and London, he moved to the English capital.

Were these *Recuerdos* real memories of a real journey, real beaches? I wondered. Where had he been? When, and with whom? With his new wife, Rosina Jordana? They married in 1883. With his children, too? They had five by 1890, two of whom, Blanca and Cristina, did not make it through early childhood. There seemed a deep sadness, an agitation, stored in that music. I wondered about Albéniz's grief for the loss of his children, about its magnitude and influence when he wrote the music. Whose or what murmurs were we hearing?

Reconstructing my photo of Dad's music stand using the sheets tucked inside the Bach volume, I could see that behind 'Rumores' was a fragment of the Chaconne from Handel's Suite in D minor HWV 448. A footer on the music revealed it was bought for download the month before Dad died, on 7 March – learning the Handel seemed to have been a recent plan. He had made notes on it; annotated it with fingerings and chords. 'JUMP' in his handwriting, with an arrow. A movement for the hand? Originally this was harpsichord music. It's a maritime overture; I wondered, given Dad's love of boats, if he chose it for that reason. I listened to it. I didn't know it; but I also somehow did, knowing the work Dad was putting into it, and it made me desperately sad to know that he would never now play it to the standard he wanted. Another project left unfinished.

Behind that was Albéniz's 'Sevilla', no. 3 from the *Suite Española* no. 1. The holiday we never went on. 'Sevilla' was the piece we played at his funeral, as people proceeded out past his coffin. It's the piece we chose because we wanted to end with a feeling of lightness: it has a lilt to it.

As I looked through the pages, suddenly, a battering flutter behind me. Against the glass. A robin had flown into the conservatory through the open door, got caught in the fronds of the red pepper plants, Mum grabbed a T-shirt. One dog put outside, the other – mine – shut in the house, and out the door the robin went. So fragile. Thin legs, I could almost feel its heartbeat through the air between us.

I had gone into archivist mode, cataloguing, piecing together. I didn't make space for the idea that the archival object was my dad. There was no room for sadness as a researcher. It was a way of being that was familiar and masterful and easy. I photocopied the music, took photos, behaved exactly as I do when I'm in a library with rare materials; made folders on my computer and conscientiously organised the photos and PDFs with clear labels.

I went to the piano and had a go at some of the Bach in the volume that was behind the sheet music. 'Mum, do you recognise this?'

'No,' she called from the other room.

On this quick logic, we presumed it wasn't something Dad played, even though the paper was severely worn away by water damage. 'Yes, but that could mean anything,' said Mum. 'It may just be evidence of the music being left on the boat. Or spending a lot of time in the car.' He had been in Wales for a week without Mum not long before he died, though, so she couldn't be sure he hadn't played some of it there.

Two tangos tucked in the front of Bach's solo lute works: 'Oblivion' by the Argentinian composer Astor Piazzolla; 'Jealousy' by Jacob Gade.

I listened to a recording of 'Oblivion', and the tone, the strings, really got me. Hard. His absence in the music's presence. I didn't know the music, but it didn't matter. It's such a melancholy, introspective work of plucked syncopations – that is, rhythms that go against the beats, rhythms that encourage the body to move. The melody appears in relief against an undulating, arpeggiated lower line. Both essential for one another, like the weaving bodies of two dancers, I supposed, balancing synchronisation and independence.

Beaches. Maritime. Seville. Jealousy. Oblivion. Was this coincidence, or unconscious, or finding what we wanted to, and letting interpretation do the work?

I froze. I was anxious that Mum was crying upstairs. I paused, still, listening. But she wasn't.

Afterwards, we went for a walk, milky white skies, too warm for a coat, went to an Iron Age hill fort and climbed its sides surveying the horizon. And then eyes cast downwards on the chalky path ahead I felt angry and so sad, in a way I hadn't in weeks. Like a hugeness was expanding in my chest and there was nowhere to put it. Like I wanted to break things. Like I couldn't contain what was happening, and being under the sky wasn't enough, being surrounded by space wasn't enough. The feeling that you want to lash out but you don't because the release won't do anything. So you wait. You freeze. You pause for it to pass, and hope it won't break through, somehow. The blackberries were starting to come out early. Dad and I had gone blackberry picking in Wales, in Scotland, with ice cream tubs, and Mum had made blackberry and apple pie.

When we got back from the hill fort, I found myself wanting to know how things had been the moment he died. What was he interested in? Where were his books? What was he doing? I knew him, but I wanted to know him more. I wanted the house, the archive, to exist exactly as it had, so I could walk right back into it, pick up at that moment when he had gone and reconstruct everything. Revisit the world as it was that day, even though it was the worst day of my life. That was what I wanted. But I couldn't have that. There was more loss, loss piled on loss. I wanted to hold on to him so badly. And I couldn't.

I didn't really know anything about Albéniz, but now I wanted to make Albéniz – Isaac, who tried to evoke that little beach on the piano – real, and so I reached for the ready tools of my trade. Quickly, through the most basic online resources available for music historians, I had learned about his biography, his wife, the death of two of his children. There was no pathos in the article I was reading, reporting those deaths within a flurry of dates, locations, works composed, concert halls performed at, leading publishers engaged – the trappings of a musical life, a standard musical biography – but the author slipped in the names of the children who'd died, all the same. Blanca and Cristina.

The bad news for me was that the vast majority of the sources I might want to read to delve deeper into this history are in Spanish, a language I have a basic knowledge of at best. There's a little in English, I discovered, reading further through the list of two hundred or so sources. A scholar I met at a conference in the States has reviewed a major book on Albéniz. I needed to get my hands on that book. A trip to King's Cross, to the British Library would be needed. I put a pin in that for now.

From that colleague's book review, which I could access online, Albéniz sounded like a mythic, larger-than-life character, with a romanticised biography based on stories that have to be debunked in the work of the latest biographer, supposedly smuggling himself to America to do a concert tour as a child (he hadn't), making a Faustian pact with a patron in later life (again, untrue). *Recuerdos de viaje* is a dead spot in the literature. Searching it in the advanced research database, the really serious one (RILM Abstracts of Music Literature – RILM stands for Répertoire International de Littérature Musicale), which also houses all books, articles, reviews, PhD and masters theses, all languages, produced nothing. All was quiet. Not even murmurs through dark library shelves.

I looked again at the stand, pale red, at its emptiness, stripped of its many messy layers, the tumult of the music left behind so easily packed away.

A blankness. An empty frame. Dad was gone.

And without him, without those layers, I supposed I needed to work out who I was.

Maybe – just maybe (I could only just concede that this thought was here) – it was time to start putting my own music on.

The Tuesday night it happened, I had barely realised I had to go back. Dad had been in hospital less than forty-eight hours. Pancreatitis. Everything I read on the NHS website made it sound routine, and so I got on with my marking. I was going home at the weekend anyway for Easter, bringing my new boyfriend to meet my parents for the first time. I'd see Dad then, once he'd been discharged.

Mid-afternoon on Tuesday, a text came from Mum saying that Dad had been moved to intensive care. I didn't know what to think. I have a lot of medical friends, and the way they talk about it, it sounds like people go into the ICU all the time, so I still wasn't ready to be especially worried. The landscape had shifted so swiftly, and we were a family who didn't do emotion, who looked at our relationships with a degree of irony. It was easier not to engage. But then

I heard one of my brothers (the other was off-grid doing university fieldwork in Cuba) was going home that evening. I prevaricated, unsure what to do. Surely going home was an overreaction. And with my then-boyfriend's help – the one we're calling Ramin – I realised I should go now, too. He took me to Waterloo. I don't think I would have got there without him. As I left Ramin's flat, Mum texted me asking for Ol's number, Dad's best friend, and I knew then it was serious. Looking back through the barriers from the platform at Waterloo to catch Ramin's face, I walked into the path of an austere woman coming in the other direction off the train. She looked derisive, like I didn't know the train changeover etiquette; perversely I briefly wished for a terrible outcome to the travelling home saga. 'My dad's in hospital and I'm going home' didn't yet feel enough to warrant my outrage.

On the train I listened to Bon Iver's *22, A Million*, a distorted voice, 'it might be over soon', ambivalent, suspended against the synth folk drone; I switched to Radio 4's comedy podcasts, unwilling to allow the feeling that anything might be wrong to surface through the music. In retrospect, I realise this was the first time I found music too much, too overwhelming, too immersive and too full a space, as if the music was distorting the borders of the world as I knew it, a harbinger showing me the first shadows of an alternative reality. I pushed it away. As I listened, I was knitting sleeve cuffs, a dense grey wool, close to finishing a cardigan. How serious everything was going to be had yet to resolve, so it seemed better to go on as normal, even in the unknown situation of being called home (indirectly) because Dad was in our local hospital's ICU. There was no yardstick against which to gauge it.

'You're keeping him alive, aren't you,' Mum confirmed with the ICU nurse that night, after they took away all

Dad's prescription medications, even the gabapentin he was insisting on having with him in the ICU for the nerve-related face pain he'd been dealing with the past few months. They needed total control over what was going in and out of his body. They gave Mum back the bag of his overnight things, a spare shirt, his book, to take home with her.

Initially, almost the biggest affront was realising that when the worst is happening, no one actually summons you home. There's no announcement. No one is in charge, no one tells you to come to the hospital. Because sometimes no one actually knows it's happening. It wasn't at all how I imagined. I thought my parents had everything under control.

And then, without anyone ever sounding the alarm, *the worst had already happened*. We missed it. And all we could do was sit, 7.30 a.m., at Formica tables in the hospital canteen the next morning and look sickly at Styrofoam tea from a new universe that was also the same, and realise that yes, it was indeed possible that Dad could now be dead. Because he was.

Nothing about the events in the sixty hours leading up to Dad's death – from Dad going into hospital on the Sunday night to us arriving at the hospital on Wednesday morning at 6.20 a.m. to find him having died minutes before – seems hard to remember. Not yet, anyway: I'm still close enough to the aftermath that it feels like it'll be imprinted on my consciousness for ever. But I don't visit that tight capsule of memories much. From time to time, I worry about corrupting my knowledge of what happened through over-rehearsal, and so I tend to keep it closed, falsely believing my memories to be preserved behind glass. But then I worry I won't notice the quiet damage of time, will lose them through simple neglect. And when I do look more closely,

I'll realise that details are slipping away. What did Dad joke about with the nurse in the middle of the night? And was she changing a drip? Inserting a needle? Altering a medication? The consultant had told us ('It was amazing he was that lucid'), but I was too numb to retain it.

After we found our car, parked illegally outside the hospital, we drove home, my brother in the passenger seat, me in the back ('Are you OK to drive, Mum?'). I stared into the car footwell and thought, trying on this new reality for the first time, *Dad will never see how my life turns out. Know my partner. Meet my children.* An ungraspable new truth, not yet solid, watery as my stomach and the space right behind my eyes. At home Mum began to call a roster of relatives, friends, who suddenly needed to know how profoundly reality had changed – just a phone call and everything is different, again and again. Eventually I left her to have a shower. It wasn't clear if going for a shower was an appropriate thing to do after we'd just seen Dad in a hospital gown newly no longer alive, the aftermath of the ultimate transitional moment, but no one had washed before we left at 6 a.m., Mum waking us shouting up the stairs in a voice I'd never heard before: 'We need to go *now*.' She'd been on the phone to the hospital. She'd called them; she'd had a sudden feeling something terrible had happened.

'Yes, come now; the consultant is with him,' the nurse had said. Heavily loaded words I didn't understand.

He was dying right then, we learned when we arrived. I'd tugged on jeans, and managed to think to grab my deodorant, but as we got in the car I'd felt resentful when I saw my brother'd had the presence of mind to bring along his laptop bag. I'd thought we were going to be at the hospital all day, bored, now me with only my deodorant for company and nothing to keep me occupied in the periods of waiting. Life-defining tragedy playing out elsewhere as I thought about my deodorant and a laptop bag. I was a big step behind; I hadn't believed Dad could die. I'd never even seen Dad in a hospital gown before.

Instead, we were back home by half-past nine. When someone is already dead, there is really no reason to stick around at the hospital. You might think there'd be more ceremony. There isn't.

Mid-morning, I took it upon myself to call his university. It seemed easier to stay busy and task-oriented than to actually begin experiencing this new life or dealing with the granite that had made its home in my stomach, and he would be worried about the students he was meant to be travelling to London to meet the following day. 'I'm afraid he's died, I'm his daughter,' I said. 'This morning. So he won't be able to teach his students any more. He's meant to be seeing them tomorrow. Perhaps you could tell them.' Words that made no sense at all, but a message that needed to be communicated.

'This morning,' the woman on the other end repeated, alarmed, then rallying in her transition to sympathetic. 'Goodness, I'm so sorry. You really shouldn't be calling us.' She clearly thought it wasn't a fitting activity for a bereaved daughter on the morning of her father's death. I had no idea what a fitting activity might be.

Not too long after I looked through the music on my dad's music stand at our family home, I went to the British Library. I cycled. Forty-five minutes thronging through a sun-kissed late-September rush-hour London morning – perfect, a hint of cold, the seasons turning. Weaving around buses, then over Blackfriars Bridge, the sudden spaciousness of the Thames either side of me, positioned at the back of a stampede of bicycles, moving in Lycra-clad formation through the channels of a concrete wilderness. It put me in mind of the ravine scene in Disney's *The Lion King*.

The British Library entrance is cavernous. Low voices were echoing through it, blurring into a comforting hum. I was outside the café on the ground floor. It was the first time I'd visited in well over a year, since the pandemic began. People passed wearing masks, not wearing masks. There wasn't a consensus yet.

Since arriving, I'd spent two hours in the foyer complex nursing three coffees, tweeted 'Hello @britishlibrary, very, very nice to see you again', to an unusually appreciative response from the good people of the Twitterverse, worked out how to reactive my online BL account and then procrastinated even further by booking my bike in to be serviced for the first time in the seven years I'd owned it. What I hadn't, noticeably, yet got up the courage to do was brave the reading room.

The reading room. Rare Books and Music, on the first floor. I found reading rooms controlled spaces that made my chest tight. You have to put all your belongings into clear plastic bags to bring them in, think carefully each time you stand up, sit down, notice everyone watching your movements. It makes the breath catch in my throat thinking about it, the hair stand up on my neck.

It was never quite as bad as I thought it was going to be once I got in, got settled at my desk. Plenty of space. A lamp just for me. Comfy leather chairs and studious companions. But. Still. That nagging sense of control. The feeling that always made me want to get out of libraries. I Shouldn't Be Here. I'd never been the kind of academic that dreamed of beautifully quiet libraries lined with leather-bound books and ancient globes, these romanticised, perfectly cerebral spaces in which the mind supposedly could wander free. Unless for whatever reason I'd become fantastically rich and that beautiful library happened to be in my own home, and I was allowed to go around in my socks with a cup of milky tea that I might spill, and tuck my feet up on the chair, and put the radio on in the background, I wasn't interested. I felt watched.

I always, always, always preferred to work in a café, given a choice. I liked the sense that I could leave at any moment. I liked pretending I wasn't at work, even though I was working. I liked watching the world go by, and nowadays, I liked that I could take my dog. But even pre-dog, I would have chosen working in a café over a library every time. Cafés allowed you to drink coffee, and I found silence unnerving.

I collected the books I'd ordered from a man at 'Issue & Return' who seemed pissed off that I existed, and tried nonetheless to feel spry and important as I walked self-consciously back to my desk. We hadn't done this, inhabited our professional selves in this way, in public, for a year and half.

I put such thoughts aside and opened the books. *Isaac Albéniz: Portrait of a Romantic*, and *Isaac Albéniz: A Guide to Research*, both by Walter A. Clark, who seemed to be the man who writes about Albéniz in English, and who is based in California. Doing things properly (or procrastinating from the serious tasks), I started with the *Guide to Research*. You need to know how to do the research, I reasoned, before you actually do it.

Clark's *Guide to Research* is very cool, and likely a game-changer for anyone who wants to do academic work on Albéniz. Published in 1998, when one's search engine of choice would likely have been Yahoo or AltaVista, it remains just as useful for the Google era. Not only does it contain a short biography of his life, and a comment on the contemporary state of research on Albéniz, it also gives you an overview of all the books and articles that have ever been published on Albéniz, with commentary so you know roughly what they say and whether they're something you might want to look at. Then there's a comprehensive list of all his musical works, of all the recordings of his musical works, a list of the archives where materials relating to him can be found – mostly in Barcelona and Madrid – and even a list of interesting contemporary newspaper and periodical articles published about him. In short, this unassuming volume is a time-saver, a springboard and a lifeline for English speakers, who otherwise would need to foster for themselves those insider, personal connections Clark has made over a lifetime. To share them in this way is a huge act of generosity to the scholarly community.

This is one of the things I love about scholarship. When there's the sense that we are all building together, for the benefit of everyone.

Albéniz may not be a household name. But with thousands of recordings of his music, and his music printed by over forty publishing houses, he's certainly a significant composer. Looking through the discography, his music is everywhere. Yet the scholarly landscape of Albéniz research, it turns out, is a bit strange and patchy. 'Given his importance', writes Clark, 'one is fairly amazed to discover that the scholarship on Albéniz has traditionally been neither wide nor deep.' He's been very overlooked, with almost nothing done on him in English, I learn.

I doubt that Dad knew much about Albéniz as a person beyond the compositions. Often, for musicians, the music gets divorced from the human who composed it, becoming mere repertoire. Or maybe that's just me. When I used to play the trombone and the piano seriously, the composer was often nothing more than a name at the top of the music. Something like a mathematical axiom. Dad, by contrast, might have been interested in the human behind it all.

I think Dad would have liked Albéniz, or at least the idea of Albéniz: nearly every major detail is contested in the early accounts of Albéniz's life. And this is because – apparently – it amused Albéniz to simply make things up in his conversations with journalists, biographers, even friends. To tell them highly elaborated versions of the truth. For instance, in 1880 Albéniz travelled to Budapest to fulfil his dream of studying with the piano virtuoso and composer extraordinaire Franz Liszt, a rock star of his age, and he wrote in his diary that he'd played for him, and told everyone about it when he got back. But the entire thing must have been invented: Liszt hadn't even been in Budapest when Albéniz visited. Albéniz was a man of extravagant moods, prone to bouts of depression, even suicidal, as I learned. Uncovering the documents that untangle the man from the myth, the fact from the fiction, has been Clark's life's work.

From this tiny detail, I felt two distinct versions of Albéniz come into focus. The version I liked more: Albéniz the rogue, who is subversive, cynical, who sees through the media circus and the biographical myth-making around him, and plays with it, tells these exaggerated tales with a wink and a glint in his eye, realising he can say anything at all. The man who doesn't see rules, but who knows the truth and reserves it for the people closest to him. This is the man I like. The man who makes a mockery of the publicity machine, because the publicity machine doesn't matter, really, and he recognises that. What matters is much closer to home. But whose rejection of the publicity machine and its promises might in the end be to protect himself. He doesn't trust love, so he plays with the affections of the public sphere. Real love is too dangerous.

Then there's the man I like less. The egotist. The jovial type who exaggerates for effect, who can't really tell the truth from the fabrication, who needs the bigger version because he needs to be loved, adored, needs the enhanced sense of self it creates. In my mind's eye, I see this man, and he is overbearing.

I like the first man, because the first man sounds much more like my father.

I like the first man, because that disregard for reality sounds a lot like me, after my father died.

We can only ever fabricate these historical figures. Albéniz made himself a myth while he was alive, and now only the myth – or the mask – remains, with the man behind it impossible to locate. A person lost in so many words, so much music. So, for now, with only these two short books to guide my impressions, hardly impartial (history never is), I'll stick with the version of the man I like.

It was spring when Blanca, Albéniz's eldest child, died. 4 April. She was nearly two, twenty months old, and died of a fever, leaving behind Albéniz, his wife Rosina Jordana and their younger son Alfonso, born in the summer of 1885, and not yet one. On 8 April 1886, *La correspondencia musical* published its condolences to the Albéniz family. According to Clark, family accounts of the period read as if it never happened. She goes completely unmentioned in letters, diaries, even any biographical accounts – the contemporary primary sources, and he describes this absence as 'an index of the emotional devastation this must have caused'. Blanca had been named after Albéniz's sister who killed herself on 16 October 1874, a singer, depressed after failing an audition for the Teatro de la Zarzuela in Madrid. Perhaps Isaac worried that, in passing on the name, he had committed his daughter to another tragic fate. Perhaps he felt responsible.

Nothing may have been written in prose, perhaps, but what about his music? Right after Blanca's death, it seems Albéniz travelled to the southern coast of the country, to Málaga, ostensibly to give concerts. On 13 May 1886, *La correspondencia musical* reported his return from a financially successful excursion, performing no less than twenty-six selections. 'Rumores de la caleta' explicitly references a style of flamenco specific to Málaga in the title, the 'Malagueña' – and it brought me back to the question of grief and place. Whose murmurs; what beach? What was Albéniz thinking about, travelling to give concerts in Málaga, Andalusia, in the month after the death of his eldest child? Did he travel alone, or with Rosina, the daughter of a wealthy businessman in Barcelona, described as 'pretty and discreet' in a press announcement of their marriage? I feel angry on behalf of Rosina, consigned for ever to be 'pretty and discreet'. I'd be furious. Her husband's legacy is monumental and she's: what? Nothing more than: appropriate for him, confined. One man's wife, another man's daughter. Amenable, pleasant, a footnote, a mere outline visible through the paper she's written into. Were they together in grief, or did they want to be as far apart from one another as possible?

And how much of that loss, that isolation, made its way into the music, the same piece Dad left on the stand? The dates of composition given for *Recuerdos de viaje* are 1886–7; it was written at exactly the time when Albéniz would have been most deeply, acutely grieving his small daughter, the life she'd had and the person she wouldn't grow up to be. Clark translates 'Recuerdos de viaje' as 'Souvenirs of a journey'. I'm slightly annoyed with myself for going for 'memories', not souvenirs; I began by getting the translation wrong. Is that journey as metaphorical as it is literal? Is that journey a way of describing grief? I wondered whether it tracked him bouncing around the concert circuit, moving fretful from place to place, trying to escape himself.

Or maybe my 'memories' is the better translation, at least to modern ears; to me, 'souvenirs' is suggestive of taking something away, and implies travel, the idea of the late-nineteenth-century tourist. 'Memories', by contrast, might take us further into his consciousness.

*

Albéniz was well-travelled, having spent time in Cuba; nonetheless, the beaches of Andalusia would have felt far from home for a man of the north, born in 1860 in a small town in Catalonia near the French border, brought up in Barcelona, with his Catalan mother and Basque father. Andalusia, far, far south, with its North African architectural influences, and the flamenco folk tradition to which Albéniz was so drawn, would have been tinged with the exotic. As a young man, he had spent a lot of time touring there; perhaps it carried particular associations from that period of his life.

I found what I'd suspected, and it had been as easy as checking Wikipedia. 'Rumores de la caleta (Malagueña)', which Clark translates as 'Murmurs of the cove', refers to a real place, a well-known site on the Andalusian coast. I could imagine a figure, early morning, having been unable to sleep, needing to be alone, away from it all, on the edge of the world following the death of a child, eyes empty, sea swilling back and forth, murmurs comforting, bringing us back to the world, tying us into the perpetual cycles. It's a deeply Romantic image of course – does it matter? After Dad died, someone sent us a photo of a dram of whisky they'd left on the shore, letting it get washed out to sea in his honour and memory, in the name of all things ending and beginning and staying the same. In the name of the miracle that is ever witnessing the sea in the first place.

I recalled that I wrote a poem when I was eight. It was about the magnitude of the sea, and I remember the line, 'some day, my boat and I'. I wanted to sail away alone. It was doused with big eight-year-old Romantic fervour, the romanticism of someone who's never heard of – and learned to be embarrassed by – romanticism. I wanted to sail away *for ever*. And probably, underneath it all, I wanted to grow up to be like my dad.

My dad. Hunched over his guitar, playing this music, on the stand, or just laid flat next to him on the sofa. Testing the notes out one by one, before strumming his way through the opening arpeggios, slightly labouring the triplets as he got it under his fingers. I remembered listening to recordings after he died, and I remembered the fear: how I already felt the aural image of my dad slipping away into the unknown and irrecoverable. And I didn't want to go there.

Instead, at my vast desk in the British Library, I started reading about all the sources I could find, the archives in Spain. I wanted words, not music. I began to plan a trip in my mind, thought of friends in Seville or Barcelona I could stay with, imagined taking public transport to the archives. But I pulled up short, breath suddenly shallow in my chest. It didn't feel quite right. I realised I didn't know if I wanted to do this to this music. I didn't know if I wanted to do what I usually do: to analyse it, to disenchant it. Because it only took a historical fragment, a source or a detail for my mind to want to whirl it away like the wind, up and away from the messiness and ache of feelings. Up and away from the messiness and ache of the music. Whirl it away in spirals of thought like: I wonder about the idea of the south and what it is to be bereft, I wonder about the meanings of heat and absence, beaches and emptiness. I wonder about the subversion of the cold of the north, and the wasteland of grief in a sun that roasts – and how I might, like an intellectual acrobat, a trapeze artist of the mind, weave this into a postcolonial argument about release and escape and fantasy and grief and the projections we in the so-called Global North cast on to the South. The sound is nowhere in these feelings. And its absence saves me from having to feel, swinging weightless above the leaden pull of the emotions that the music wanted me to have.

I was scared of falling, but knew I needed to fall. To feel.

And so I pulled myself back from my imaginings

of aeroplanes and buses and bookings and letters of introduction to archives, unsure. I didn't want to corrupt, complicate this music. I didn't want to add these intellectual problems. But neither did I want to pretend that the music was something simple and pure. That veers dangerously close to something else. There's a long history of northerners idealising southern music, in the same way as the South, defined in different ways, has been idealised as something primitive, natural; an antidote to modernity and industry, to the problems of the North. Nietzsche, for instance, did that regarding the music of the south, when he got very excited about Bizet's opera *Carmen*, a supposed light and simple and healthy French-Italianate antidote to the intellectual problems, the *sickness* of Wagner's German operas. To do so essentialises the south, views it as a mere resource. We don't seem to be able to think our way out of these oppositions rooted in self and other, no matter how many centuries pass. And this music was far more than a resource for my grief.

So much thinking, so much mental noise. I just wanted to keep its connection to Dad.

Chapter 9

UNFINISHED SYMPHONY

Even with the bursts of human contact unavoidable with a dog, I still felt unmoored from the outside world. We'd made our own one, tiny, self-contained and confined to my flat, filled with bin bags and cardboard and dog toys. As spring turned to summer, I continued to traverse the park with a sense of light-headedness. We passed the personal trainer working his victim, press-ups against a bench, a loaded barbell on the ground. Under the bridge. That's where I let her off the lead, far enough from the road, and although Datch was fully terrestrial, nose in intimate contact with the tarmac and grass, I was just floating: I felt no connection to this reality of which I seemed still to be a part. A couple were sitting on the next bench sharing a takeaway. I needed encounters at the park to ground me. Dogs meet one another, and immediately begin to wrestle. Imagine if humans were that direct. Instead, we wrestle mentally with one another and our internal codes. I asked a huge don't-mess-with-me man with a muscular dog straining on its leash 'How long have you had her?' and his eyes misted, and his shoulders slid together as he gestured, said: 'I got her when she was this small', and, just for a moment, I saw the tiny puppy in his arms, and the care, and there's someone else, a glimpse under the armour we apply for public spaces. A dog was a licence to trust, to get to the heart of things, to elicit secrets and longings, a door opened on to people's vulnerability, a thing between you that allowed closeness.

I discovered that, had I wanted to date straight white women, I would have been spoiled for choice.

But they weren't quite who I was looking for back then.

Luckily, around that time, I met someone, J, through means that weren't my dog. An old-fashioned drinks party. I wasn't ready, but neither was he, so we saw no reason not to stick with it, and find out whether we would start to feel differently.

'Is she an especially cute dog?' he asked me, unable to fathom the reactions of strangers. J was completely clueless vis-à-vis the world of dogs, and the peculiarities of those of us who reside there. Did this happen to all dogs? Was everyone apart from him in a permanent state of readiness to express their delight at every dog they saw? Baffling.

Time continued through various lockdowns in a new routine governed at both micro and macro level by Datch, and at some point in all of this, as was always inevitable, my birthday came around. Against my better judgement, on my birthday I was getting my music stand out again, placing it in the middle of the room. Because J wanted to hear me play the trombone. As a treat. He'd never seen me play the trombone before. For all he knew, I might have invented this slightly bizarre capability.

'Only if you want to,' he said.

I didn't want to: I was afraid of knowing how bad I had become. I was afraid of how little joy it would bring me. To hear pale echoes of how good I used to be behind the crackle and messy articulations of which I was now capable, and to know how much work it would take to get back to that standard, and to know that I no longer had the time or the motivation to do two hours of practice a day so I could access that glorious feeling of fluidity and power when the instrument comes to my lips.

It was dispiriting.

But none of these seemed like good enough reasons not to play for him. Not to show him what I can do.

I knew that to an outsider, I would still seem very good at the trombone. I knew even before I began to play that J would be impressed. A woman playing the trombone is a cool thing, and still mildly startling. Surprise: I have this wildly unexpected talent. But I knew that to me it would still feel awful and unsatisfying. Before I made the mistake of harnessing my identity to musicology, I had previously made the mistake of harnessing my identity on to how well I could play the trombone. I thought I could be a professional, longed for that life, gaze fixed on the conductor over a sea of heads, or swaying to salsa, or spraying my slide with water during a quick pause, bringing the instrument back to life, then all senses fired to the microtunings and timings of my neighbours as we played a chorale. Now everything short of that was a kick in my stomach.

People who haven't fallen from these heights find it hard to understand why this relationship would be so fraught.

'But surely you love music! Have you thought about joining an amateur orchestra?' well-meaning friends, acquaintances, colleagues, friends of my mother, people at the gym, police officers, supermarket checkout assistants, would ask.

It offends people to no longer play. I'm not sure what exactly you are offending, but it might be their unfulfilled dreams. Suggesting that you wouldn't want to keep doing it is an affront to the standard you have reached, to how much work you have put in, to who they want you to be, to who *they* might want to be. But that's precisely why you don't want to keep doing it. Amateur orchestras can mean you have to attend weeks of rehearsals for repertoire you've played several times before; you'd rather be invited to dep in a concert – that is, to play a part at the last minute, in the way you used to be called on to do for money, but that won't work, because you'd be too out of practice to play well, and even if you could play the notes, you'd hate the sound you made in performance. You're a victim of your own success, now too good to properly enjoy amateur music-making.

'My relationship with music is so complicated,' my friend Helen said to me recently. Her feelings are different to mine, but we share a complex nostalgia. 'I'm a musician, first and foremost. I'll always be a musician.' Helen did a year at a London conservatoire, focusing on playing the oboe, before studying music at university, and after she finished, she worked at a charitable agency supporting exceptional young classical musicians at the start of their solo careers. 'It's how I see myself. And yet my daughter has only ever seen me play the oboe twice. I worry that I need to play more often, so she associates it with me. So she understands. And now we're thinking about what instrument she might start to play – she's five – and it's bringing back all the old longing to play, to be, above all, a musician.' I remember, ten years ago, watching Helen play incredible concertos in a huge concert hall; hearing her solo on the cor anglais, the opening theme of the beautiful second movement of Dvořák's *New World* Symphony. 'I think about my relationship with music a lot. Whenever I introduce myself to someone, I can't help it; I stress the fact that until recently I worked in classical music.' Helen now works in the civil service. Among other things, the maternity leave is better. As is the pay.

I felt differently. I felt I'd been ruined by the quality of those orchestras and big bands I played with in my twenties, made up of people who really did go on to become pros, where only the best was good enough, where everyone was practising the hell out of their instruments, aiming for the stars. Everything since has felt thin compared to those heady experiences.

It's hard not to slip into thinking that being good at music has ruined music.

Chris's instrument is also the oboe (not all my friends play the oboe). He's played in numerous professional orchestras, but mostly these days he only plays rarely, and he teaches the piano. I've known him since we were teenagers. He *loves* music. When I texted him out of the blue to ask if he had time to talk to me about his relationship with his oboe, he replied that he was feeling a bit raw about it, and that he might cry. There was an emoji, but I didn't think he was joking.

When we spoke, he said, 'I'm disappointed I don't miss it more.'

But he's afraid of giving up completely. He's afraid of what that would do to his sense of self. Every time he's asked to play professionally, though, it means weeks of advance preparation to get his stamina back. He doesn't think it's sustainable.

No one wants to hear that musicians don't miss playing. I'm not sure why.

I know betrayal is a key ingredient in the slurry of feelings here. I loved – love – my trombone. It's *mine*, and it's storied with everything we've done together. And I've abandoned it, neglected it, like a former lover, but with a slightly different flavour of shame. I'm conscious of all the adventures we could still be having together. I feel deep guilt that something so alive could be inanimate, boxed away. But it's still out. It's not packed away in an attic. Like so many of my friends who are former musicians, we keep our instruments within close reach.

These were the sorts of thoughts not-exactly-warming my soul as I went through the second-nature motions of taking my trombone out of its case. My trombone is a marvellous instrument, and one with a backstory. It was once anecdotally fished out of the canal in Manchester with sudden regret after its previous owner hurled it in after a gig with the Hallé, frustrated by his inability to get a permanent seat with an orchestra, a familiar fate for excellent musicians. It's a Conn 88H, mass-produced as all brass instruments are, which makes them, unlike strings and woodwind, relatively budget friendly. The Conn 88H is a favourite among professional orchestral players across the UK and US, and mine has a trigger adaptation done at a brass workshop in Yorkshire, giving a smoother action than the standard Conn. It's easy to put together. A trombone comes in two pieces; I screwed the slide to the bell section, and popped the mouthpiece into the slide section. I sprayed the slide with water; considered using the slide oil that has the double entendre brand name 'rapid comfort' and looks like semen (it's long been a boys' game, this); but I wouldn't be playing long enough, I thought. I wouldn't have the stamina.

Datch pottered around my feet, flopped on to the ground in a puddle, and looked up at me. Cocked her head to one side, inquisitive. I was curious what she would make of this noisy metal thing I was about to plant on my face. I'd had to gradually acclimatise her to the vacuum cleaner. Who knew how she was going to cope with this.

She wasn't sure. *I* wasn't sure. She scooted away as I lifted the instrument. It was worryingly bulky. Safer to be out of the way and ready should any barking be required.

The last time I had played was in Boston, three years previously, a concert of Schubert's 'Unfinished' Symphony with an amateur orchestra attached to the university, and for which I avoided nearly all the rehearsals, and turned up for the concert, and, yes, hated the sound I made. I had bought a special reinforced hard case to ship my trombone out to the US for the privilege of playing in that single concert during the two years I was there. I had taken all three of my mutes, each as large as a flower vase. I didn't want to give up the idea that I played the trombone; nor did I want to actually play it.

This love-hate-ambivalent-can't-admit-how-I-feel-maybe-one-day-I'll-play-again and when-did-these-other-priorities-get-so-big? story is one many of us know all too well.

The cold of the mouthpiece on my lips. I inhaled the taste of metal and tentatively started with some slow lip slurs, moving between harmonics without changing the slide position. You can do these on any brass instrument because they all generate sound by vibrating a column of air, and you use the vibration of your lips to change the frequency of the air vibrations within the metal tube that is the instrument. It's simply a standing wave. Amazingly, what I hadn't fully lost was my sound, and my sound had been the thing that was the hardest to develop. This was encouraging. My lip flexibility was shot, though. So was my articulation, which is all done with the tongue. So as not to bore J, I fished out some orchestral excerpts, those being, as I've mentioned before, the famous moments for trombone from big orchestral repertoire, which we learn alone in practice rooms without the rest of the piece, so we're ready for them when they come up.

The trombone is cruel to those who don't practise regularly. Serious players complain bitterly about a three-day break. It's all about the muscle conditioning.

I didn't play 'Mippy'. I couldn't face it, it was too personal. I'd played it in a recital once; worked at it day after day after day in a white room tucked at the top of the music department, a window looking over the drizzle and brick of the university library, a soprano in the neighbouring room cycling through each of the Italian vowel sounds, the scents of the oil on the valve and the slide lubricant, familiar and reassuring, the old-blood metal air filling my lungs. Rehearsing not until I got it right, but until I couldn't get it wrong. And the feeling of promise, if we all only worked hard enough, put in enough hours. A sense that drove us, aged twenty: the world would be ours, hundreds of possible futures rolling out ahead. So I didn't want to hear my inability to do it now. Couldn't face knowing what I'd become with a piece that I'd once been so close to it had become part of me. The orchestral excerpts, they didn't belong to me in the same way. For J, I played the trombone solo in Wagner's 'The Ride of the Valkyries'. Music off the rack, I could tolerate.

J thought it was wonderful.

I didn't feel as awful as I thought I would. I felt as if I was standing at the bottom of an enormous mountain I didn't have the inclination to climb, only there was a vague and pervasive sense that I really should be making time to climb it; that I had some duty to the mountain. That at the top of the mountain was someone else's joy – or maybe even my joy – a satisfying life of trombone playing in my spare time in high-quality amateur ensembles, and an unidentifiable obligation to that dream.

Chapter 10

CASTLES MADE OF SAND

'The fifteen twenty-nine South West Rail service to [beat] London Waterloo via [beat] Sherborne is delayed by [beat] eleven minutes. We're sorry that your journey will take longer than planned.' Mmm hmm. Longer than planned.

If there's a station that really does make Clapham Junction look like a place of dreams, it's Yeovil Junction. Which was where I found myself stuck that day. Contemplative solitude under empty skies in the August heat of the arse end of nowhere.

And an hour to go.

I was sitting on a blue metal bench with oval holes in it waiting for the next train. I checked the display above the platform: fifty-eight minutes. Fifty-eight minutes of birds tweeting, a light breeze through my hair, still trees, train tracks on both sides of me, a feeling of *nothing ever happens here* and, the *pièce de résistance*, a silent railway centre with a classic locomotive on show, glossy green. The sound of a drone became an aeroplane, and a man coughed at the other end of the platform. Which was godforsaken-levels of empty, and flecked with chewing gum. The slatted underside of the awning (nineteenth century?) was grubby, except it was festively edged with upside-down jelly-like shapes, recalling beach huts at the seaside. A feeling of hot-weather haunting, a long-forgotten jolly Victorian holiday.

I was on my way to spend some time alone in Sherborne, a small market town in Dorset. One night booked in a hotel. Because Sherborne School – the old boys' independent school in the heart of the town – had hosted an annual music summer school, for which I'd worked as a steward throughout my twenties, free food and dormitory board and participation in three weeks of orchestral courses in exchange for moving kit around, setting up rooms for rehearsals, working in the music shop, changing bed linen between the influxes of people: in short, keeping the hidden wheels oiled. Dad had learned about it through my stewarding job, and several years in a row had taken the week-long jazz course they offered.

Despite having spent so many summers there, it would be my first visit in seven years. It was an August playground where I'd had many formative musical experiences, and it was a place I closely associated with my dad.

As I'd left my flat that morning – usually I cut trains fine, but the magnitude of the day meant I arrived early – I had felt excited, but also curiously on the verge of tears. I had passed the man I always wave at who works at the Greek supermarket, and because I didn't have the time or inclination to stop, felt some explanation was needed in lieu of small talk. 'I'm off to the station,' I said, as I kept walking. Where was I going? 'Down south,' I said. And then I told a half-truth, because the actual truth was too complicated, and a bit embarrassing. 'My mother lives there.' She did. But that wasn't where I was going.

'Are you staying?'

'Just one night.' I held up a finger, like an idiot, as if 'one' needed clarifying.

'We'll miss you, darling,' he said.

I did the thing I do when men say things like this, and smiled. I tried not to dwell on the fact I felt I had to justify myself and my actions to a man I didn't know.

The truth *was* complicated. And a bit embarrassing.

I was undertaking what some – not me of course – would refer to as a pilgrimage. A word J had used when he suggested the idea, and of which I disapproved. *Real people don't go on grief pilgrimages*, I thought. But it was hard to come up with concrete ways in which the activities differed, other than I don't think mine was religious. Not being religious didn't stop it being a ritual. My self-consciousness was a way of avoiding how emotionally dangerous it felt.

Wheat fields and buddleia hedgerows had raced past on the 12.20 to Exeter St Davids, flossed August clouds against bluest sky and sun diffraction on the window as a woman had organised a toddler with some crayons. That was when I'd felt the uncertainty crowd in. This was expensive and a ton of effort and I hoped I was going to get something out of it, but I wasn't at all sure what that would be. Sitting with my memories and feeling weird? Perhaps in Sherborne Abbey, feeling like the mysterious heroine of a melodrama, daring people to look at me, wanting them to avert their gaze. I had a vision of myself in Victorian mourning gear, something that featured a lot of crêpe and maybe a veil, me looking pallid (even more pallid than normal) and interesting. Or would I be trying to remember what those memories were? Hoping that the place would stimulate memories I'd forgotten? All of those things. *Possibly I'd be trying not to cry,* I thought, as someone wafted to their seat from the bathroom, smelling of talcum powder. Or possibly I'd feel fine and the whole thing would be a disappointment.

I was afraid of trying to stir grief into action, and not having the right response. Or, worse, any response.

This purgatory at Yeovil Junction, however, hadn't been part of the plan. I'd managed to miss my stop, overshoot.

Not wholly my fault: my carriage's electronic display had been out of sync with the physical reality of the journey, and I'd locked myself in the loo at what had turned out to be the crucial moment, i.e. arrival at my destination. Now I was waiting for the same train back in the opposite direction.

Sherborne School was a fairy tale I inhabited through my twenties, after I'd left school, the backdrop to my summers as I shuttled between universities and got more and more education, specialising further and further. They'd filmed parts of *Wolf Hall* there, I recalled. A place of ochre limestone: corners and quadrangles and churches and cobbled streets and walled gardens of grass for late-night secret telling, truth or dare and a bottle of rum, or for lounging and reading through your orchestral parts in the morning break. A community that re-formed every summer, different, refreshed, new faces and bodies, but with a core of staff whose identity shifted much more slowly, impervious to the community's surface-level chatter. A heady mix of twenty-somethings like us studying music at conservatoires or universities, but also professionals, amateurs, conductors, composers, singers, school ground staff. Not forgetting the contingent sent over each year of army, navy or air force bandsmen and women who brought a more athletic demographic and military mentality to proceedings. Or the members of the Royal Oman Symphony Orchestra, who also regularly flew in from Muscat. And what these people had in common was the desire (or, in some cases, if I'm honest, contractual obligation) to dedicate a week to music-making. In the case of us working on the stewarding team – and some of the military – it was dedication to music-making combined with extreme all-night socialising on a schedule that utterly exhausted me even then. An image of myself playing 'pick up a cardboard box with your teeth' while at a staff party, dressed in gingham as Dorothy from *The Wizard of Oz* arrived unbidden in my mind.

But in spite of the opportunities for fancy dress, the music was what really mattered. And you had to bring your A-game.

There was nowhere to go and visit Dad, because we hadn't got a grave, or decided what to do with the ashes. These things often take a long time. We hadn't decided whether to have a memorial stone, and it wasn't at all clear to me where we would put it. We'd talked about where to scatter the ashes, and there'd been a strong consensus that it would happen at sea. I suppose we don't want Dad to be fixed in one place, either.

I'd like to have a place to visit, though, so maybe I'd make my own.

His ashes still lived in the duck-green box the crematorium gave us, on top of the piano in the hall, under his childhood collection of butterflies on the wall. His name, date of death and his age are written on its label. Mum turned the container around so that the label wasn't facing outwards. It's a good, easy place to live. Last time I visited, I didn't even remember to notice he was there, or to feel complicated about it.

But for now, we didn't know where Dad would be, and we hadn't had a ritual scattering of the ashes at sea, and that meant Sherborne was as good a place as any for me to go and do some thinking about Dad, because it was a place that was just ours, and was suffused with music.

I was going back. This was a mere hiccough.

And maybe, I thought, in a way that didn't quite voice it directly even within the safety of my own head, not quite looking at the idea – maybe once I was there, I would try listening to some of the music I associated with my father.

Maybe.

Flat toddler feet ran down the platform. 'We've got loads of time,' said her mother. *Indeed*, I thought. I felt sad. I admired the half-empty car park. A white butterfly half floated, feather-like, half fluttered, its pattern of direction seemingly generated at random over the tracks by an agent of chaos. Dad loved butterflies. A tortoiseshell joined it, tracing an arc that went up and then dropped down like a weighted see-saw. There were pink, white and yellow flowers in green window boxes; weathered doors painted royal blue and turquoise. The colours of house fronts at the seaside. Green weeds forcing life through the railway tracks: we'll be here too, thanks.

My eyes continued to follow the haphazard activity of the butterflies as nothing continued to happen and minutes seemed suspended in the beating sun.

All my snacks were gone. The moment I got on the train at Clapham Junction, I'd eaten the best thing in my bag: the banana bread J had made me all parcelled up in foil.

I regretted this now.

It was August, the time of year we used to go there. Everything felt right. In a normal year, I'd have arrived right in the middle of the summer school. But it wasn't a normal year. There was a global pandemic.

Humans are resilient. When a friend who's a psychologist and I had mused the impact of the lockdown, she had reminded me: 'There was a time when they kept babies in a closet just to see what would happen. Sure, it was bad when they came out. But it wasn't as bad as you think.'

I hoped this was true. Either the world on pause was a world with more space for grief, or I was going to come out of all this deeply, deeply messed up.

I'll admit it pleased me that the summer school wasn't on. Dad was so dead that the world couldn't continue without him in it. He'd booked on the jazz course for the summer of 2019. We'd received emails to him after his death about his booking (again, lucky we'd known his password. Do tell someone you trust your passwords). I'd had to email the organisers, as I'd had to email so many people, to explain. Emailing someone on behalf of your late father's email account to say 'Sorry, he won't be replying, he's not being rude, but, well, he died. Unexpectedly. Please don't feel too badly about it. Actually, I wouldn't mind if you did. But I didn't mean to spring this on you, it's just true.'

And the cancelled summer school meant I didn't need to see anyone I knew on this journey.

Sherborne School for Boys wasn't an especially long drive from the school I had gone to, but they were not alike. Mine was two storeys high, constructed in the 1970s, and not exactly built to last. When I first went into Sherborne School's library to set up stands and chairs for some string quartet rehearsals, I realised why so many of my peers had felt at home as undergraduates at Oxford, where I'd briefly gone to study maths and philosophy before realising my mistake – both in terms of choice of course and my sense of belonging – and dropping out to pursue the things I actually loved: music and drama, off in the north. The lamps were the same, the polished wood was the same, the feeling that outdoor light was foreign here was the same. There was a large courtyard outside. There would have been no sense of aesthetic transition for them to contend with, as I had. At our school, the tables in the library were the same tables we had in classrooms, grey desks for two, grouped together in the middle of the room to make space for four on institutional but perfectly acceptable carpet. Strip lighting. The books were to one side, on metal racks. At least the carousels of books, the displays were the same, I thought. It amused me that the Dewey Decimal System transcended all. That was more or less the extent of what they had in common. But I hadn't thought there was anything lacking in our library. And yet the grace, the solidity of Sherborne. Imagine being used to this. Imagine not feeling the wonder I felt.

My dad would have felt no such wonder. Instead, something else. Cloying air, closed-in walls, visual trappings of history and bloodline and behaving right. A deep sense of oppression. Later, I looked up his school. It had never occurred to me to do so before, so unconscious was the taboo around it. But it's remarkably, disorientingly real, and easy to see photos – it's still a school, it has a website. Although I think of it as such, it's not a historical relic. It's been a real place all this time. Red brick, gardens, quads, a large chapel built on the grounds. One of the first schools to have a purpose-built place of worship. Any secondary school founded in the mid-nineteenth century is likely to still be standing, and to still be expensive.

By sending us to comprehensive schools, our parents kept us as far away as possible from the world they'd grown up in. But that made it hard to relate to what my dad was reacting against until I was much older. Because I'd never experienced it, bar the glimpses of girls with swishy hair on netball teams who, in the rare tournaments where state and private schools mixed, would always beat us. By a significant margin. 'Don't worry,' we were told by our PE teacher. 'They train every day. And they have to go to school on Saturdays.'

Occasionally, I would get flickers of images and I didn't know what to make of them, or where to place them on a matrix I didn't have. Chapel. I'd never gone to chapel, couldn't really picture a school having its own place of worship; but I sensed – or knew – it was something pointless and suffocating. How Dad reacted to embroidered kneelers when we went to church weddings, so irrelevant as to barely be worth observing. Bewilderment, if his attention lingered on them, laced with dismissive indifference, not curiosity.

He'd liked cricket and been good at it. I knew that. Possibly he was even the cricket captain. But the misery of that time was all I understood. He would convey it through talking about his O levels, a sense of failure. A fixedness of expression. I believed that my dad had done terribly at all his exams.

When he was nine, he was sent away to live with a French family for six months. So he would 'have French'. He and Yves, the little boy in the family he lived with, didn't like one another much. They used their catapults to bombard each other with conkers. At school in northern France, he spent his days idly drawing boats during his lessons.

He hated that time, too.

Only after he died, at his funeral, did I start to hear more, as I was introduced to school friends of his I hadn't previously met. It felt like I was doing something illicit, entering a time my father didn't want me to know about. I learned that, at his school, my dad had been well-known and respected for his talent on the guitar. That he was peerless in English and history. I'd only ever been peddled stories by my dad of his failures in mathematics and science – failures which I'm sure would have disappointed his own father, a consultant paediatrician. Who would have wanted him to be scientific, in the family tradition. When I was fourteen, my grandfather wrote to me on crisp letterheaded paper in indecipherable handwriting to suggest I pursue a medical career. He included an NHS leaflet detailing the process, the school qualifications I'd need, the academic pathway.

I wasn't keen on blood.

But now I think the mention of those exam results wasn't really about the exams. It was about the despair, about anger, about the quiet sense of failure that comes with feeling unwanted, that you didn't belong with your family from the very beginning. What had you done wrong? Why was this what you deserved?

Everything I know about my father's school, I have pieced together through his reactions to other things. Unconscious associations with that world's tropes appear to me as if fully formed truths. Churches. Oxbridge. Hymns. Monarchy. Titles. Rarified environments that suggested money or The British Establishment. His distress during my Oxford graduation, telling my mum he couldn't breathe. His decision not to set his sights on a career in the London Stock Exchange, or as a lawyer, but to travel to New Zealand. To get as far away as possible. To become a local news reporter; to live on an ancient yacht off the west coast of Scotland, as far from that southern Wiltshire English establishment, from croquet sticks, as far away from the confines and blinkers of class as he could get.

But my dad loved music. Just not the violin. Not the piano. I never saw him play it.

The music my dad loved was blues.

The music my dad loved was unsanctioned. An escape, a way of being something else.

At my dad's funeral, his friend Mark told me a story.

1968. Dad and Mark are meant to be doing English prep in their shared study. Instead they're listening to Jimi Hendrix's second studio album, rocking back on their chairs as the summer of revolution unfurls far beyond Wiltshire boarding school walls. *Axis: Bold as Love*. It's all about the guitar. Making his routine checks, the housemaster opens the door; Hendrix stops. Music is forbidden during prep, and so, ingeniously, they have rigged up a circuit breaker: drawing pins as contacts on the door frame, and the action of opening the door silences the reel-to-reel tape player. Dad leans over ever so slightly, surreptitiously, to turn off the quiet hum, all that could have given them away.

I hadn't really known Dad had loved Hendrix when he was young. Hendrix was a mystery to me. I first listened to the album months later. I was drawn to 'Castles Made of Sand', midway through. It's tuneful, begins with the album's signature psychedelic backwards guitar sound-world. The bass paints thick, precise lines, then bass and kit cut out in a way that feels just right before Hendrix sings the chorus, how castles made of sand will always eventually collapse into the sea: freewheeling, spinning, a guitar texture picked out behind. It has a superb guitar riff. On the first hearing, you don't really make out the words, except for that chorus.

Doubtful what Hendrix intended, it took me mittened to a Scottish beach with Dad, making sandcastles, the plop suction of bashing grey sand with a plastic spade, and then running, running free for the distant sea, desperate to swim, although I couldn't. A lengthy pause, Mum and Dad watching the tiny figure that was me receding with grand intentions towards the horizon. Dad, with a sigh, 'Right, I suppose I'd better go and get her.' And I'd be swept up by Dad, into his arms, screeching indignant as I was transported against my enormous four-year-old will back to safety, away from the foaming water that was all I wanted.

There's a photo from that day framed in my flat, me sitting on Dad's shoulders, grinning, hair windswept, gloves with the faces of lions (they each had names) secured with elastic threaded through my sleeves, across my back, visible hanging below my hands; Dad holding my ankles, me gripping Dad's hair above his ears. The sky is flinty slate behind us, the shore wet. He would be thirty-nine, perhaps; his hair was already completely grey. Thanks for those genes, Dad.

The shore is pebbly, and according to Mum, it's not in Scotland at all. The distinctions of memory always fade, melt into the sea.

Sandcastles must have been some other time.

*

Once the frustration lifted, Yeovil Junction was quite a beautiful place, and I had it all to myself. It had one of those lovely clocks with Roman numerals.

A train pulled in, pulled away, and Yeovil Junction resumed its primary function: a habitat for butterflies.

In some ways Sherborne was a peculiar place to go because although Dad and I were there together, our paths crossed while we were each doing two separate things. He was participating in a course; I was on the staff. For a moment I wondered whether this whole plan was totally misguided: whether Sherborne had enough of a connection with Dad for me to feel whatever feelings I thought I might want to feel or not feel.

And then I realised it anew. He died. It was too late.

I only have the experiences I've already had. There wouldn't be more, wouldn't be a right one. We went to Sherborne together and he clutched crumpled scores getting out of his car, contrasting with the nice, neatly ordered folders of his colleagues, and it wasn't going to get any better because there wouldn't be any more experiences. I couldn't wait for something that more closely fitted my picture of what it should be like, and I felt the faintest prickling behind my eyes, but it was so beautifully sunny here and I was too on edge to know what these physical signals meant. I think I was approaching the feeling I had when he died and there were phases of *Why do I feel OK? Am I doing it wrong?* before it flooded back in and don't panic you're really really really devastated, it's just sometimes you're also functional.

Six minutes to go, assuming I could trust the delay. Those butterflies were singing in my stomach.

It was always really comforting to know Dad was there, even if I hadn't admitted it at the time. He used to come and visit me when I was working on the till in the music shop in the breaks. But he never wanted to cramp my style. He would leave the course-mates he couldn't connect with and get drunk on the steps to the dining hall. He'd be joined by my twenty-something-year-old friends. 'Your dad's an absolute legend!' a tall percussionist bounded up to tell me at breakfast the following morning. I was proudest when Dad joined a regular group of us who'd been playing squash together in the sports centre – I have a clear image of him limping towards us on court with his kit – and he beat everyone by miles despite being in his mid-sixties and needing a hip replacement. We stewards had been playing every time we got an unscheduled moment to ourselves, when we weren't rehearsing, or moving music stands between buildings. That's *my dad*. He might look harmless, but he's not like anyone else you know.

Moving again, on the very short train back to Sherborne in the wrong direction, I didn't know if I needed a ticket. I didn't have one, didn't know how I would have got one. Who cared really, some things are beyond our control.

I walked up the hill from Sherborne Station. All of a sudden it was a three-dimensional place again. I felt excited and a bit weak. I remembered how small the town was, how it felt like it was ours all those summers.

The station was much closer to the abbey and the school than I recalled. Doves flew out of the eaves. I walked past Digby school house, where we used to change the bed linen, and we didn't always like what we found.

A sign outside the abbey told me it was closed to visitors until tomorrow. Bother, as my dad might have said. I'd looked up the opening times in advance; but there had been a service going on, possibly a funeral, which I didn't want to think about. I smelled the church darkness as I dallied in the entrance way, regrouping, and decided to head up towards the school instead.

My plans scuppered for now, I dropped into a coffee shop and ordered an elderflower cordial. It was quiet. The staff were comparing how good their teeth were. 'Did you have braces?' A young woman with a limp bob and a nose piercing looked blankly out the window while saying, 'You've got nice teeth, though,' as if the matter was settled. 'Do you want to clean the kitchen?' she asked her colleague, as she sprayed the counter.

When I left, I was the last customer.

Chapter 11

BELLS

I left my things at the pub doubling as a hotel where the carpet was herringbone and the corridors smelled of garlic bread, and wandered back into town. I bought a takeaway pizza from a pop-up pizzeria in the garden of an antique shop, a horse box trailer with a pizza oven on its folding-out door. I took it down to the abbey. It was an absolutely perfect evening. The light was exactly how it's always been, grazing the tops of the buildings on Cheap Street. The sky was empty, translucent at the edges.

I might not have been able to go in yet, but I could eat outside the abbey on the gently inclined lawn in front. The grass was damp, so I looked for a bench.

I wasn't sure I'd ever really looked at Sherborne Abbey, but I looked at it then as if I were going to draw it, thinking of my mum and her sketchbooks. Black birds were perched motionless atop its Gothic spires. Probably crows? Too far away to know, with my ornithological skills. A square tower with fourteen spires punctuating its perimeter, and one on each corner. A gargoyle with the face of an owl. And the whole structure, sandy in colour, verging on amber in this sunset light, higgledy-piggledy stonework, was all sharp lines against the sky and curves within and thin windows (for arrows?) and lichen. Lines rounded ever so slightly by centuries, edges worn away, but no less imposing cut against the milky purple-blue of sundown.

I was sitting at some distance from the abbey on a park bench where, I remembered only as I sat down, I once kissed a long-forgotten conducting student in the middle of the night. I watched a couple investigate the entrance, now closed up for the evening. Even the door arch was vast: she could stand on his head, I thought, and they still would be nowhere near reaching the top. Not even if I went over and helped with this absurd project. I got a sense, all of a sudden, of its true magnitude, sitting here alone. It's harder to notice in our age of skyscrapers. *This is magnitude on a human scale*, I thought. I tried to imagine how staggeringly enormous it would have seemed in the fifteenth century, when you likely wouldn't have travelled far in your lifetime and it was almost certainly the largest man-made structure you would ever see. The abbey dominates its surroundings, dominates fragile little people. It inhabits a deeper time; the people passing it by, myself included, are transient. The abbey will still be here.

Aurally too, it has dominated people, disciplined them, with those bells ringing out every fifteen minutes. Apparently, this is the heaviest peal of eight bells in the world. Each weighing around a tonne; the largest, the tenor, weighing more like two-and-a-half. I read later that it had been a gift from Cardinal Wolsey, a powerful figure in the sixteenth-century government of Henry VIII. You always know where you are in this town in relation to the abbey. There's no forgetting it.

A bell does far more than tell us the time. It builds a community around it. In early modern England, each parish had different bells, different codes. They bound together the people who recognised the messages of that precise peal, making a spiritual and emotional community.

And that community was also shaped by those who were excluded: those from elsewhere, who would not know the codes; people for whom the peals were unreadable noise. In those days, elsewhere could be as nearby as the neighbouring parish.

That's probably still true, actually. Rivalries between neighbouring villages where I come from are fierce and borderline bloody. Depending on how seriously you take cricket.

Specific bells rang for death. Bells have rung for death almost since the very beginning. According to a 1725 publication about the habits, opinions and ceremonies of 'the common people', a work that deploys historical, and therefore fairly random, conventions of punctuation and capitalisation, 'The Ceremony of Tolling the Bell at the Time of Death, seems to be as ancient as the having of Bells themselves'. In early modern England, the bells might ring several times around a death: while a person was dying, then to signal that the death had happened and again for the burial. Samuel Pepys observed in 1665 during the Great Plague of London: 'Sad news of deaths of so many in the parish of plague ... The bell always going.' Before the Reformation, when Henry VIII shifted the national religion to Protestantism, and the idea of purgatory was done away with, the bells were one of the ways in which the living intervened on behalf of the dead, smoothing their way to heaven, lobbying on their behalf. The bells weren't primarily a signal that someone had died. Instead, they were a call to action for the community: pray for the soul.

Sometimes the bells would ring out all day and all night.

The precise peal would signal the status of the person who had died. It didn't come free, unless you were a monarch, or a leading figure in the aristocracy, or unusually pious. If none of those categories applied, you would have to pay. When Queen Elizabeth I died in 1603, the parish bells worked like an aural semaphore network, the code passing from parish to parish, the news rippling right across the country, sound waves, shock waves from that first church, that first set of bells. Change in the air, the country on a precipice.

What that endless clamouring all over the country must have been like. A once-in-a-lifetime's experience, an extraordinary soundscape bringing people to the streets like a solar eclipse.

Death was closer then. Constant. Now we clear it away. We don't question that the body has to disappear; our world is for the living. We don't need to signal a death to the community, it's not their business in the way it used to be.

Sherborne Abbey's bells still ring out for deaths, I learned later, although these days most people choose not to have bells rung at funeral services. With the wind in the right direction, the bells can be heard far outside of the town.

This was an old, old place. It had seen more than my nocturnal teenage misdemeanours.

I thought then about putting on some music. But I was afraid of my response. And was also afraid of not having a response, that the power of that music to take me to the emotions would have worn off, and what would I have then? I wanted to still be able to feel, and I wanted that feeling to be the musical sadness that is pleasant and bearable, and *I miss him*, not the anger that is big and unendurable in my chest and makes me want to run or break things.

So I didn't get my phone out.

I could hear the distinctive cawing of a seagull, and a little girl, like countless little girls before her, ran bare-legged across the lawn.

I was cold from sitting still for so long. My pizza was long finished. I had earned a pint.

*

It wasn't an especially nice pub, and since I wasn't eating, and it wasn't warm enough to sit outside, I'd been shunted into an uncomfortable corner area by the bar. Away from other clients, but right in the swim of it, listening to the waiting staff and bartenders, just where Dad would have liked to be. Knowing what was going on. Hearing staff complain about tables that were difficult, hinting at something dark and threatening under the surface – 'I hate going over to table ten'; people splitting their bill inconveniently, drunk; overhearing staff calling me 'the lady' who wants another half-pint. At the pizza van I'd been 'the young lady', but I supposed these people were about eighteen and I was nearly thirty-four. How did that happen?

Around me were the West Country accents of my teens. It was my youth rendered strange, yet oddly comforting. *Verfremdung*, the Germans call it – I'd learned German when I lived in Berlin during my PhD, and sometimes it gave me a useful extra vocabulary. I knew these people. I'd worked this job, waited these tables. Blokes (definitely 'blokes') at the bar were talking about exercising for their mental health. This is Britain in the early 2020s. 'It's not even about the fitness. Get out on your bike for ten miles first thing in the morning and you are—', and his hand signal indicated perfection.

After I'd arrived in Sherborne it all felt completely different to how I'd imagined before I'd arrived. You can't grieve right in some places. Places are generative. They bring on the thoughts and the emotions. And we'd all been stuck in place for two years, travel forbidden. I tried not to worry about blocked grieving, and worried about blocked grieving all the same.

I was slightly drunk now, and it was a nice feeling. A feeling appropriate to my memories of the place. I'd adjusted. 'Do we do Jägerbombs?' asked a waitress, coming back to the bar. I hadn't thought about Jägerbombs in years. She was on her second ever shift, I had gleaned. Learning the ropes. The pub did not stoop to Jägerbombs.

I'd always taken the abbey and its magnificence for granted. For me, it was a functional space, mainly: a space of arranging chairs and lugging instrument cases and timpani around, and I had needed no permission to enter because it had been simply another venue associated with the summer school. Albeit the grandest one. Its majesty had been an ancillary feature, far behind the pressing problems of its expansive acoustics, and the inconvenient placement of the various structures of worship (altar, lectern, pews) when you're trying to set up a symphony orchestra.

The next morning, though, I inhabited it differently, sitting on a wine-coloured pew cushion, now feeling more relaxed about being in a town so unlike London, but also dull, hung-over and slightly bewildered at the feelings and memories and urges crowding my body. I had bought a guidebook at the abbey shop across the flat lawn from the main entrance, and learned about the abbey's history, and was interleaving it with my own.

Sherborne Abbey is a palimpsest, I thought. Time written on time written on time, and here we are, inhabiting a paper-thin film at the very top like ghosts waiting to happen. I watched a woman with a backpack admiring the Tudor marble tomb of John and Joan Leweston, magnificently supine, tucked away in a recess, and surrounded by all this stone her bare legs looked terribly flesh-like; terribly corporeal, captured in a moment in time preceding their decay. For well over a thousand years, the abbey had been a site of Christian worship. It was founded in AD 703, and it has significant portions from the twelfth, fifteenth and nineteenth centuries. Layers, seams, revisions, a living document of human history. If you knew where to look. I never had before.

The thickness of the past. A wedding was happening later on; a florist was making ready in the nave with huge displays of white roses that nonetheless seemed small in the yawning abbey. That wedding would be another moment, the centre of some lives, unmarked by others, witnessed by the abbey, then receding into the abbey's history, its many, many human moments spanning centuries.

We had laid white roses on Dad's coffin after the rest of the funeral-goers had left, before they took the coffin away. A few years ago, Dad had planted a white rose bush at the end of the garden. Somehow, white roses here, today, felt nice, like the abbey expected not just the wedding guests, but also expected me.

We look for meaning wherever we can find it.

It's easier to tell someone your dad has died when you imagine them as the abstract idea of a dad that the other person might be thinking of, not your actual person. It's a great trick for blocking it out. I inhabit the story I know they hear. The same story I know I once heard other people tell – one that felt like it only happened to other people, like time (and death) was a thing that could be held at bay, that only started to apply once the starting gun had been pulled, and it hadn't – or at least, not before it happened to me. I try to make it easy for them, yet all the while I'm fighting and kicking under the surface for them to feel the pain with me, to be angry along with me, to feel things through combat. I've never been this angry before. I don't know what to do with the anger. It makes me unsettled and restless. I want to be alone; I want to be with J; I want to be at home; I want everything and nothing; nothing can respond in kind to what I'm feeling, which is something, in itself, that is being mis-expressed, coming out in fury and the need to keep moving, in contradictory needs for security and lonely silence.

My dad's older sister once told me that death was like the incomprehensibility of black holes. You know about black holes, but you can't imagine them, not really, because they are beyond imagining. So you assimilate the knowledge in tiny increments, scratching away at the stone, a brief glance to see what it might be manageable to look at, today. Allowing yourself to sit for just a moment with the reality of the person, which precipitates the knowledge of their death, and the sickening depths. *Perhaps this*, I wondered, *is how it happens*. Perhaps this is how I learn it happened. So far it had been numbness and alcohol, and dogs and coronavirus, and isolation and emergency: deferring my own reality. And maybe that's how you do it.

It takes so much time. Now was the first time that I'd been able to think of him, to really think of him, to remember what it was actually like to hang out, to drive to our local market town, to search for free parking spaces, to sit in cafés, me working or applying for academic jobs, him doing his German homework, to leave the swimming pool changing rooms knowing he would be waiting in the foyer for me – I would have been holding him up. To revisit the grain of our lives, to alight on the smallest moments. And every time I do it feels like being punched, like something falls away in my stomach, like it can't possibly be true that these things will never happen again. Or perhaps more importantly, that he is not out there thinking of me any more.

Parents are hard. You don't notice how vital they are until they are gone, and then the specific memories aren't there, to hold on to, to pull out, because the memories don't work that way. They are something else. Continuous. Parents track your existence, necessary, inevitable, a string resonating with your own that you took for granted. The people who first taught you to be.

Sometimes I do understand that he's died.

The pew I was sitting on was about a quarter of the way back, roughly where I might have sat if we were rehearsing there but I wasn't involved in that movement of music. Close enough to the action, but distant enough to get away with reading my book. The spatial make-up of the abbey that made sense to me. My abbey, as it were, reorganising it around how I knew it, personalising it from the tourist space where kind volunteers at the entrance ask you if you need help and provide free information leaflets. My history of the space, layered on all these other histories of the space.

But I wasn't feeling anything in particular. I didn't think. Not the feelings I'd both hoped for, and feared. Maybe I was in the wrong place, I thought, wildly. I needed to go to his boat. Was that where I would get the feelings I needed? So old it was virtually unsellable, it was still in the boatyard. A valuer had declared it unseaworthy, which I knew wasn't true: I'd been at sea on it *loads*.

I felt a bit panicked that my father had died, not just my dad but my best friend, and that I couldn't work out how to feel truly, deeply sad about it in the way you're meant to.

I tried some more quiet sitting. I hadn't been patient yet, I told myself. Maybe if I sat here for long enough.

I sat some more, felt self-conscious.

And that was when the music came out. Maybe, I thought, music would hurry things along? I got out my phone and put on some Handel through my headphones, tried the piece that had been on Dad's music stand when he died, but it was being played on the harpsichord and coming direct into my ears it felt shocking, confronting, contrived, embarrassing. I wanted to get away.

Perhaps I should leave this for now, try it again later, once I was alone.

I paused it, put my phone away.

Got my phone out again. Partly out of a feeling of conspicuousness: I wasn't used to sitting in churches.

I tried 'Freddie Freeloader'. The piece we played as people came into his funeral. And it was fine. It had lost its effect, I worried.

I put on the Jimi Hendrix album Mark had told me he listened to with Dad in sixth form. I had never heard it before Dad died, so it wasn't exactly music I associated with my dad in that way. I'd been listening to it a bit lately. 'Castles Made of Sand', the one I liked. And somehow, it was what worked. Oh: all of a sudden it comes. Hello Dad who was eighteen and I don't know what he wanted or what he thought the world might hold and I don't know if he dreamed it was full of possibility. His expensive school sounded less freeing, counter-intuitively, than mine. The abbey bells rang, blanketing the music. The feelings. Wondering where he's gone. The pain. They were there all along. I hadn't needed to worry.

I missed my dad so much.

I kept my eyes straight ahead. It's a religious place so it's probably fine to stare, I reasoned. And to cry. People might just think I'm a Christian.

Music is about the looping around of time, the return, the revisiting. And grief, well, it's all about what you've lost. And when you can envelop yourself in the music, just forgetting for a moment what you've lost, because time is repeating, and once again, he's right here, just like that moment when you see him, that hair-fine split-second when you know-don't-know, before the real task of kidding yourself comes crashing in and it's all over and he's gone, again, as he always was.

Music lets you inhabit that past, just briefly. And as it enfolds you, it pushes you, strives always towards the next note, the end of the phrase, and you strive towards it too, and you live in that music and live in a time where there's a future and that person's in it as well.

That little tug of *Oh, Dad's not here any more*, even in my twenties when I was cool and independent, when Dad's course would end and Dad would go home. That's what came back.

Albéniz's 'Recuerdos de la Alhambra', though, suddenly made me livid. It brought the slide show at the funeral vividly to mind, where all those gestures had got nowhere near him. Music. Photos. Not Dad. All not Dad.

Perhaps it was my anger that had kept me away, I thought. Anger, and fear that the music wouldn't trigger enough emotion and I wouldn't be able to feel, rather than what I thought I was afraid of, the easy thing to fear, which was that I'd feel too much.

Is this anger the root of the aggravation? My rejection of music after his death? The fear that it wouldn't work its magic, that it wouldn't reliably help me feel, that it wasn't trustworthy. Sometimes music still aggravates me. I don't know how else to describe it. *Ätzend* is the German word, the one I reached for. Corrosive, biting. Something like that.

Without realising it, to try to get myself to feel in the cathartic way I wanted, I was going through the playlist. 'Dad funeral'. The music we had marked out as potential things to use that day – not all of which we did. The playlist I hadn't dared to go near. Ever so quietly, my subconscious had taken me by the hand and brought me without ceremony to this thing. I forgot the people browsing the abbey like it was a library, or maybe they didn't matter.

'Sevilla' and I could see the coffin and everyone walking out. And as I kept listening, I could hear his hands on the strings, as if sitting behind me, and it caught me again. A choke of tears. Now the Villa-Lobos Prelude: it conjured Dad before me, sitting facing away from his desk, looking down at his music, and playing, sequestered away on the attic level, escaping whatever it was he needed to escape into music.

In that moment, I realised that I didn't want to overplay it, because I didn't want to lose the effect it was having on me. I was afraid that if I played it too much, I wouldn't be able to bring him to life from it any more; I was afraid, I think, that the shock wouldn't still be there, that the music would burrow its way into my mind and become part of the normal furniture. And that loss would be unbearable, because what else did I have?

I guess I didn't want to use up the connection I feel. I wanted there to be plenty left in the bank. Storing my relationship with my father in this music.

I didn't mean to confront this music today, but here I was, and here it was, and it was OK. Nothing happened really. I had a lot of thoughts, and a lot of feelings. Angry, sad, uncomfortable, and then the music was over, because of course everything ends at some point.

Why does music do this to us? Why is it the thing we can use to control our emotional selves, like a dial, like a safety net, like a mask, when we don't want to show how we feel? Why is it the thing that undoes us when we do?

The music had ended. I took out my headphones, and I listened. A murmur. A space this vast diffuses sound. I had wondered what I would feel, and I was feeling very sad, like coming into this quiet space removed me from the world. It was calm and empty and out of time, and it allowed me to feel. I had worried I would feel nothing. That wasn't the case.

The laced ceiling soared above me. Intricate cross-networked mathematics. I looked hard at the space where we always set up the orchestra, in front of the pulpit. I thought of my parents coming here to see my concerts, dutifully, always. Always. By this point, I did so many concerts that they felt everyday, but my parents came to the ones in Sherborne. They were an annual fixture, a proxy for my performance life at university. And I thought of the many trips my parents did separately, too: Dad coming north to see a production of Bernstein's *Candide* that I assistant-directed as a first-year undergraduate; Mum coming to Oxford to see me play with the university orchestra. So much love in all those journeys.

A performance happened here, once, fleeting. I wonder if anyone else remembers it. I'm sure they must, but I'm thrown that without any written sources to hand – programmes, for instance – or other people here to remind me, I can bring to mind so few of the pieces we played here over what must have been seven concerts over seven years.

I remember it, though, because of the galloping adrenaline. Stravinsky's *Firebird*. First trombone. Waiting, heart pounding, for my risky momentary displays. We'd had to work bloody hard to counteract the abbey's acoustics. Spiky attack, as short as could be. The abbey had been filled with noise, with power, energy, excitement. So far from the contemplative, quiet space it was today. I remembered the last movement's horn solo sailing out into the expansive acoustic, its depth, strings swelling below, the movement of scales joining from the brass, building, building, until the abbey was all sound, warmth, bells, and the conductor looked at us with delight as he held us right up to the end of the final chord, and we looked back at him and we'd pulled it off and the feeling was ecstasy, rushing downwards, and the abbey was thunderous with applause.

There was a golden statue of an eagle under the altar, so familiar she had been lost to my memory. A shock of recognition. A Victorian addition, perhaps. I had sat in front of her, beside her, moved chairs around her for years, without really taking her in.

And under her, the candles. Exactly where the trombones used to sit.

An elderly woman in a loose blue and white printed blouse ahead of me stepped up and lit one; that was how I noticed them.

It made me feel deeply sad, looking at those candles, and the tears came again. I wanted to be part of the ritual, but I didn't want to draw attention to myself. I wanted to straightforwardly feel the sadness, but Dad was here, complicating things, making me feel like probably candle-lighting was silly and emotions were unnecessary.

It hit me. Dad had been here, and now he wasn't. A quiet spasm of grief. The problem with crying while wearing a cloth mask is that you risk getting it damp with snot. I let my mask hang from my ear. I figured that maybe exceptions applied, and even if the abbey wasn't well ventilated, it was vast.

Dad had been here. *Here.* He had come to see me play. Once, at the summer school, he had dropped in to listen to a rehearsal that I wasn't involved in. The conductor had seen someone was listening, and asked him about the balance; could he hear the harpsichord all right? Dad had felt rather put on the spot. He wasn't sure what a harpsichord sounded like in an orchestral texture.

This was a space Dad had been in, dropped in to have a listen, and now he would never come here.

I didn't really decide, it was just no one was sitting there any more and I felt unobserved. I took a candle, slim, creamy white, and I lit it from the tea light burning next to the shelf. I sat in the front row of the pews and cried, hot and silent.

Dad's was now the tallest candle.

Dad wouldn't want to be a candle.

What was this?

Now I had done it, I felt self-aware of my new role, but pleasantly so: grieving woman staring at candles. People would be kind to me in this contemplative, peaceful space. Several minutes later, another woman added a candle. And Dad's was no longer the tallest candle, and I no longer had the special status I craved. Which was really about being special to someone, unconditionally, and it was a thing that had dropped away the moment my dad stopped existing. And afterwards, I noticed something about this feeling. If I wasn't special to Dad any more, because he couldn't think about me any more – he'd stopped being able to think about me – I'd imagined that I could at least be special *because* he was dead. Desperate not to let go of that feeling, I thought I could be special in a different way. But in this space that held me close, that, cavernous, had space for the enormity of my feelings, that could contain everything and more, I was beginning to realise that being in a community was nicer than being marked out.

In the cosy abbey shop I bought two pencils, sharp and new, as if I'd been on a school trip.

Over the days that followed, I found I heard snatches of the beginning of 'Freddie Freeloader'. The first time I had Dad music in my head since he died.

Chapter 12

DIES IRAE AND HARDCORE DEATH DANCES

Chloe is a funeral director. She's roughly my age. On a typical day, the first thing she does when she arrives at work is to go to the mortuary to collect her person. Her colleague who cares for the person who has died, known as the practical lead, comes with her. The mortuary is in an old chapel. It's beautiful, airy, high ceilings; a far cry from the stainless-steel spaces of television drama. She does a final check: first against the wristband, to make sure it's definitely the right person – not something anyone wants to get wrong. If they are being cremated, she does a pacemaker check, since batteries can't go in.

She takes a moment to say hello. She checks their hair is neat.

Often the family will have visited and dressed their person with the help of the practical team. Sometimes they'll do their hair, paint their nails. This is a particularly important element for many Caribbean cultures. From time to time, people are buried in their favourite football shirt. She and the practical team try to pay real attention to personal details.

Before Chloe started the job, she wasn't sure if she would be able to do that part. The mortuary. She wasn't sure how she would respond. She'd only ever seen one dead person before, her father, and that was within an hour of his death.

She worried about seeing someone who looked like him.

But what she has learned is that when she visits someone in the mortuary, she no longer feels that person is there. They are somewhere else. It's about caring for, loving and respecting the body that carried them.

She checks that everything they need is in the coffin. Sometimes people are buried with a childhood teddy bear, or clothing, or books, frequently photos. Often, people will put in blankets and cushions, comforting things. Recently, a man was buried in a natural burial ground along with the ashes of the five dogs he'd owned throughout his life. There are some limitations on what can be buried with someone; usually it's to do with environmental questions about what can go into the ground.

Unlike the funeral directors my own family used, the coffin option vibe isn't 'Here's a catalogue, pick a coffin'. Instead, people can do whatever they want with the coffin, source them from wherever they like. Sometimes people decorate them.

'Today', she told me when we met for coffee, 'we had a coffin from comparethecoffin.com.'

She will always see the person in their coffin before the lid is closed that final time.

Then she works with her colleague to make sure the flowers are arranged on top, before they drive with the coffin, sometimes to the family's home to pick them up. This won't be her first contact: she'll have spoken to the family before. In this, her company differs from more traditional organisations, where the funeral director is usually just the event manager on the day. They might have a limousine, or a cortège of other people's cars might follow the hearse. But sometimes they take the person into the house, just to spend some time in their family home. On occasion, this has meant taking the coffin in through the sitting room window.

'If it's legal, we'll do it,' she said wryly.

And then they travel on to wherever it is that they're going to hold the funeral.

They hire hearses from a separate company; the hearses are mainly driven by retired police officers. They reminisce about the ease of driving hearses in London during the pandemic. Because of course – it never stops. For ever, travelling around this country, and in every country, cars carrying people, and people caring for those who've died. It's a hidden world. There is always someone on call in Chloe's company. Twenty-four seven. They have a special phone they pass around the team, even at Christmas.

From that point, her job becomes event management, not only in terms of getting things to start on time, but also making sure everyone has everything they need. That can really differ depending on whether they are in a church, or a crematorium, or a temple, or if they are doing the ceremony outside. If they're in a woodland, for instance, she'll have a Bluetooth speaker, and her phone in her pocket, with Spotify and all the music preloaded as a playlist. Otherwise, things depend on the individual space. The music will usually be lined up on Obitus, the online platform for managing funerals, the same one whose name, and indeed, existence had seemed so surreal when we organised my dad's funeral.

If people are going to carry the coffin, she briefs them on how to do it. Most of the time in the funerals she manages, family and friends bear the coffin, and it's rare that any of them will have carried a coffin before. It's heavy, and it can be quite dangerous. They also have a team of professional bearers drawn from some other companies, so bearers can be easily organised.

From there, it's about melting into the background.

She thinks you're doing well if you're not noticed, or only noticed in a supportive way. It's nice for the family to know you're there, standing at the back.

She doesn't hold the image of the person in the coffin in her head; as soon as the order of service is handed to her, that image is quickly replaced. Instead: a sense of their life, from all the people in whom they are reflected, speaking, singing, playing music.

A sense of them within their family. Who they are.

All the things they've done, from the ordinary to the very extraordinary.

Afterwards, she goes back to the company offices, which are next to the cemetery, makes a cup of tea, chats to colleagues, decompresses. She made the mistake at the beginning of treating it like any other freelance job, and driving straight home afterwards. She doesn't do that any more.

Chloe works for a forward-looking funeral company with millennial branding. When I spoke to her, she'd been working there for eighteen months, and in that time, she'd directed around seventy funerals. 'I do probably four or five a month.' These are funerals of all denominations, although given the local demographics, most often the funerals are humanist or Christian, with a number rooted in Caribbean traditions, plus the occasional Sikh or Buddhist funeral thrown in for good measure.

Chloe had arrived straight from a Caribbean Catholic funeral. She was dressed in black, and slightly delayed because the family had wanted to do a backfill at the burial.

'A backfill?'

She explained that sometimes people will get involved in throwing the soil back on to the coffin after it's been placed in the ground. With shovels. Not all cemeteries allow the family to participate. In this particular instance, the daughter had made a special cushion to lie on top of the coffin to dampen the sound as the soil went back in. 'Family and friends can find the sound quite upsetting.'

Chloe had moved into the funeral sector from working full-time in classical music, particularly event management. A friend who'd studied music with her had put us in touch. Chloe's love of music comes from her background playing the oboe (yet another oboist. I promise this is coincidental). Now she works part-time in both industries, making her a unique person to talk to for insights on music at funerals. She'd never yet been to a funeral without music. In twenty-first-century London, every single one of the funerals she's directed has had pre-recorded music at some point, and the vast majority only had pre-recorded music. Around a fifth of those funerals have been in churches, and they have had organs, and – very rarely – choirs.

'It's usually during the music that people really break down,' she told me. 'That's the moment when you see most people's shoulders shaking.' She reflected for a moment. 'I suppose because music is in the present tense.'

'So music can bring the person who's died into the space of the funeral?'

'Exactly. In a different way to a family member telling stories,' she said.

So much of secular funeral music is about recreating the person's identity, I thought. I remembered searching blind in the depths of my dad's record collection, examining the CDs, his unconscious, those discs that received frequent play stacked by the CD player in the kitchen, pulling out and inspecting what were my own memories, not his, lost within the magnitude of the endless track lists; and yet desperate, frustrated that I could no longer know what he wanted, what he saw as the music that represented him. That there wasn't an answer that would do justice to the multitudes of the person he had been.

Music, Chloe thinks, is the moment in the funeral when the line connecting us with the person who's died is unbroken. People are trying to really get their person in the music,' said Chloe. 'And they're trying to do the right thing for their person, while not screwing themselves over by ruining a song for ever, or playing a song that they won't be able to handle on the day. There's no forgiving it if it's wrong.' With a poem, if listeners think it a strange choice, they can focus on how well it's being read. In general, her clients worry about getting the music right more than they worry about any other element.

'They are the barest moments, the moments where everyone's listening.'

But music, of course, hasn't always been used in this way at funerals. Because only relatively recently have secular funerals become mainstream.

It was murky outside, that barely-there drizzle that's like standing in a cloud, and I could smell the rot of nearby bins. I locked the front door to our building, dodged the traffic as I crossed the main road midway between pedestrian crossings and headed for the bus shelter.

I grew up in rural Scotland and, later, rural England, where standing in a cloud is the default climate. It leaves you soaked through even though you might not think to put up your hood, and so it was with religion. Even if we didn't go to church, even if my parents were strident atheists, religious history nonetheless seeped into everything. There was no doubt that we were culturally, if not intellectually or spiritually, Christian. The minister was a frequent presence at our school. He felt like another teacher. His title confused me for a long time: I was five, and I was convinced someone very important in the government spent a surprising amount of time visiting our village. As we sang hymns and prayed in morning assembly – hands pressed together flat in Scotland, fingers curled over in England – as we returned to our classrooms to craft cotton wool sheep for our wall display of red-haired Katie Morag's fictional Hebridean home, we were learning that there was a deep past at work that was all in the entwining, the inseparability of religion and state, and history and geography, and science and art altogether, and that it was also our past, and that we wouldn't ever be able to fully repel this mist that blurred our British edges, even if we were pretending it had nothing to do with us. It validated us. It gave us a template for our rites of passage.

Until relatively recently, *all* funerals were religious funerals. When we, beings of our time, looked for music that summed up my dad, I knew, somewhere old, that we were doing something new. And at the same time, something ancient.

But I didn't know this history, and I'd made a new place home. I wanted to take a thread from myself, and cast it backwards into the history of the places and communities in which I'd been a child, where my mind began to form. To find a depth of place. To know how death might have sounded here; there. To know what work music did or did not do for people who mourned through the centuries.

Walking down the south London high street, I was about to take the bus into town to meet my colleague Matthew in our university department. Matthew studies the music of the eighteenth century. The air was dank, soapy with fumes, and I wove past people with crunched-up eyes walking fast to beat the weather, people whose ancestors came from all over the world all on their phones, umbrellas, heads down and hoods up on technical rain jackets and loose sweatshirts, being pulled along by King Charles spaniels, or by Staffies, a pair drinking beer under a canopy outside the newsagent, all of us who'd wound up here together because of the choices made by us and made by others over the centuries, stepping around puddles containing grimy chicken bones and the plastic from cigarette filters. It wasn't glamorous here, but it was home. I watched a bus driver doing some stretches, arms above his head, as he waited at the stop opposite. And on my right, set back behind the wall, was a church I'd never even noticed, surrounded by dry cleaners and nail salons and the Wetherspoons and estate agents and the halal butcher and the Polish supermarket. Old, quietly present, obscured. A graveyard. I paused; I was an adult in this familiar-unfamiliar city, and yet this church was part of something that had always lived on the very edges of my field of vision.

'It was only with the Enlightenment that the idea of death and grief sending people on an individual journey of self-realisation kicked in,' Matthew told me. 'It's a relatively modern idea'.

Matthew was wearing a Paul Smith T-shirt. On it were printed two multicoloured skeletons. They were dancing. He indicated his chest. 'Before then, say in the medieval period, there was a skeleton in every painting, a skeleton in every room. The reminder that it's going to happen to all of us, and that we coexist with the dead.' The memento mori, *remember you must die*, like the decaying apple, the wilting flower. Something that, at least in Christian doctrine, was intended to focus your attention on the afterlife, on the fact that to be human is to be impermanent.

'I wore this on purpose,' he said mischievously. 'It's the early modern *Totentanz*, or dance of death. Death comes to embrace us, he carries us off, as if in a dance, something like a suitor. Death is a lover, a comedian. He attends our festivities. He is particularly fond of brides.'

Bringing the dead, death, into the room: a nice touch for our conversation.

And like the memento mori, the music for grief rituals was also intended to focus your attention squarely on what was to come after your death. Matthew sent me off with a list of books to read.

If you had lived in Europe in the late medieval period, the big grief ceremony was the Mass for the Dead, also known as the Requiem Mass, a title taken from its first line 'Requiem aeternum, donna eis, Domine' (Grant them eternal rest, Oh Lord). These Requiem Masses all used music – but the music wasn't intended to console listeners; this music was for the dead, not the living.

There were several occasions for the Requiem Mass: the funeral, yes, but Masses were also held regularly for a stretch of time after the burial, as well as there being a yearly Mass marking the anniversary of the death. If that wasn't enough Requiem Mass for medieval you, there was also a Mass for the commemoration of *all* the dead on 2 November, All Souls' Day.

Briefly, the Mass is the standard Catholic bread-and-wine church service, also known as the Eucharist. If you go to a Mass today, you'll be attending a service that has a great deal in common with the medieval Mass, even in Anglican churches. The music you get during these services is the Mass setting, and then there are hymns in addition, which are largely free-choice wildcards in the service (OK, not *that* wild: they come from a book). The Mass is made up of a set of texts called the liturgy, for instance, the Kyrie, the Gloria, the Agnus Dei and so on, and today, churches usually have their own favourite house setting of the Mass. For special services like baptisms, weddings and funerals, particular versions of the Mass are used.

Not dissimilar in this regard to the present day, medieval Masses for the Dead were effectively special, extended versions of the more routine Mass. In the sixteenth century, the liturgy of the Mass for the Dead was unified – before there had been a lot of regional variation. The result of this unification of the liturgy was a core standardised set of liturgical texts that a composer could set to music.

And set the liturgy to music composers did. The purpose of the music was to advocate for the deceased, giving them a leg-up into heaven come the Last Judgement (the day when bodies would rise from the ground to join their spirits), since at the time it was commonly believed that the actions of the living after someone's death could affect how they'd be judged, and this music formed part of the ongoing lobby for mercy come Judgement Day. For the same reason, rich people would leave large sums of money to the Church, on the condition that Masses be regularly held in their name.

Well-known classical works like Mozart's Requiem (1791), Verdi's Requiem (1874) and Fauré's Requiem for orchestra and choir (1887–90) are all settings of the standardised Requiem Mass, even if today you're much more likely to find them performed in concert halls, rather than in the churches they were intended for. Requiems tell a story, that of the soul's journey after death – awesome, terrifying, and especially awesome and terrifying because, according to Christian doctrine, this was the journey awaiting all who were listening. Listening to a requiem was a time to reflect on the magnitude of what was to come; the final reckoning, and whether you would be saved or cast down. A bit like Matthew's sartorial skeletons, the music was there to ready the living for their own death. Nothing about this offered any degree of comfort.

In Mozart's Requiem, for instance, the listener accompanies the soul of the dead person on its journey through the Last Judgement to their acceptance into heaven. The music of Mozart's Requiem is mostly written from the perspective of the person who awaited judgement, alternating with more 'objective' passages describing what the deceased person will encounter, according to scripture, and moments where the perspective of the divine judge can be felt in the music; like many of these such works it features a great deal of emotional turbulence: angst, longing, guilt, fear (particularly around facing the Last Judgement) and – from time to time – hope. After the uncertainty of the journey, these settings end with mercy from a higher power for the deceased person, and therefore their ascent to heaven.

Although, in the Catholic tradition, Mozart's work is for the dead, there are a couple of interesting twists that make it the stuff of legend: people also think it was a requiem for his own imminent death, which he (correctly) anticipated. He also didn't finish it, having died before he had the chance: one movement famously only consists of eight bars in the manuscript. The best-known completion of Mozart's Requiem was by Franz Xaver Süssmayr. Mozart's work also has the claim to having been the first requiem to be performed in a non-liturgical context, when Baron van Swieten, a patron of Mozart's, arranged a performance in aid of Mozart's widow and his offspring. This might be obvious, but as soon as a requiem is performed outside of a church Mass, it starts to have a different purpose. In the words of the musicologist Wolfgang Marx, it allows listeners 'to reflect on the concept of mortality in a more abstract, sublimated way.'

I've only ever heard Mozart's Requiem in concert settings, where the movements are performed back-to-back, rather than, as in a church service, being interspersed with readings, prayers, the Eucharist, even other music. In fact, most of the times I've heard it, I've also been rehearsing or performing it, and rather than having sublimated thoughts about my own mortality, I tend to have been feeling petrified: the 'Dies Irae' fills me with dread, with the memory of the knowledge that I'm waiting to play the terrifying solo in the 'Tuba Mirum', which, incidentally, is the movement that mimics the tones of the trumpet heralding the Last Judgement.

Less than a century later, the German Romantics started writing funeral music to be used in a way that's much more recognisable to secular funeral-goers today: Brahms's *German Requiem* of 1868, for example, is not for the dead, but for – and about – the journey of the people left behind. The main currency of Brahms's Requiem was consolation. This is a shift towards the experience and value of the individual on earth, reflecting other cultural changes around this time, and the diminishing certainty of religious tenets and religious truths for organising modern life. 'God is dead' Nietzsche declared; Darwin had published his *On the Origin of Species* (1859) not long before; the novel, with its stories of individuals on journeys of self-discovery and self-actualisation, was the dominant literary form. With such important challenges to religious certainty, and in particular to the carrot/stick certainty of an afterlife, it makes sense that, as the musicologist Nicole Grimes puts it, 'Brahms was concerned with the individual here and now, rather than the notion of the beyond.' 'German' refers to the German Bible in Luther's translation. What Brahms meant was that it was for everyone, that it was human, that it wasn't specifically Christian, instead aimed 'at people of all faiths and none'. For him, 'German' and 'human' could be used interchangeably. Indeed, we might call this the first humanist requiem; it would be followed by others in the twentieth century: Benjamin Britten's *War Requiem*, for instance, which interleaves the Latin Mass for the Dead with a number of poems by the English poet Wilfred Owen.

In England, the nineteenth century saw a significant culture war between the Tractarian reformers and the previous Anglican practices in local churches, practices which had little of the polish and sheen of cathedral culture. The reformers eventually won out, introducing a more sombre and elevated tone to church proceedings, as well as a more sombre and elevated style of music, using professional musicians who stuck to the liturgy. Popular eighteenth-century funeral hymns were suppressed, but the old church bands – motley crews of local musicians – didn't give up without a fight. A literal one, with street brawls between old and new choirs.

At one point, in the Norfolk village of Little Walsingham, someone blew up a church organ.

Chloe was much younger than I'd always expected a funeral director would be, and I hoped she wouldn't mind me asking why she became one. She told me that many people assumed it was because her dad died. 'But it wasn't Dad really. My dad dying just showed me I could. I think. And then doing it showed me I could. It gave permission. If I could stand up at my dad's funeral, I could probably manage it.'

Her father died suddenly, like mine. There was around a week between them learning he had cancer and his death, from sepsis. They think they'll never know the full extent of it. 'He wasn't even in the oncology ward. He was still in the lung ward.'

She got into funeral directing through arts and event management. When friends asked her to officiate over their marriage at Glyndebourne, a country house that hosts a famous annual opera festival, she thought: *Maybe I'd like to train to be a celebrant for weddings.* She was interested in what it means to mark life occasions in all senses. But at the time, she was too busy to do anything about it. After her dad died, though, things were different, ambitions in sharper relief, and her mum said 'Dad'll pay for the training.' That moment of death is a moment of change, when anything's suddenly possible again. Something like childhood.

A year after she trained as a celebrant, she saw an advert on an arts job page for people with event management experience to work as a funeral director.

Within three minutes she'd sent an email. 'It was such a gut reaction.'

She'd spoken at her dad's funeral. She'd always thought that should her parents die, 'which, by the way, seemed inconceivable', she would be a mess, that she wouldn't be able to function, but when it actually happened, she went into work mode. There was an event to plan. She often presented broadcasts for the Royal Opera House; she was used to standing up and reading scripts. So she spoke. Despite what she'd always imagined, she knew she could do it.

'I found that day – as horrible and weird as it was... it *happened*. And I'm always fascinated by how things happen. You watch TV and think: *How did they do that shot?* And I had the same feeling about wanting to know how it all works.'

She thought maybe she could use her event management skills in this setting.

'So I saw that job advert. And here I am. No two days are the same. It really is the most amazing job.' She looked away, as if checking whether what she was about to say was true, and then she said, 'It's my favourite thing to do.'

More changes to funeral music came with the advent of cremation in the late nineteenth century, which, crucially, began to change where funerals happened. Up until that point, funerals in Britain were held in churches and presided over by ordained ministers. The music for the service would either be sung, or played on the organ. Once cremation became widespread, though, chapels were purpose-built for crematoria, so there was no need for funeral-goers to change venue after the service. But organs were expensive, and so, early on, few crematoria had them. Nor did these crematoria have in-house choirs. Since only a minority of crematoria had an organ, which was needed even to accompany hymns, any music for the service would need to be available as a recording.

In 1933, two hundred delegates to the Joint Conference of Cemetery and Crematoria Authorities gathered at the chapels at Tottenham and Wood Green crematoria in London to hear HMV equipment playing recordings of Handel's Largo (the popular title for 'Ombra mai fu' from his opera *Xerxes*) and Chopin's funeral march. Attendees were impressed by what they heard, even though the sound quality was likely pretty ropey. One wrote:

> One needs but little imagination to realise what a lasting impression it leaves upon the mourning relatives. It brings for the first time beautiful music into the burial service for every class, rich and poor ... It ... take[s] away the cruel silence that precedes a funeral service.

Many crematoria distributed lists of suitable music, their contents presumably decided by cremation managers and their organists. These included oratorios, and well-known works by Chopin, Dvořák and Mendelssohn. But as early as the 1930s, debates began about whether the traditional repertoire really reflected the times. Pieces like the 'Dead March' in Handel's oratorio *Saul* and Chopin's funeral march were apparently 'out of date'; some believed 'brighter funerals' would be more in keeping with Christian doctrine. It wasn't until the Church reforms in the 1970s that broader opinions shifted in a way that had a significant impact on funeral culture, and music that reflected the personality or interests of the person who'd died started to be used – another important shift in the music's purpose, from consoling the bereaved to personifying the individual. People often mention the funeral of Princess Diana as a cultural touchstone that relaxed broader attitudes to playing non-religious music at Christian funerals in the UK. I was too young to understand the cultural significance, but I do remember the non-stop strains of 'Candle in the Wind' that autumn.

One thing Chloe had noticed at the funerals she presides over is that families often pick a piece of uplifting music, something with a beat. 'It's a moment of relief and release, introducing light and shade into the funeral's narrative,' she said.

Funerals are stories. The stories that help us to process who we are, and what has happened to us, and the thin membrane between life and death that's always right next to us. Not long before, she had done a funeral for a very young man. They'd had a huge church service. But afterwards, at the crematorium, it was just his mum and a handful of close male friends, some in army uniform. They'd all got through it: the part where you do a big show. Now it was just them, escaped. No one's talking to you, no one's looking at you. The celebrant read a very short committal. And then from nowhere all was thrown elsewhere – wrong – no, *right*, deeply familiar. A memory of raves: blistering heat, dancing, sweat, vodka Red Bull, European festivals, glittering Mediterranean. A hardcore dance track. 'DLMD'. Darren Styles and TNT. Aftershave, girls in damp strap tops, hair slick to their necks, arms held high, thirst, flashing lights, all here in the crematorium.

And everyone began to laugh, and then immediately everyone started to cry. The music of closed teenage bedroom doors. Of yelling to 'Turn it down'.

Laughter and tears. Physiological reactions, necessary reactions, a hair's breadth apart. The distance from life to death and back.

It seemed this music, this dance track, granted those present permission to feel all those contradictory things.

I kept my cool as Chloe recounted this story. But later, as I listened back to my recording of speaking to her, the tears came and they wouldn't stop.

Chapter 13

GUSTAV MAHLER, ALMA SCHINDLER AND SONGS FOR LOST DREAMS

We were surrounded by marbled rose-rust walls. The proportions were those of the Enlightenment, somehow more rectangular than other rectangular spaces. Her voice was magnificent: there was no other word for it.

I had felt ready, I had thought, to try it out.

Gustav Mahler's *Kindertotenlieder* – a work with a reputation. *Kindertotenlieder*. 'Songs on the death of children'. A title easier to stomach in German, with the foreign veneer. This is music with an aura. Music that's dangerous, feared, revered. Near mythic in its capacities to affect people.

Not a requiem; something closer, breathing down your neck.

Even the critics were afraid of this evening's concert, a piano and vocal recital. One had mentioned on social media that it was the one piece she'd vowed never to be in the same room as again – and yet she'd agreed to review it. When I'd read that, a thrill of nerves had rushed through me. 'Mahler's *Kindertotenlieder* does what it does much too well,' she wrote. 'I just can't deal with it.' A prickle of anticipation, something like fear, something like hollowness, something, too, like the PE lesson glow of being picked first. Because when I'd listened to the *Kindertotenlieder* before, when I'd been on a Mahler binge at university, I was sure it hadn't had any effect on me beyond how I experienced Mahler's other songs: vaguely detached appreciation. (His symphonies are another matter. Those, I love. Those were an undergraduate obsession.) But back then, no one close to me had died. Death had seemed remote. Now things were different. Had I become one of the chosen few, the people who hear this music deeply? I got the sense that this song cycle might operate in its own class once you'd been bereaved, that this was the music – not my dad's music, something different, something less personal, bigger in the community and connections it forges – that would unlock something else for me.

Out in the world, back in London, a scattering of masks in the audience a reminder that the pandemic hadn't fully released us, I was chasing the feeling of sitting in Sherborne Abbey. The connection with people past, and people future. The reassuring sense of our impermanence, insignificance, and the comfort of the enormity of everything beyond. I wanted that again. But I wanted it from music.

'Tell me about the piece by Mahler,' J had said as we waited to order dinner beforehand. I was dragging him along for company. He wanted me to do my music historian act, and it felt good to oblige.

Gustav Mahler began the *Kindertotenlieder*, originally for voice and orchestra, in 1901, when he was forty-one. They are his settings of Friedrich Rückert's desperately painful poems of the same name, which come from a much bigger collection of four hundred or so that Rückert wrote in the bleak, boneless agony after the deaths of two of his own children in the winter of 1833–34. There had been a big shift in attitudes towards the death of children between the time of Rückert's poetry and of Mahler's music. Around 1800, half of all deaths were of the under-fives. With the nineteenth century's medical advances, between the time of the poetry and that of the music, the death of a child had become a significant and terrifying personal tragedy.

Gustav later said he could never have written the *Kindertotenlieder* if the experience had been one he'd had himself. He told his friend, the conductor Guido Adler, that 'I placed myself in the situation that a child of mine had died.' People often worry that it's a curious choice of subject matter for a man who was not yet married, let alone a father. Gustav had known the deaths of children, though, having lost multiple of his siblings in childhood, in particular his twelve-year-old brother Ernst, younger by two years, to whom he had been very close. Now having turned forty, he was at a point in his life when he sought stability and a family of his own; he'd perhaps begun the *Kindertotenlieder* as part of his psychological preparations for becoming a father. Reflecting on the precariousness and transience of those young lives, contemplating the risks he would run, should he himself have children. The danger that it is to hope, to dare, to invest in new life. And not long after he began the cycle, he met the woman who would become his wife, Alma Schindler.

When the waiter came, we ordered a vegetarian meze platter and tap water. He warned us that we might get bits of mint in our water. 'Look,' he said, leaning towards me to show me the inside of the copper jug, 'it's all mint.' He was right. It was. Like a garden had been compressed. He left it on our table.

Maybe the *Kindertotenlieder* is a work that explores the possibility of feelings, tries them on. A work that links past griefs to the knowledge of the inevitability of new ones, and a work that points to a man unable to close his eyes to potential loss, a man who thought steeling himself might be enough of a defence.

I refilled my water from the mint-filled jug.

And then. It was just two years after finishing the *Kindertotenlieder* that Mahler's own daughter Maria Anna died, swept away at the age of four by diphtheria and scarlet fever. The work feels like an omen, a prediction.

'When I really lost my daughter,' Mahler told Adler, 'I could not have written these songs any more.'

People are afraid the work is, if not exactly cursed, something that sits very close by.

I know that there's an emptiness and a delicacy in the opening piano line, sparse, like small, polished bones, the keys weighted but fleeting, stones dropping one by one almost traceless into a pool.

An atmosphere you could slice open, as those tones begin to interweave in counterpoint, a sense of circling, trance-like, inert, the lazy rotations of a children's mobile hanging from the ceiling.

Like the beginning of a fugue that not enough voices will ever join.

I understood all this rationally as I listened. But somehow, I felt nothing yet. It was so far away, locked in a different medium. Only distance, irritation and the Edwardian discomfort of the angular seat. I felt like I was posing.

I stared at the singer. I willed myself to feel. But it wasn't working. It wasn't working at all. Not like I'd imagined it might, hoped – feared – it might. It wasn't working in a way where I couldn't get time to run properly, to settle in this moment, to gather around the music and make a space in which to hear it. I was too keyed up. By the experience, although I wasn't sure by what aspect: by being in this public space? By all the observers around me? I couldn't get my past self, who had anticipated this concert, who was afraid of this music, to mesh with my self in the present.

My mind wouldn't rest in the here and now, and even if it would, it seemed there were no feelings to be had. I watched the singer in her Shiraz dress and the pianist, all length and angles, with his matching velvet jacket – knowing camp – and his socks visible under the piano stool. There was nothing to say, although I wished profoundly that there was.

The walls loomed starched and fixed around me. I'd sought out this music: I wanted the promised effect. Real music experts should be deeply moved. What was wrong with me?

But Gustav Mahler, this piano, this famous singer, this opulent dress, his musical cosplay of profound bereavement, had nothing to do with my dad. Nothing at all.

And as I listened, I began to feel the presence of the woman whose grief is shimmering at the boundaries of this music, never seen head on. A long-forgotten crystal of grit in the gears of what I knew about Gustav Mahler had wedged itself where it couldn't be ignored.

Alma, his wife.

And my profound dissociation from this music.

A different story. Or the same story, refocused.

Alma had a four-year-old girl with wide blue eyes and black curls, a girl who looked so much like her father. Maria Anna. Known as Putzi. Who would visit him in his cabin in the mornings, and chatter away with him – what on earth they were talking about is anyone's guess – and emerge inexplicably covered in jam.

But now Putzi had been buried. Something all parents feared. Scarlet fever. Diptheria. A failed tracheotomy the day before her death.

Alma was distraught. Shut down. And furious with her husband. Furious. Who writes such a thing? And now it had happened. Maria was dead. As if this was what he'd always wanted. All that time spent writing his miserable music, when his children were alive. When they were real. When Maria Anna was chasing Alma through their summer orchard, her tiny sister Anna trailing behind, fierce concentration, tiny dusty hands outstretched, roly-poly-grass-stained skirts and shrieking with her sister – there he was – her *husband* – preparing for his children's death in his cabin at the end of the garden. Wallowing in emotions he'd never felt, emotions he wanted to ready himself for, mitigate, insisting on his family's silence when he worked.

The *Kindertotenlieder*. 'Songs on the death of children'. A curious form of avoidance. The safety of emotions that are contained and detached by art.

And now Putzi was gone, and there would be no more chasing through the orchard. No more playing the piano – or, she thought bitterly, telling her not to. No more wiping jam-smeared faces.

What was wrong with the man? Who does that? Why tempt providence?

It was incomprehensible.

She was furious.

Over falafel an hour before, I hadn't told J much about Alma. When he'd asked about the *Kindertotenlieder*, I'd rolled out the standard history. We'd come here to hear Gustav's voice. But now, suddenly, I was livid that she wasn't present in this music. That we all conspired in the idea that Gustav's grief, or his music, or both, spoke for everyone, would affect everyone, spoke for us all.

Because it didn't. It couldn't. Where was Alma?

Where was I?

My feelings were far too personal and too painful for me to let someone like Mahler anywhere near them. His music was not my grief. And yet it seemed there was some diffuse social obligation to agree that it was. I was winded by this realisation; it wouldn't let me look away. It seemed suddenly to matter a lot.

If I'd told the other story, this is how it would read.

It would begin much earlier.

Alma was a woman who desperately wanted to become a composer. Who lived and breathed music, composed non-stop. Who wanted to outrun her sense of abandonment after the loss of her father, her idol, when she was on the cusp of her teens, who wanted independence from her mother's second family, from her mother's new baby, twenty years Alma's junior. Her mother's 'new toy', Alma wrote with anger and fear. To escape her mother before she in turn rejected Alma, before the pain of the betrayal, the starting anew, became too great. For whom, unlike for Gustav, self-realisation, escape, had meant not the boundless exploration of her artistic potential, but marriage.

A woman who bore Gustav's children. A dangerous breech birth for Maria Anna.

A woman who yearned to be herself, not to lose herself to Gustav, not to become his shadow. His foil. Who dreamed of writing a 'really *good* opera, something no woman has ever achieved.'

She wanted more from life than to reflect his brilliance back at him, and yet little else was available. Somehow, I knew these contours of being, of being only in relation, as a memory in the twitch of my muscle fibres. Mahler would always get to be a man in a suit; Alma realised young that when she grew up, she would be transformed into something quite different.

Alma met Gustav when she was twenty-one; he in his early forties. Director of the Vienna Court Opera, and recently appointed, to both acclaim and controversy, conductor of the Vienna Philharmonic, the pinnacle of Viennese society. He had a mythology around him, celebrity, seniority. He was the incarnation of masculine creativity, bold and boundless; he would later famously describe his symphonies as 'like the world'. All-encompassing. He wanted to write everything there was in art, and no one would stop him. Not the Vienna elite who didn't like the idea of a Jew conducting their most prominent orchestra. No one.

When she met Gustav, Alma was under extraordinary pressure. She already had several marriage proposals. Described as being the most beautiful young woman in Vienna, she turned heads. Serial suitors. One had already threatened to kill himself if she didn't give him an answer. She had to choose somebody, and soon. A young woman at the heart of bohemian Viennese society, she was bruised from a long flirtation with the ever-unavailable painter Gustav Klimt, and uncertain of her feelings for the famous composer Alexander Zemlinsky, who had been teaching her composition, and of whom she had grown very fond.

She missed her father desperately. He was the painter Emil Schindler, widely exhibited, one of the most prominent painters of the Austro-Hungarian Empire. He had died when he was fifty, she only thirteen years old. As a child, she had lived for the wry smile of his approval, the warmth of his eyes. For how seriously he took her and her ideas. Her mind. He gave her Goethe's *Faust* when she was eight, much too young – inappropriate reading! – according to her mother, who took it away again. She read books, secretly, hid them, books deemed unsuitable for women. Philosophy: Plato, Socrates. Nietzsche. She was convinced she had what it took, and at the same time, was plagued by self-doubt.

When Gustav proposed, she wrote in her diary that she: 'must do everything *now* to stake *my* rightful claim ... particularly in artistic questions. He thinks *nothing* of my art, and much of his own ... Now he talks unceasingly of safeguarding *his* art. I *can't* do that.'

But in the end, Gustav made her choose.

They couldn't, in his opinion, both be composers.

Gustav said it wouldn't work between them. And he said more.

During their engagement, Alma wrote him a letter. Mindful of her need to stake her claim to her art, she indicated that she would have to cut her letter short, as she needed to get back to composing. She wanted to show he was not her only priority. His reply was brutal, and crushed her ambitions to be in an equal creative partnership built on love: 'How do you picture the married life of a husband and wife who are both composers? Have you any idea how ridiculous and, in time, how degrading for both of us such a peculiarly competitive relationship would inevitably become? What would happen if, just when you're "in the mood", you're obliged to attend to the house or to something I need?'

He impelled her to give herself up entirely to him, told her she was still nascent, developing, had no intrinsic sense of self. 'Would it be possible for you, from now on, to regard *my* music as *yours*?' He was infuriated by what he described as her compulsion 'to be and to remain true to herself'; he made it clear he found it childish.

It was his red line. Marriage to him, or her compositional ambitions. The glow of being appreciated by, standing alongside someone else's brilliance, or her first love: music.

He gave her two days to decide. He would send a servant to collect her answer.

It was the interval, and I was distracted. We descended the stairs to the overlit bar, where we met friends. While I'd been thinking about the terror this music held and my capacity to experience it, their priorities had been forensic music criticism. They found the singer's voice tired, and the pianist wooden.

They were unimpressed by the programming choices. Bar the singer, they observed with resignation, there were no women on the programme this evening. Five male composers. Unremarkably. I made my excuses, and I wove through the crowd in search of a drink and space. I hadn't thought, felt about Alma in this way before. This raging, surging way. This *thing*, systemic sexism, is in your face *all the time*, but mostly, day-to-day, you manage by deliberately forgetting to remember, because there is not enough time and are not enough people in the world for the anger it needs. Deliberately forgetting is another effort that wrings you out, another self-effacement, like smiling up at men and nodding when they tell you things and noticing that if you're not agreeing, or projecting agreement as you disagree, you get talked over. You get further by agreeing, right up until your life has passed and you realise: actually you didn't. You stayed where you were, or maybe it was more accurate to say your edges became blurry and one day, you couldn't find yourself any more.

Alma shone bright for me that evening, because I think in spite of everything, some part of Alma refused to agree to what she had been told she could be.

At the end of the bar, I took a tiny glass from a stack and poured myself a tap water. People never leave out big enough water glasses. Blocking the dispenser, I drank it straight down and poured another.

I thought of another story about Alma, aged nineteen, not so very long before she met Gustav, at a concert of works by French composer Cécile Chaminade that would have taken place in an intimate hall in Vienna not dissimilar to this one. A concert of music written by a woman. Alma knew of no good music by women: finally, she hoped, Chaminade would be 'an exception to support me': someone who could be a role model, who could prove to her that women could compose too, that her ambitions were not fanciful.

I could taste her anxiety. The hope. The thrill of recognition, of kinship.

But she was horribly disappointed by Chaminade's music. She found it 'coquettish, affected, Parisian.' And that settled it. She wrote afterwards, 'I [now] know that a woman can achieve nothing. Never ever.'

The tables were all occupied. I found a gap on the wall and leaned against it, sipping my water, watching on the fringes.

Without doubt, Alma was brilliant. She wanted more from life than life seemed to offer someone like her. She wanted things for herself. Self-realisation as an artist and as a human being. Love, not the strictures of Viennese mating rituals. Greatness. To be 'a somebody'. And while she believed deeply in her own brilliance, she also could not help but internalise the particular misogynistic flavour of her era; hers was a constant internal struggle against what she had been taught, 'scientific beliefs' about her female insufficiency – 'It's a real curse to be a girl, there's no way of overcoming your limitations,' she wrote, in a moment of frustration – and her profound sense that no, actually, she was the exception. Since she was the daughter of a great artist, she reasoned, she was the exception, because genius flowed in her blood. A conclusion characteristic of the heyday of hereditary science. She *was* exceptional. This smallness she perceived in women's lives could not be true for her, too.

I surveyed the crowd. The struggle was expressed differently today. But it hadn't gone anywhere. Hard to imagine yourself doing something with so few examples. Easy to assume you can't.

The Viennese society straitjacket of expectation was more clearly drawn. Right on the surface: women could simply not be creative. They were not accepted to the Vienna Conservatory, where composers, musicians, conductors honed their craft, gained prestige, nor were they admitted to the Academy of Fine Arts. They were not even able to attend the gymnasium – secondary school – much less graduate from university. Skills on the piano were highly prized, sure, but these were about being an accomplished and impressive wife, about containment rather than expansion. In contrast to the pioneering expanses of male creativity, female creativity was assumed to be small, domestic, lacking in vision. Alma was caught between impossible beliefs: that she was destined for greatness; that there was something wrong with her mind. You can see her struggling to believe it.

She had impressive credentials. She studied rigorously with Alexander Zemlinsky, one of the major opera composers of his day, a man whose image in my mind is staid and bearded, but to her, was always the youthful 'Alex'. She was told of her compositions: 'a most respectable accomplishment, for a girl'. Barriers at every turn, especially the psychological ones that she came to internalise. When her songs were performed at family soirées, 'The general opinion was that they didn't sound like they had been written by a woman.' High praise that reinscribed her as inherently inferior. 'Why are boys *taught* to use their brains, but not girls? ... My mind has not been schooled,' she complained, certain of her capacity to overcome the limits everyone believed held her back.

But after Chaminade's concert, yet another instance of the barrage of assertions that she'd never make it, you can see her thinking: could she *really* be the singular exception to her sex's apparent limitations?

Men, for Alma, as she left her teens, were a way out. A means of self-expression, the path to self-realisation. The sort of self-realisation open to her. An escape from the life she lived then. The best she could do, I think, as a way out. When there was no way out.

A bell rang decreeing we should head back to the hall, take our seats.

Some other German or Austrian composers were billed for the second half, but I was somewhere else: I didn't care what we were listening to; I was still with Alma. I'd known her story since I was an undergraduate, but I'd never given it this kind of sustained attention. Because I don't think it had resonated back then. Life had looked impossibly big and exciting and I don't think I had fully understood that the limits that were applied to her, especially the covert ones about who you saw doing what kinds of things, would be limits I would also have to reckon with. I had still naively thought I lived in an era where, for the most part, things had been fixed, and that generally, what people wanted for the future was for society to become more and more equal.

There was more singing, but I was busy running a thought experiment. Gustav had asked her to give up composing, give up her creativity.

I put myself in her place.

She couldn't accept Gustav's demands. Could she?

That evening, after reading his letter, she didn't know what to do with herself. This was an impossible situation. She was distraught, manic. She dressed up and went to the opera, tears streaming down her face. Late into the night, she talked it over with her mother, who was scandalised by these demands and urged her to break with him.

And yet, in the Vienna of 1901, if Alma wanted to follow her dream of a life dedicated to music, she would have known this offer was probably as good as it was going to get. To be married to the director of two of the most significant musical institutions in Vienna, a man at the centre of the musical universe.

Dedication to someone else's art.

The next morning she pulled herself together and she changed her mind. She accepted it. She had to. She made herself, tangled herself into a new logic to reconcile impossibilities. 'What', she asked herself, 'if I were to renounce my music *out of love* for him … Yes, he's right. I must live *entirely* for him, to make him happy. And now I have a strange feeling that my love for him is deep and genuine.'

She wasn't sure where she belonged. She was twenty-one. She needed music, and she also needed, I think, to be needed by a significant male personality. A creative genius. Enough at this point in her life to give up her burning ambition to *be someone*, to compose.

She gave herself up in the hope that it would raise her up to his level; she searched for another sort of self-realisation when the first had been denied. She convinced herself that living through him would give her 'life meaning'. And she was so very young.

I got it. I could see the powerful narrative like a force field around Gustav, and also, in the background, feel her uncertainty and her knowledge, whether she admitted this to herself or not, that the deck was stacked completely against her own compositional career. Nagging, inculcated anxieties about the lack of training, about the limits everyone else believed curtailed her female mind. Later, looking back, she admitted the depth of her belief, one she tried to resist for so long, that this self-renunciation was the fate of women. So why not reach for the next best thing? Why not settle, when you were settling with greatness, greatness by proximity? She, like so many, was trapped in uncountable ways.

Of course, you might say, at least her cage was gilded. Unlike the cages of many others.

I got it. The appeal of a man who was brilliant. Great. Who you might learn from. The appeal, the sexiness, even, of their approval, of being chosen by greatness, *almost* as good as having power. These were dynamics I recognised from my time in sexy France.

My dad and I used to argue about this. 'But women have loads of power. They can seduce their way to the top. That's just not an avenue for men,' he would say. He thought it gave women an advantage in the workplace. It was like arguing with a wall, but a wall who wilfully misunderstood me. Couldn't he see that this meant that all female power was bestowed in relation to male power? Couldn't he see that you had to reduce yourself in the process of flirting, that you had to make yourself desirable, an object, not a person? Wasn't he my ally?

He would challenge my belief that power relations were structural. 'What about psychological explanations for people's behaviours, for what they want? What about their psychological drives?' Possibly he was being antagonistic; he knew exactly how to wind me up and had a deliberately contrarian streak. But I wished so badly that he understood what it was to be a woman, that he didn't need all this convincing. I wasn't interested in psychological drives, and especially not the kind that suggested men and women were fundamentally different. I wanted all difference to be a product of nurture, of societal values training us to be one way or the other, rewarding us girls when we put other people first, when we listened, when we didn't make a fuss, rewarded us for being good. When we fitted whatever mould had been carved for us. In the early 2000s, thin, ladettes, drinking as much beer as the boys. Thinking this was equality, when instead it was meeting others' expectations, squeezing and starving ourselves into someone else's image of cool.

Alma was quickly to regret her decision to marry Gustav. It was the turmoil that drove her sense of self in this difficult marriage.

'It feels as though my wings had been clipped.'

Later, she wrote: 'He has taken so much away from me that his presence is my sole support.'

Alma's music is mostly lost. Of the songs she wrote, over fifty of them, only seventeen remain. The price we pay for going along with it.

And if you try to find Alma, who she really was, within the pages and interviews of history done throughout the twentieth century, she's indistinct behind the many words of others. Behind all the mistrust, the sexism – from both men and women – setting her in place like a great distorting glass paperweight. Warping the only view of the only way we have of reaching her: in documents. The sharpness of her voice in her diaries. Her letters.

It's possible that what I wanted most wasn't limitless possibility for my own life (although I wanted that too, of course), but simply for my dad to understand what it was to be a woman. To be me. To be as bewildered and furious about the world as I was. To be angry too. Because if he was angry too, if he recognised my experience as real, it felt like it would make it all OK.

It's quite possible that I wished my dad understood even more than I actually minded about how shit it all was.

And herein lies the problem. It was a yearning to be validated by men. To have my experiences made real by my dad.

How pathetic, and how very human.

Because the thing is, it was me who knew how it was. Not him. He didn't ultimately get to decide how things are, what mattered, and I'd never needed to convince him.

But it would take me a long, long time to come to terms with this truth.

J had come straight from work, so had his bike with him. After the concert ended, he cycled home and I walked alone along Oxford Street, following my lazy avatar on Google Maps to the Tube in a city centre with which I still wasn't familiar. I found myself thinking about one of the first-year seminars I used to teach in Oxford during my doctorate. A seminar about Taylor Swift, in which I would counterpoint her album *1989* against the moody cover of the same album by a soulful-sounding, introverted man with a guitar, the man in question being Ryan Adams. At the time both albums were newly released and I hoped my use of Swift in particular showed the undergraduates how in touch I was with contemporary popular culture, which was a masquerade. I played the students two versions of 'Blank Space', first Swift's, then Adams's. Which sounded more 'authentic'? Interesting when students acknowledged the pull they felt towards Adams's version, his oak-rich voice crooning over lonely guitar chords, tapping deep into a learned cultural sense of musical exposure of the soul, how the soul's exposure, we think, sounds. Because, well, she wrote the songs. Even if there are synth beats, and even if her voice is sometimes electronically altered. *It is her music, it is her intellectual property.* Surely there is no greater claim to authenticity? But no – something catches us lower down. Authenticity has weevilled its way right into our guts as a man's voice and a lonely guitar; it's the unmediated exposure of (white) male pain. Raw sound, no electronic interventions.

The images accompanying their respective promotional materials were: for her – glossy, manufactured; for him – gritty, realist, black and white.

There's a lot to say here. Even more so given that, a few years after I taught that seminar, in a *New York Times* report Adams was accused by several women of sexual misconduct and manipulative behaviour.

I would then play footage of Marin Alsop giving her address to the audience as she conducted the *Last Night of the Proms* in 2013. The first time a woman had ever conducted it.

When I taught that seminar, we usually wound up talking about why we thought of flutes as instruments for girls, and trumpets as instruments for boys. Plenty had never considered this before, which blew my mind.

I think the connections I then made between Adams and Beethoven, putting him in a lineage of idealised Romantic artists seen as expressing the Truth of Subjective Experience went over many, but not all, of their heads. The gendering of musical instruments was safer territory. If they were anything like me when I started university, they wouldn't have known much about Beethoven anyway.

And it was this idea of music communicating the Truth of Subjective Experience that was bothering me so much here.

Is listening to this music really an opportunity for everyone to feel, together? Or does it reinscribe the idea that some people's feelings matter more than others? Gustav Mahler's more than Alma's. Gustav Mahler's inalienable freedom to compose, to express the Truth, more important than the idea that we hear, trust Alma's historical voice.

Where is Alma's music? What I want is to hear Alma's *Kindertotenlieder*. But I can't. And mostly, we don't notice it's missing.

In the confines of that concert hall, I realised, the problem had been an anger so deep I couldn't even recognise it, so internalised, so nimble, it slips around the mind's corners whenever you try to face it square on, and leaves you with something quite else: a sense you should be trying harder to get the world to work for you. I was angry about how men are allowed to have universal experiences. For what the world does not expect of them.

That is to say: as I heard this song about the loss of children, it was hard for me not to feel some difficult things about whose voice we still hear through history, as we listen to the music of a man who had not lost any children at the time he wrote it. I'm so angry on behalf of Alma. *Stop writing that fucking music,* I hear her shout. *It's not poetic. It's fucking insane. Stop it!*

Either she's shouting it or I am.

This was somewhere my rage could belong.

Because this made sense. Being angry on behalf of Alma made sense.

And what didn't make sense, what I couldn't acknowledge, was how angry I was with my dad. Because if I did, it would break our pact that let me believe we were the same. Being angry with my dad wasn't an option. Being angry with him would bring everything crashing down.

But if I were to be angry, it would be an anger that he was the context for the choices I'd made. I hadn't realised he was. And now he was gone and those choices made fuck all sense when I was just me. Anger that he'd encouraged me as a child to know things and to understand things and to reason and to play music, that through him I'd seen a glowing world of infinities. A world that didn't exist. Anger that he couldn't see how constrained our choices were by gender. Anger where I wanted to bring him with me into this painful, rageful place where I lived at the limits of being, where the boundaries are and say: *Look! It's real! Those things we thought, agreed, weren't coming for me: they are still fucking here, despite everything. No one's fixed it. Look!*

My dad thought I could do anything, and didn't understand that I couldn't.

I slept deep and dreamless that night, spent on fury.

And of course, still I hoped. That in spite of it all, *Kindertotenlieder* could hold something for me.

*

Much later, I listened again. At home, a recording of the original version for voice and orchestra that had been recommended by someone knowledgeable: 'If this doesn't do it, nothing will.'

There's a line in Mahler's songs – Rückert's poetry – that is infinitely sad. It is about kidding yourself that the person you've lost has just run on ahead. You're on a walk, a walk you know well, and they've just left you behind for a bit, but this time, you won't see them again, later, back at the house. Striding off, giggling, flurry of scarves, a flash of burgundy, a welly maybe, and they've gone to the top of the hill. Seeing them back at the house is infinitely deferred; you put yourself in the suspended space between you and their return, prolong it for ever. Because they *have* gone on ahead without you.

And what's the difference, really? They're off. They're away doing something else, doing their own thing. Just hold that idea, stretch it out. It will hold you as long as you can hold it, until it snaps apart once again, like it always does, astringent, brittle. Shattered.

When you remember where they really are, the fear is that they are lonely.

The text, Rückert's poetry, speaks exactly to feelings of loss that I know. The innards-emptying ones. The ones that transform hastily taken photographs into sacred objects. 'They've just run on ahead of us / And they won't be coming home. / We'll join them up on the sunlit hills. / It's already daytime there...'

As I listened, my chest tightened hearing those lines about the walk. But it was the words, I think. Not the music.

For many, this music of Mahler's connects us with something bigger. A space in which we recognise all the generations of people who have been here before us, and who will come after us. In the sentiment, and in the performers.

In the solo voice: there are people as yet unborn who will sing these songs of loss for people as yet unborn who these songs will affect in ways that they can never affect me. And we keep going, we keep living. We keep trying.

For many, it's the music of longing, of searing living with that edge that is the discomfort of life, the very fact of the living on and the not-having and the coping and making do and the knowing of the absence and the knowing that you have to continue through the untenable and the only way of doing it is to tell yourself stories, lie to yourself, hide parts of yourself *from* yourself, conjure beautiful images, reckon with the absurdity of a world in which everything ends and loss is ever-present and we will all be both leaving before long and living too long. As we gingerly, imperfectly, brokenly, pick our way around the debris and *immer wieder*, once again, step into our lives.

I had wanted a lot from this music. I wanted it to provoke some feelings that would signal I knew some deeper truth, I wanted some feelings that reflected and justified the enormity of my existing experiences, that reflected them outwards, that made them count for something. And then I'd finally be allowed to stop, to be allowed some kind of exemption from the endless churn that is life and grief. Because this music would render my grief recognisable, bring me into a club.

I had wanted so much from this music. Too much. And, I realised, I'd fallen into the trap of thinking this music, the people around this music, would give me permission. If I could only show them I belonged.

And then. Right at the very end. A glimmer. Of something else, of the easiness of feeling, like the opposite of thirst, clear water on a hot day, maybe. Like magic, it just happened. And then it was gone again, a flash of fins on top of the water as I let the sound hold me, as I leaned against it, or maybe all it was was simply there and I was also simply there, unguarded, and I let it be beautiful and I let it be cathartic without worrying too much about what emotions, exactly, were being catalysed.

As if it had been waiting. The quiet and the still, and the singer's voice soaring, trembling, contained:

'They're resting, as if in their mother's house / Not frightened by any storm. / Covered up by the hand of God / They're resting, as in their mother's house.'

They haven't merely left for the hills any more; they are somewhere safer, as if at home.

Home.

It's heartbreaking. Because they aren't.

I nearly cried, but I didn't.

I had to admit: Mahler knew exactly how to write an ending.

There was no reason to show anyone anything in my reaction to this music. I – it – could just be. Here I was, listening to music. The closest I'd been to myself. And I was finding the music to be alienating yet enormous, infuriating but capacious, able to provoke and contain and hold many, many things. Mahler's sadness, his fear, Alma's anger, my anger. It could be all these things. Music can be all these things. Anger, injustice, frustration at a world that isn't free. Sadness. Connection. Alienation. Consolation. Anger. Both/and. All at once.

This was what I'd wanted. Been searching for. I wanted music to let me have that softer, purer, gentler grief that I believed was out there, the one that feels sad and feels good and mostly eluded me. And here, I got it. Briefly. Before it dispelled, crowded out again by the anger, the sourness, the despondency and the recklessness which was what my grief was made of. Because the world was just so shit, and there were so many places to put my anger, and because so much of my grief made me feel things that had nothing to do with the person I was missing.

And I still wished for Alma's voice, Alma's music. Because I wanted to find a home in this world of music, with its canon of dead men and blokes in turtlenecks and plaid. Somewhere I made sense too. Somewhere no one was surprised by me. Somewhere where the prefix 'woman' wasn't implied. Where I could once have been a trombonist, not a girl playing the trombone. I'd understood since I first picked up the instrument that I was a surprise, an incongruity. And I was so, so done with that feeling.

I needed somehow to make myself my own world where I, where we, really could be at home.

Chapter 14

PLAYING CHOPIN (BADLY)

One summer's day towards the beginning of my doctoral studies, I took a sheet of A1 cartridge paper and I decided to make a wall chart. I was staying at my parents', probably for the weekend, and I sat down at the kitchen table with a mismatched collection of biros, a pencil that, in a household where pencil sharpeners had a habit of disappearing, had been whittled to a point with a knife, and a long ruler. The light that streamed in left everything overexposed and me squinting, and, with dates proceeding horizontally, I mapped out key periods in German and Austrian history, a smattering of French history, the lifespans of philosophers and writers, and then the dates of birth and death of some of the best-known German, Austrian, French, Italian and Russian composers (all men). I was shamelessly Teutonic in my historical focus, and shamelessly canonic in the figures I selected: these were the ones I felt I needed to know to be taken seriously. Afterwards, I made a deck of learning cards on my computer, and I memorised some useful-seeming dates: things like the birth and death of Verdi (1813–1901); the beginning of the North German Confederation (1867); the publication of the second edition of Schopenhauer's *The World as Will and Representation* (1844). Friedrich Nietzsche's nine-year professorship at Basel University

(1869–1878) gained undue significance within my account of the nineteenth century because of the colour of the biro that was closest at hand when I marked it on the chart (red).

Once Dad realised what I was doing, and once he spotted this particular Nietzschean quirk of my wall chart, a testing game evolved that might as well have been called: 'Did it happen before or after Nietzsche's professorship at Basel?' Here is an example of how you play. Person A: 'Did the Franco-Prussian War happen before or after Nietzsche's professorship at Basel?' Person B: 'Um... 1870–71, I think... so... aha! Trick question. It was during it!'

Another key – and perhaps more historically standard – point of reference on my chart was the various European revolutions of 1848. A variant we developed on the 'Before or after Nietzsche's professorship at Basel' game ran like this. 'It's 1848. You're on the barricades. You need back-up. Can you call [composer X] to come and give you a hand?' And the correct answer for Chopin was 'Yes' (d. 1849) and for Mendelssohn 'No' (d. 1847). This had nothing to do with their politics; I was simply being tested on my knowledge of their death date.

And here, roughly, my knowledge of Chopin ended. Unlike the lines of other composers, which I had annotated with crosses for major works, Chopin's line (1810–1849) was still empty, bracketed by the words 'Poland' and 'Paris'. (Yes, I know I gave a country for his birth and city for his death – lazy – but the chart was just for me, and I didn't trust my ability to learn his actual birthplace, Żelazowa Wola, given I also knew next to nothing about Poland.)

That wall chart day was the most productive day I ever spent in my career in academia, and the secret to how I was so confident of Mozart's death date at that pub with my colleagues.

*

We were in the park. The air was tangy with concrete, dried grass, birdsong. I could hear the far-away rush and rhythmic thud of a passing Overground train. Life felt small. A year had passed, somehow, since I'd been to Sherborne, and now a high-profile musicology job had come up in the Midwest. America. I'd received an email inviting me to apply. It was the kind of job that, before, I would have gone for in a heartbeat. One of the most exciting research departments in the world.

The problem was that I knew I didn't really want the job.

And that meant I didn't know who I was any more. Or, more importantly, who I wanted to be.

The uncertainty thrummed incessant like the planes crossing overhead. It was what was behind the clouds that had formed, that made me feel claustrophobic, oppressed, like my life in London wasn't quite right, that made me grind my teeth and want to stretch out my neck and shoulders.

I lifted my arm, ready to throw Datch her ball. Held the ball up high, where she could see what I had for her clearly. *Down. Dooowwn.* She lay. She had to lie down before I threw the ball, that was part of the agreement. She knew about this, but always tried on the first instruction to get away with *nearly* lying down, so that she had a head start on racing off. Lying down put her at a disadvantage. I thought it looked cool; a friend whose father had gun dogs had told me about how they were trained to do it.

Datch wasn't a gun dog. She was a fluffy cannonball. A fluffy cannonball covered in stray bits of yellow grass. The mower had just left the park.

And she ran for it. With a bounce for good measure. And rolled past the ball like a commando soldier puffball. Grabbed it. Bowed, ball on the grass ahead of her. Threw it in the air for herself, playing. Monitored it rolling along the ground, like a cat with a mouse.

Immediately, I felt better. Life decisions could wait.

I crouched, and she barked. Time for a bit of chasing each other. Well, Datch chasing me. That's the way round she likes. Sure, it was probably the reason she sometimes chased runners, but it was all good fun.

Datch rolled in the long grass with pleasure, as if she was rubbing her back, getting right into the itchiest places.

We arrived back on our street and the clouds were still heavy in that late summer way: change is coming, but it's taking its sweet time. When we entered the flat, the piano was there. J's piano.

Our first, battered piano was one my parents had got free somewhere. I was seven when they got rid of it to make way for a slightly better one they'd bought in a local auction, and no one had warned me. The piano I learned to be a child beside, that I learned 'Chopsticks' on long before I could read music, the piano that was part of how things were, that represented what things would be. I sobbed on my bed. *Our piano*. I don't think anyone had expected the strength of the loss or the sense of betrayal.

J's piano was the smallest upright you can buy. He'd brought it with him when he'd moved in. Square-shaped men swearing their way up the staircase, taking the plaster off the wall in the tight turns. 'Hope you don't think you'll be moving again. This piano is never leaving this flat.' It had been here several months by now. But I'd ignored it. *It's not mine, music's not for me.*

But why not for me? I pulled the velvet piano stool back against the carpet's friction and sat down. Opened the shiny lid. Placed my hands on these clean, cold, unfamiliar keys. Like meeting someone new, someone I might get to know so well I'd know their voice as well as my own. Growing up, we had never closed the lid of the piano, and the backs of the keys and those at the extremes of register were powdered with dust. To close the lid was to stop playing. I was always playing, or about to play, an all-day on-and-off relationship with the piano. My piano.

And it felt like the idea of Chopin came out of nowhere.

I don't know why it was Chopin I came back to. Maybe it was because his Prelude was the last piece I had studied in depth for that interview for the job that evaporated (it had been the Prelude in E minor, op. 28 no. 4, I'd looked through my notes). Back then, I'd searched its surface for patterns, symmetries, deviations from the norm. As if this music were mathematical. As if it were little more than a frame for demonstrating my abilities, for getting myself over the professional line. I hadn't been ready to let the music be anything else.

And maybe it was because he represented a fresh start for me, unfreighted by everything else, and by everything I'd been taught, everything I'd internalised. A fresh start with classical music, like brand-new sheets.

I was ready to get to know someone new.

Most of Chopin's music is for the piano, so our paths hadn't really crossed. I'd never worked professionally on repertoire for the piano (I studied orchestras); and although I'd played the piano, I wasn't a good pianist, at least not by the appallingly exclusionary standards of musicians. The trombone had given me few chances to get to grips with Chopin's music, since (foolishly, of course) he didn't write for the trombone. Why was it him? Because I knew lots of people thought his music was very special, and there was a chance for me too. Because I'd never be anything like him, and that was compelling. Because I could never master Chopin's music, and that seemed healthy. I'd never made the mistake of staking my identity on being a good pianist, so there was one less neurosis to unwind.

And because his music is beautiful.

After I'd studied that Prelude without knowing the first thing about him as a person, I guess we had unfinished business.

And now I was craving the cold, smooth weight under my fingers as the keys made hammers thud strings. Itching for the shapes, the addictive flowing motion that translates into the right notes. Longing to dive back into the scores, the papers, the elegant books with their thick card bindings, turn the pages and animate those scores on the keys, smell the metal of the strings. And somehow, through all of this tactility, what results is both elsewhere and rooted in those mechanical actions: music.

There's a piece of music that sounds to me so much like death – or the idea of death, deathness, pomp and ceremony – it sits on a plane that's nowhere near sad. When it echoes in my mind, it sounds like a parody of death, generic, an announcement or a signifier. Pointing at death, while believing death will never touch you, with the certainty, the confidence of the never-bereaved. (To live in that world again.) It doesn't even sound like music; it's lost the depth and detail. It is grotesque, comic, the piece we jauntily hummed as children when we did pretend-death, giggling, dum dum dum dum-de dum dum-de dum. Holding death at arm's length, lest it become too real.

Chopin's funeral march.

Which Chopin didn't refer to as a funeral march. At least not after the beginning. It is part of his Piano Sonata in B-flat minor, the third movement. Although he wrote it earlier, as a stand-alone, once it was in the sonata he deliberately dropped the word funeral from the subtitle, *Marche funèbre* becoming simply Marche, and he never referred to it as a funeral march in his letters.

It didn't stop everyone else. Or stop it being played at Chopin's own funeral after he died young, just thirty-nine. On 30 October 1849, the funeral march would resound in the Madeleine in Paris, played by an orchestra as his body left the church.

Chopin was sickly and frail, diagnosed with tuberculosis, and a mythology of weakness has been created around him that bled into how people thought about his music. A man known for his miniatures, for delicacy; many believed that he didn't have the strength, manliness or indeed virility needed to develop extended musical forms like symphonies, and therefore be a proper composer (read: man). This march was probably written around 1837, when Chopin was in his late twenties and his health was beginning to deteriorate more seriously. It is an emblem, a portent, a foreshadowing of tragedy; and, in reverse, his early death shapes our perception of this music, giving it, as the Chopin scholar Jeffrey Kallberg has it, 'an aura of regret over a compositional trajectory cut short'. But it wasn't only a meditation on his own mortality (and did he drop the subtitle so as not to tempt fate?). It was also a death march for his beloved Poland in the wake of the failed ten-month military uprising of the Poles against their Russian occupiers from 1830 to 1831. For those like Chopin who believed ardently in an independent Poland, this was a profound tragedy, and it led to the death or exile of thousands of Poles. The march is thickly scored, all notated in the depths of the bass clef, dense, dark, sombre.

And if you actually listen to it, if you don't just give it a jolly sing-through in your head, if you put on a recording of the piano sonata, it is chilling as fuck.

I didn't realise this. I don't think I'd ever actually listened to it, just heard the surface representation. The ubiquitous Frankenstein grotesque thing unzipped from the original and sent out to make its way in popular culture.

Anecdotally, in his thirties, on tour in London, Chopin would sit down in the evening at the piano and play and play and play, ever more feverish, ever more pale, and the only way to get him to stop was to ask him to play the march. When he was done, when the march was finished, his mood turned, spent, nothing more left for him, he would take his hat and retire to bed.

The trio middle section is something else. It takes us away from the ceremonial genre of the funeral march to something with fewer sceptres, less military garb, more introspection. It has a beautiful melody – one of the most graceful and simple in his whole *oeuvre*, and it sings and glides as arpeggiated broken chords undulate below in the left hand. He gives us not a fanfare, but a quiet prayer. A private space. It is a passage that has been described as sorting the poets, the storytellers, from those who were mere pianists: hearing Chopin play it, Wilhelm von Lenz wrote, 'Nothing is easier than to reduce this trio to the tritest platitude; nothing more difficult than to raise its melodic spell to the level of sorrow that hangs over the whole poem that this "Funeral March" is.' And perhaps herein lies the enduring appeal of Chopin's march. It turns inwards to the humanity of grief; it's about humans caring about their own experience in a way that feels very contemporary, a moment from which we can thread a line to the present and our sense of the personal in funerals and funeral music. How radical, to tell us that grief belongs not to public spectacle, but somewhere internal, somewhere alone.

All that said, they also performed Mozart's Requiem at his funeral. A bit more traditional, some good solid Journey-of-the-Soul stuff to get Chopin into heaven.

I wanted to play Chopin, but I didn't know where to start. Obviously not with the funeral march. How on earth would I find something to play? It seemed to me that it was worse being an expert. *Expert: expectation*. People thought I knew what I was doing, and I was at a complete loss.

It paralysed me. There is *simply so much* music to choose from. Even if I just limited it to one composer.

And then I remembered. The feeling when I was small, when my piano teacher would play me selections, to see what I liked, to see what I wanted to learn, and something would catch in my throat and start to burn. A powerful sense of who I was going to be. Who I wanted to be. *That one. That's the one I want to be able to play. I want to be able to do that.* And then, hours and days at the piano, and the fluidity would increase.

That was how you start. You just listen. I'd thought I should already know which pianist to go for, because I'm an expert. This was stopping me from moving, stopping me from doing anything from curiosity or pleasure, from admitting what I didn't know. The freedom, the exhale of not knowing. I'd thought I was willing to admit such things openly (I haven't read *Heart of Darkness*, as I declared to all those academics in Boston), but there were plenty of things I was still hiding from myself.

I would start like everyone did these days: with Spotify. And because I was tumbling into this project – the marvellous feeling of giving up control: *I don't have to worry about it!* – I searched 'Chopin Etudes' and let the algorithm do the rest.

12 Études, played by Jan Lisiecki. I'd never heard of him.

I listened to the first few. It was wonderful music. I kicked myself for not having spent any time here before. This was fantastic.

And then something began that felt like arriving. I flicked back to look at what it was: *this* is what I wanted to play. Op. 10 no. 6 in E-flat minor.

That's right, it was in bloody E-flat minor.

E-flat minor is the relative minor of G-flat major, and G-flat major has more flats than anyone can ever remember. Because I didn't have a piano under my fingers right then to remind me with the familiar muscle memory of playing the scale, which would reveal to me exactly how many flats it had, I was going to have to look it up.

It's six. Six flats. That's nearly all of them. Everything flattened except F. Straightforwardly, what this means is that even something that sounds fairly simple was going to be an absolute nightmare to sight-read.

Flats are the black keys on the piano, and are conceived as modifications of the white keys. Whenever I see one, I have to remember not to press the white key, which is where my brain lands first, and instead play the black key to its immediate left.

On the trombone this issue wouldn't cause me concern. *Six flats. Whatever.* Key signatures on the trombone are second nature, as is playing in all different clefs: bass, tenor, alto, treble in B-flat. Clefs being the symbols at the start of a line of music whose purpose is to explain which pitches are signified by each of the lines of the stave. So, depending on the clef, the lowest line of the stave, for instance, will signify a completely different note.

Probably the reason I'm looking for is easy: I'm much, much better at the trombone. I've spent much longer practising it. And there might be another reason: on the trombone, you are only ever playing one note at any one time. On the piano, you are playing up to ten. Or, I suppose, you can technically play even more, if leaping hands and pedals that sustain notes so you can play others on top of them are involved. My brain goes into a sort of panic-freeze when it sees multiple notes that don't spell out a familiar chord shape – there are a few I reach for without thinking, but not that many. Working in the world I do, I have many friends who are truly excellent pianists, and they tell me they see everything as a combination of these shapes and patterns that my brain has never developed the software to process properly. It amazes me.

I don't necessarily want to insinuate that with the trombone I picked an easier instrument that won just as much glory but it's hard not to reach that conclusion. I'll also refer you back to all that time we spend in the pub rather than rehearsing hard with our colleagues, because some composer or other didn't want to use us in the orchestral texture. We are sort of a special effect. It would cause offence if it didn't come with some rewards.

Maybe op. 10 no. 6 in E-flat minor wasn't going to be my spiritual home, after all. Too high a pain threshold for learning it. I kept listening, in the hope that something else would strike me in the way that étude did.

I found a collection of the preludes; played those instead.

And here it is.

Preludes. Op. 28 no. 6 in B minor. My one true love. And only two sharps.

I'm in a minor mood, of course. My dad died. Nothing flashy and virtuosic for me.

As if I could even play anything flashy and virtuosic.

I found the B minor Prelude in J's sheet music collection. First read-through: Datch had come to sit under the piano, at my right-hand side. Her nose touching my shin. She wanted my attention. Eventually she lay down flat, hips splayed outwards at improbable angles, then curled into a croissant. I made liberal use of the pedal, as I always have. I thought about how I hadn't played the piano seriously since I was a teenager, and how this was a blessing. I connected straight to my teenaged self, the person who stayed out late, hung out with the boys, went to after-show parties, played piano in my grandparents' hall. I missed an accidental; played the wrong note, corrected myself out of time. I thought of my dad shouting 'Wrong' from the next door room, constant antagonism. It was faltering, but this was my speed. I got right through it with the kind of rubato you use, loosening the strict regularity of the pulse, when you don't know something at all, and kid yourself it's musical, but really you're giving yourself time to cope with whatever the hell is coming up next. Pleasing octave leaps; repetition of spare intervals in the right hand, descending bassline that climbs right back up again.

We were trying again. I held tiny pieces of Cheddar scrunched up in a piece of foil in my left hand, ready to pick off morsels with my right. But it was dusk, the clouds gossamer behind 1930s flat fronts, and that meant only one thing to a person as sensitised to the ways of dog as I had become.

The foxes would be out.

Three fox cubs now spent the evening winding up and down our street, darting through fences, from behind bins, dodging between parked cars. Louche, stunned when we caught them, then curious eyes, sometimes approaching us, trot trot trot hello? in a way that made me giggle. But to Datch, foxes were purest enemy. They sent her wild, transformed her into the vigilant, fearful, ferocious creature within, fully concealed by her daytime act. The dog who needed to howl.

This was the most difficult time of day to train loose-lead walking, the witching hour when foxes and cats abound and animals become wilderness versions of themselves, all heightened senses and dusk awareness.

I forced myself to walk at half the pace I normally do. *Yes.* Accompanied the affirmation with a piece of cheese. Arc of my arm moved Datch back into position at my side. Responsive. We continued for a few paces. *Yes.* Shoot my cheese-wielding arm downwards, feel her tiny teeth as she scrapes it from my fingers. *Yes.* Cheese. Eyes peered up at me, hopeful, accomplished. She was tempted to walk ahead; the scent of fox had caught in her nose. It was lucky I had

Cheddar today. No other treat will work against vague eau de fox. Not even the fancy ones with chatty packaging they sell at the pet shop. I curved her back around once more with a twist of my wrist at my right-hand side. She obliged. We repeated. We connected. *Good* dog.

With a breath-catching suddenness, she pulled away, standing, straining on the lead, the full force of her body on the harness. I winced on her behalf. She'd seen the fox before I could prepare. And sure enough, it made itself known, emerging from behind a car on the other side of the road. People say foxes saunter, because they do. The fox stood there, in the road. The noise Datch made was piercing, a complete affront to the sleepy civilisation of the street. A noise that did not belong.

As we headed back towards the flat, I felt the foxes eye Datch with disdain. This well-fed, grotesquely cosseted creature, all soft-fur glossy, tripping down the street at my heel after the ever-suspended promise of cheese. How pathetic to live with cheese above your nose. On a lead, but your every need met, without you ever knowing the alternative reality. I felt their disgust at her need to please, and then I felt instantly protective.

The second time I played the B minor Prelude was because J asked me to. He was feeling sad that morning. Datch was playing with her squeaky bear, the soundtrack to many a work call. He mock-announced my performance: 'Emily at the piano, accompanied by Fluffy on the squeaky.' (We call her Fluffy because it is an accurate description.)

I started off too fast, overconfident. *Squeak-y, squeak-y,* contributed Datch. The first time I had played it, it had gone better than expected. In my memory, that had transformed into a sense that it had been a success; now was a classic case of the disappointment of a second play-through. I faltered.

I came close to swearing. My slowness, my pauses frustrated me. *Squeak-y, squeak-y, squeak-y* in the background. My finger strength was badly lacking; my wrists complained, reminders of an old computer overuse injury. Nonetheless, there was still that satisfying bass line A-G-D-E-F-sharp, sitting perfectly under the hand, the beauty of how the texture falls away at the end, now stitched of gaps. The absence by the end of the B from the opening is so subtle. Beautiful, painful loss. Everything still works without it, a descent has happened, but it's missing.

Datch came and curled up by my feet.

Chopin would also have likely worked with a poodle curled up under the piano sometimes. The poodle was called Marquis, and he technically belonged to Chopin's romantic partner, the author George Sand. Her claims to fame extend far beyond being the owner of Chopin's favourite dog. One of the coolest women in the early nineteenth century, Sand didn't care what other people thought of her. Sand had a huge following in the 1820s and 1830s, selling better in Britain than either of her major contemporaries Honoré de Balzac and Victor Hugo. So: a literary megastar. She was born Amantine Lucile Aurore Dupin, and experimented with a new name in her twenties to help her literary profile, and to sow confusion about her identity. She refused to give up wearing trousers, even after being arrested for doing so, she smoked in public – taboo for women – and she was referred to by a mix of male and female pronouns throughout her life. No one quite knew how to place her. She protested against the institution of marriage. And none of this detracted from her success.

Knowing about Chopin's relationship with Sand made me far more interested in him.

Anecdotally, Chopin's 1847 composition the 'Minute Waltz', or the Waltz in D-flat major, op. 64, no. 1, immortalises Marquis chasing his tail. Chopin was besotted, writing to his family about Marquis when he was looking after him at Sand's residence 150 miles south of Paris during what was to be his last visit there, in 1846:

> That little dog, Marquis, has stayed behind with me, and is lying on my sofa. He is a remarkable creature: his coat is like marabou [a fluffy feather trimming], and pure white. Mme Sand herself brushes it daily, and he is as intelligent as can be. He even has originalities which are quite enigmatic. For instance, he will never eat or drink from a gilt vessel; he pushes it away with his head, and overturns it if he can.

Dogs belong in that same secret world of the home of pianos and music lessons, the familiar culture of music. The 'Minute Waltz' whirls around, that repetition lower down, how long will it last? And then a sudden racing, spinning up into the higher registers, and back again. Always ready to go again at a moment's notice. What Chopin would play to accompany Marquis's doggy antics. You can see Chopin sketching it out for Sand at her residence, Marquis there, tail wagging frantically, Sand crying: *Play it again, I'll get the stick*, and baiting the poodle with a toy in time to the music, the poodle bouncing in the air in pursuit of its quarry as the music cartwheels upwards. If the funeral march is a dark veil hanging over Chopin's life, the 'Minute Waltz' is joy, is living. Is a game.

Chopin first performed it publicly at the very last concert he gave in Paris before his death.

I inhaled, exhaled and decided to do things properly, mindfully. I'd need to be careful not to inculcate bad habits. I took the prelude's opening arpeggio in the left hand, and played it over and over, as a dotted rhythm, first one way, then the other, to cement the placement under my hand, to finesse the motor action, to teach the regularity. The opening left-hand arpeggio, with the first finger smoothly crossing over the extended hand at the end in one smooth motion, reminding me of 'Für Elise' and childhood holidays at my grandparents', and the delight of first mastering how to do that, and the thrill of how real my piano playing had suddenly looked.

With Datch below me, it was easy to see the parallels. Training a dog, training the body, training the mind. Training your own body seemed to be the most important part of dog training. It was clear that the dog would respond, if only you would do the movements right, time things perfectly. The dog trainer made me think of a virtuoso violinist; her skills and dexterity teaching any puppy to lie down immediately, coming around and correcting our form.

The trick, though, is not to get lost in technique. Because sometimes it's about curiosity, about trying something new. Sniffing around. Pulling away from restraints, from discipline. Doing things just because they feel good. For no other reason. Than because it's nice.

Datch nudged my lower calf with the squeaky hedgehog she had in her mouth. Nothing, surely, could be as important as throwing the squeaky hedgehog across the room for her. And she wasn't wrong, I supposed. I chucked it into the hallway, and she – ping! – bounded away, disappearing out the door before her smug reappearance.

She doesn't play fetch, really. Fetch is too basic for a dog of her calibre. Instead, she's developed a game I call 'My Toy Now', where, in a modification of many advanced team sports, like rugby, she gets possession of the toy – and then retains possession. Sometimes putting it down on the floor, tempting me with it out of my reach until I make a move and she grabs it and replaces it slightly further away. She rarely gets it wrong: she knows exactly where she should leave it unattended (just in front of her paws); exactly how long she needs to win against this cumbersome human.

The look of triumph she sports is hilarious.

I turned back to the music. I looked at the score properly after I played it this time. The Prelude in B minor, I noticed, reminded me, at least superficially, of another: the one I analysed for the assistant professor job. Same minor mode; same descending line operating in the deep harmonic background of the work. I wondered why I was drawn back to these descents, these cadences.

I put my hands back on the keys. Once more from the top. This is how the music happens.

I was exploring, learning again. Losing myself to the flow of practising.

Finally, I was playing.

Chapter 15

OPEN STRINGS AND
UNDERWHELMING FLAMENCO

Earlier, I claimed that when Albéniz wrote *Recuerdos de viaje* (the set containing the piece left on my dad's music stand), he probably hadn't meant to leave behind a scavenger hunt around southern Spain for a thirty-five-year-old grieving British woman. I will now admit that I left out some major characters for reasons of aesthetics.

In fact, we were a party of four: not one but *two* thirty-five-year-old grieving women (one British, one Basque and pregnant), a Spanish man with an Irish accent and a hot black woolly dog. Both the women were musicologists. The man was a historian. The dog was a Spanish water dog, named Ulía, and had no particular academic specialism.

It was July, and I was in Cádiz, Andalusia, an island city and the south-westernmost tip of Spain, with my old friend Lola, an assistant professor at the University of Seville, and her partner, José, of the University of Salamanca, where Lola and José were helping me with what, without anyone really discussing it explicitly, had spontaneously developed into a quest to visit some of the sites Albéniz wrote music about, while also providing high-level historical commentary. Sometimes, being friends with mostly academics pays off.

'Sure, I know La Caleta. It's a famous beach in Cádiz', Lola had written back when I first emailed her with my plan to visit her in Andalusia. 'I love Cádiz, it's right on the coast, only an hour and a half away. It's where I go when it gets too hot in Seville.' She would book us an apartment.

Cádiz is all apricot walls and saturated greens and sky blues, shady streets in which you need to breathe in for passing cars. Built from a soft beige stone made of the eroded fragments of shells and sea creatures and underwater pebbles, people say it's a city that has risen out of the sea. It has a special place in the cultural imagination. Not only as part of Andalusia more broadly – 'Welcome to the North African–Spanish borderlands,' said Lola, as she and José picked me up from Seville airport the previous afternoon in the 'fantastic red car' Lola had promised as a flurry of emails preceded my visit – a place where the dust from the Sahara coats your skin, settles as a pale film on the roads and parked motorbikes, fast giving things a disused feel. Cádiz is a city with an important relationship not just to what lies south, but also to what does – or does not – lie to its west. It's long been considered, since before even the ancient Greeks occupied it, to be the very end of the world, the limit, the furthest place you can go. *Non plus ultra*. Beyond which point, exiting the Mediterranean Sea through its westerly mouth, sailing past the Pillars of Hercules, you would fall off the edge of the earth. To remember this deep history requires a reorientation of the world map I hold in my mind. And then, once the world became bigger, it became not a limit, but a gateway. The way to the New World, and the possibility, and the fear, and the riches – the economic potential – that could bring. A stepping-off point, a place of loss, of change, of endings and beginnings.

But first, a bookshop.

Bookshops are my first port of call whenever I visit a new city, no matter how nice or famous the beach. This was an especially good one. An absolutely gorgeous and tiny L-shaped bookshop-cum-café – La Clandestina – tucked into the mazelike streets, the kind of place I dream of, the kind of place I can barely believe exists in this city that feels so much like a holiday destination, my perfect workspace, elbow to elbow at the counter with people breakfasting on bread and ham with the sauce of fresh tomatoes and olive oil they all eat here. A breakfast I could get used to.

I'd left the others at the apartment and was on the hunt for a serious book about the city's history, complete with all the details about treaties and constitutions Lola and José had told me about in the car on the drive down from Seville: Spain's first constitution was signed in Cádiz in 1812. This search came with some anxiety; such a book would inevitably be in Spanish, and my Spanish leaves a lot to be desired. But I wanted to understand this place, and its meaning, and what it was like in the late nineteenth century when Isaac Albéniz had visited. Because I was finally here, in Cádiz, on the Andalusian holiday my dad had suggested. On the trail of the music my father had on his stand, following Albéniz's journey, attempting to understand the music my dad left behind. I wanted to see the beach, La Caleta of 'Rumores de la caleta', with my own eyes, understand the effect it might have had on the grieving Albéniz, know the sounds of the south.

In my hands I was holding a thin and enticing Spanish-language volume about Cádiz I'd just spotted on the shelves. The front cover bore an illustration of a pair of pale children engrossed in building a sandcastle on the beach for which Cádiz is best known, all vivid colours in a stylish gouache and pen design.

Cádiz: Descubre la ciudad con la guía turística infantil was right at my level, because it was pitched at 6 to 12 year olds.

And good news: there would be puzzles.

It was at this moment, beguiled by the children's cute pin-dot eyes, that I abandoned my plans to get a serious historical book.

The opening pages of 'Cádiz for Kids' (my translation) revealed that the children on the cover are Iván and Carmen, and that they were going to be my guides through Cádiz. With his finger raised as if in instruction, pointing at Cádiz's location on a stylised map of Europe, Iván informed me that Cádiz is at the base of Spain and is a port for leaving for Africa. Carmen, who was smaller, sporting a natty shoulder bag and a dress with pockets (progress!), invited me to discover La Caleta, one of the most magnificent urban beaches, known for its cleanliness and facilities, and added that Cádiz's most popular festival is the Carnaval. So far so good. My Spanish was holding up – just. Although Carmen was clearly more fun (beaches! Carnaval!) I was also already annoyed by the little sister vibes. Must Iván speak first? Why does he tell me about geography, when Carmen's stuck with frilly topics (entertainment), and care-related ones (cleanliness and facilities). I was disappointed by the unconscious bias evident in the division of cartoon child labour.

Nonetheless I pressed on. After all, perhaps they would share their educator roles in a less gendered fashion further on in the book. I learned that there are five more cities in the world that are called Cádiz. And four of them are – where else? – in the United States! (Also home of 627 cities called Berlin.) I'll bet that doesn't feature on page one of the earnest local history book I had been imagining buying. This is a fact reserved only for us privileged readers of 'Cádiz for Kids'. Save for my ongoing reservations about gender stereotyping, this book was fantastic.

Space was constricted in the bookshop, and it smelled like coffee. I felt like I could talk to anyone, language barrier

notwithstanding. It was colourful and narrow with a handful
of tables and a long counter at the entrance, which you had
to pass by to get to the walls lined with books behind. There
were gorgeous toys, plush sable octopuses in different sizes,
a blue dog, things so lovely it was enough to make you want
children just to be able to have them. Displayed by the till
were long-limbed soft-toy mice dressed as ballerinas in Breton
shirts and sparkling skirts. One barista had a pulse tattooed
on the inside of her wrist. The line on a hospital heart-rate
monitor. A poster – 'Reading is Sexy' – for the Spanish
publisher Gallo Nero, with a young Audrey Hepburn sitting
cross-legged with a book on the floor in front of her, a bed
in the background, black coffee and a striped shirt. Maybe
it was the early 1960s; that was the feel. She had a pixie cut,
black hair, large hoop earrings and bare feet. Now this was
what I call sexy France. This was a poster for the bedroom
of any self-respecting Deleuze enthusiast.

People sat at tables reading books they'd just bought, or
they were working, or eating with their families. Reading
was sexy.

A young German family were colouring in with their
toddler at a table near the door.

Rather surprisingly, in this café they sold PG Tips. PG
Tips always made Lola laugh. She loved British tea, as did
her mum, who always had some in her kitchen. 'Pay-Hay'
was what she called it, because that's how you pronounce the
letters in Spanish.

'Cádiz for Kids' starts by busting the myth about the
origins of the city's name. On the drive here from Seville,
when we'd begun digging into Cádiz's history, Lola had been
keen to impress upon me that Cádiz is known as 'la Tacita de
Plata' ('the little silver cup').

'I'm not sure why,' she said. A beat. Googling was in
progress.

'Ohhhh,' said Lola, looking down, engrossed in her phone. It turned out that *kado* is the Greek for cup (the Greeks were one of many civilisations to occupy the region), and the primitive Iberian diminutive of that is *cádiz*. But apparently it's also about the view of Cádiz from the sea, historically, the main gateway to this port city. The sea looked like a pool of silver. Lola passed her phone to me in the back seat, showing an image of the city from 1856, a vista from some imagined high point above the water. 'I suppose the white buildings trace a line along the sea, like a cup on a watery saucer,' she said. The city was lined with walls. Completely fortified. Teeming with industrial activity. Cádiz is effectively an island joined to the mainland by a narrow strip.

Well, who knew what website Lola was looking at in the car; I had found a much more convincing history in this kids' puzzle book. In its long history of occupation, Cádiz was know as Gadir by the Phoenicians, then Gadeira by the Greeks, then Gades by the Romans, and Qádis by the Arabs. In retrospect, that story about looking like a cup and saucer seemed suspect. No city looks like a cup and saucer. It's amazing what you'll nod along to when someone tells you something authoritatively abroad.

Cádiz is an important node city for relationships between Spain and South America, and of which José happens to be a historian. In the car he told me it's very near where Columbus left on his westward voyage that took him to the Bahamas. It was the main port to mainland Spain in the eighteenth century, when it more-or-less monopolised trade with the Americas. Hercules's Pillars, he told me, are on the Spanish coat of arms. The geographical inspiration for these pillars marking the end of the world has been disputed. Perhaps mountains, one probably Mount Hacho, on the northern coast of Africa, the other, Gibraltar, on the coast of Spain, barely a hop along the coast from Cádiz. (In 'Cádiz for Kids', this explanation is accompanied by an illustration of a skinny-looking Hercules pointing to his bicep.) These days, the quickest ferry crossing the Strait of Gibraltar takes around thirty-five minutes, ten minutes faster than taking a ferry from the UK mainland to the Isle of Wight.

I was now sitting on a high stool at the counter with my brand-new book and a milky coffee. The café's doors were a wall of windows, and through them, jostled into the narrow street opposite us, I could see a music shop. The shapes of the guitars lurked behind the reflections on the glass, lines and lines of curved wood, waiting for me in the corner of my eye. I could imagine Dad disappearing off into the guitar shop, leaving me to write for half an hour, like we always did. He would have loved it here.

Seville is in the same province as the town of Écija, known as the 'frying pan of Andalusia' for reasons that were abundantly clear as we sweltered in Lola and José's Seville apartment after dinner the previous evening. Lola and José told me this with a mix of glee and resignation when they picked me up from the airport. Seville is in a valley; it traps the heat. The platitude locals use to begin conversation is not 'How are you?' but an exclamation about the unrelenting temperatures: 'Qué calor!'

'They do this stunt every year on TV,' said José, his eyes dead ahead on the main road, as palm trees passed our windows and the air con blasted through my T-shirt. *(Palm trees!* Just three hours ago, I had been in *London.)* 'The first day of the heatwave, someone fries an egg on the pavement. It's a staple of the news weather coverage.' José's accent was much more Irish than I remembered. Flawless, in fact. It was a bit disconcerting, arriving in Spain to an Irish concierge. He grew up here, but he has Irish family. The accent made it all the more unnerving when he occasionally couldn't think of words in English.

Not only were we basically in the frying pan of Andalusia (lucky me), it had also been the hottest day of the year so far. Forty-one degrees, according to my phone. Television presenters told us in fevered tones that temperatures had reached 44.5 degrees in Granada. I felt the heat in my eyeballs. It was a dry heat, so you could cope. But it was still like stepping out of the car into the mouth of a furnace.

Seville is the kind of place where if you have a dog, one of your primary activities is going to be spraying said dog with a fine mist of water several times a day.

The sun demands total subservience. Humans can only surface in the narrow pockets when it relents. Everything is organised around the heat. The cool stone architecture. It had been the hottest time of day when I'd arrived at Lola's apartment building: a wrought iron gate in a wall right on the street, behind which was another world that assaulted the eyes with its glare and contrasts. A too-bright white-walled courtyard filled with matt green foliage, the kind of greenery that was as far from verdant British flora as can be. With the exception of the roses: white, red, yellow, pink. Hot-place greenery in raised beds that lined the walkway, plants with long and structured leaves growing upwards like a brush. Plants in individual pots, tied to the black railings, plants that clearly need a lot of active watering only somewhat disrupted the cut-glass geometry of the lines and shadows. Terracotta tiles on the roof, and ornamental tiles on the walls, a local specialty: royal blue geometric shapes on white; azure baroque S-shapes on yellow ochre. This is the kind of architecture that lets you know that you're a heartbeat from North Africa. One cultural chess move, maybe a knight. The kind of architecture that knows how to guard from the sun.

It is taboo to send text messages between 3 p.m. and 7 p.m. And then people re-emerge, and life continues again until 2 a.m. Sleep 2 a.m. to 7 a.m. Repeat. Arriving here, it felt suddenly like life had no distinct rhythm. Like anything could happen at any point in the day. OK, we eat now? Cool. Oh, now is a time for sleeping? Right, fine! In Seville, children are out in the streets after midnight. All the patterns of life, scattered, scrambled, reassembled. It took me back to those undifferentiated weeks after Dad died, when no one knew how to be asleep at night, or awake in the day. It gave me a sense of the arbitrariness of my life and the rules I follow without thinking. This, I thought again, was Dad's sort of place. No wonder he wanted to visit.

Around half-past nine Lola and José had returned from Carrefour in a burst of holas! They had been to buy emergency supplies for Spanish omelette (to be made – thank goodness, given the lateness of the hour – 'the fast way'). 'Donde esta Emily?' José asked Ulía, and she and her long eyelashes galloped over to find me on the sofa. She was all black coils and bounce, named after a mountain beside the Basque city of San Sebastián. I think I should be commended on how well I did to hide my dismay that, come nine in the evening, *ingredients for our evening meal had still needed to be bought.* The rumours about Spain were just as I feared. They eat in the middle of the night.

'By the way, Emily told me she felt the heat in her eyeballs *unprompted*,' Lola said to José with the air of having won a bet, repositioning a coaster so she could put down the teapot. José rolled his eyes. 'José doesn't feel it in his face; he thinks I'm making it up.'

I'd like to note at this point that English, annoyingly, is Lola's fourth language, hot on the heels of Basque, Spanish and French.

The tea had been poured. We picked at the now completely melted mini chocolate chip cookies left over from our dessert as the fan blew our paper napkins on the floor to be chewed up by Ulía. There had been a lot of changes since I last saw Lola. The flat. The dog. Her early pregnancy. And the death of her father, eighteen months previously. Because the loss was so big and so recent, because there were two of us now, it was what we talked about.

Lola explained the sense of being between two states: rationally understanding that people have to die – it's part of the deal. And the complete disbelief: where did they go? Surely all there is that is a human cannot have disappeared?

We talked about the nihilism. Lola bought a flat. Got a dog. Let's do it all now. (This sounded familiar.) José said he'd never known her like it. Although maybe she missed out a bit on the timing of the puppy, because everything was too dark, and even a puppy didn't make her happier in the final weeks of her father's illness, as he lost first walking, then talking, then swallowing. She had a whole year to prepare, to imagine it before it happened, to know what it would be to lose someone, to wonder who she could possibly be without him.

We talked about our fathers. Their physical tics. Her father was always moving. Gesticulating, in your space talking to you. Tapping the table while he spoke. Talked right into Lola's ear at the market. You were absorbed into his world, there was no space for you to think when you were with him. Once they walked the dog without the dog, left the dog at home, so involved were they in one another. A person who would like to eat precisely eleven pieces of tortellini and look surprised and worried about you if you ate the rest of the packet. *Are you sure you want a whole peach? We should share one for dessert. They are so fleshy!*

He was an academic too. Lola's own research work was influenced by his.

I told Lola and José more detail about my plans than I'd been able to in the airless space of email. I explained to Lola about the music my dad left behind. I had brought photocopies; I showed them to her. We talked about what we might have done if my father and I had travelled to Seville.

I wasn't sure. On the flight over, I had envied the woman next to me who'd had the foresight to buy a guidebook to Seville and had been reading about the cathedral. I had no such guidebook. For reasons that it wouldn't take a psychoanalyst to figure out, my unconscious had been avoiding thinking about this trip.

'Would you have gone to see the flamenco with your dad?' Lola asked me.

I paused. I didn't know. I imagined Lola and José thought flamenco shows were tourist traps. I said I didn't think so.

'We went, didn't we?' said José. 'It was interesting – there was a sort of crew of people who go every night. Regulars.'

'What did you make of it?'

Lola made a face. 'Honestly, most of the show was rather dull. But then, at the very end, a man came on stage who completely took my breath away.'

She had mixed feelings about the local variant known as Sevillanas. Everyone in Seville knows how to do it. She told me it's not that complicated; there are a fixed number of steps, and you just keep doing them. 'We can look them up tomorrow and do a beginner's tutorial on YouTube.' But it's so ubiquitous in the culture that it's really hard to find someone who does it really well. 'You should see the women doing it at parties. They are so... disappointing. They do it just like they are going through the motions. Seeing a virtuoso at work is another matter. It's just incredible.'

We talked late into the night, and when I went to bed, I positioned a desk fan pointing directly at me, and I lay under a single sheet, and even that was too much.

I didn't think I'd yet seen a single orange. Weren't oranges what Seville was famous for? *Maybe I had that wrong*, I thought.

As I left the bookshop, and approached the window full of guitars, I felt a sense of longing, and I felt self-conscious. Like people might notice me and my longing. I didn't know if I could go in. It seemed an elite space for guitar connoisseurs; I was not one of them. But then, right inside the entrance to the guitar shop, I spotted the same German man I'd seen in the café with his family, sandy-haired, trying out classical guitars. Spanish guitars, flamenco guitars. He tuned the one he had to hand, twisting the pegs, those painful, familiar tones I recognised right in my brainstem. And I couldn't do anything but go in too, steps down into the shop, pretend to browse. 'Hola,' I said in a gesture towards the three men who worked there. The guitar player sat in the doorway. I had to pass him and his toddler's pram, parked just inside. All I wanted was for him to play some more so I could hear the tones I missed. I feigned interest in some patterned ukuleles to justify my continued presence in the shop. He tried another guitar. The shop was so small inside, low ceilings, just like the café, so there was nowhere for me to be, doing my fake browsing. Electric guitars lined the back wall, three horizontal rows, brighter colours, pale turquoise, racing-car red, ultramarine, gleaming, lurid, polished like smooth beans.

My dad had a chestnut-coloured guitar just like the one the German man was holding. Has? It was still at my mum's house. A really beautiful instrument. One he was proud of, one he hadn't bought that long ago, maybe the newest in his collection. With a filigree design concentric around the hole in the soundbox, and the edge of the guitar's body outlined in fine black, the wood so lacquered it reflected the light. The sound of this man just strumming the open strings took me right into my deepest self of childhood. It was the sound of being. Not just of being at home, safe, but of being. My dad tuning his guitar: the fourths that stack uncomfortably, but fall in order like a sort of rain, a sound I heard always, and that I rarely heard any more. Out of nowhere this man sounded just like him. The closest thing I'd yet heard to him being here again. Just the open strings, played by this German man in various combinations, plucked, strummed, as he hunched seriously over a potential new guitar, assessing the sound of this instrument, its feel, the precise press of the strings, the resonance of the soundbox, learning its voice and deciding if it was the one he would live with, as his toddler, watched by her mother, played on the cobbled streets outside. Like me, that child will have those open strings engraved on their bones, bones that are still soft and bendy, like sapling branches.

Open strings are new beginnings.

And then he stopped messing around with tuning and he tried out something real, a full piece, something I didn't exactly recognise, but I also did. Something that was exactly the sort of music my dad played.

It got much closer to my dad than the recordings I had listened to in Sherborne.

There was only so long I could keep up my sham browsing without feeling like a creep. This man was not giving a concert, he was doing something private, which made it all the more compelling, gut wrenching. I needed to leave before one of the shop assistants asked me if I wanted help, which would break the spell and spoil everything. I smiled at his wife on my way past. I wished I had the courage to speak to her to say: *My dad used to play guitar just like that, your husband sounds wonderful.* The toddler was racing up and down the street on stumpy legs. What was I doing? I was a strange woman searching for an experience she couldn't have any more.

We went to bed early that evening – well, early for Andalusia – after dinner outside at a fish restaurant, where I'd had alarmingly large whitebait, the kind where you can't pretend you're not eating an actual whole fish, bones, guts and all. I wanted to get up early to catch the beach, La Caleta, at the brief time before the world wakes, when it was raw and new and only mine.

A fresh day. Clear morning light. Sandals looped over my fingers, rucksack rubbing one shoulder as I walked barefoot down the beach to find a place to sit in those shadows cast long across it, the sand cool under my skin. Broad water rushing back and forth, empty bar the sole woman doing sun salutations in her bikini and the tiny boat coming in.

Here I was. Finally sitting on an empty beach. Wondering how it might make me feel.

Here I was.

Well. What now?

I was procrastinating as I felt a keen lack of clarity about whether this was worth it, about what I was supposed to be feeling.

It seemed that first the beach wanted something from me. The thing that beaches are for. It wanted me to swim. It seemed I needed to do that before I could settle and go near the music.

One problem: I'd brought my laptop with me, ready for whatever I would do next. I had assumed this would be a swimming-free visit, and it did not seem particularly sensible to leave my laptop unattended on the beach.

Motionless, staring outwards, I dithered. The water looked so fresh and clean. There was barely anyone here.

What you can't let go of, owns you, Lola had said over dinner the previous night, prodding grilled fish with her fork, and casually quoting from Machiavelli's *The Art of War* (note not the better-known book of the same name by Sun Tzu). *The Art of War* was a text she'd found pertinent to the process of selling her dad's home. This tells you a lot of what you need to know about Lola. 'It was a beautiful apartment. But it would hold me back from forging my own life.'

Fuck it, I thought. My laptop could take its chances. I was going in.

There were large fish. Actual large fish in the sea. And tiny fish too. They darted around my feet. The sea was cool in the perfect way you dream of when you grow up only ever holidaying in Scotland. Slightly green. Water from the Atlantic–Mediterranean threshold. I swam short lengths of breaststroke back and forth along the beach, although I couldn't stop myself anxiously checking every few seconds that my stuff – all the valuables I had brought to Spain save my passport, in fact – were still happily unattended on the shore. I was banking on the fact that any budding thieves would imagine that only an idiot would leave all their valuables in a bag on the beach, and therefore that the rucksack would merely contain a picnic and some sunscreen. Because generally, it's agreed that leaving all your valuables on the beach is very stupid.

Without a shadow of a doubt, it's what Dad would have done. Dad was the sort of man who left banana skins on top of laptops. Left his bank card on his car's dashboard. Distaste for middle-class pride in possessions, and for our unconscious defensiveness around our possessions. This is *mine* and that is *yours*. Distaste for the world of accumulation. This didn't prevent him from being incandescent when things went wrong, and his wallet was stolen from his car. Dad believed that he was the specific and sole victim of a cruel world that wouldn't allow him to park wherever he wanted. Parking tickets – and misery, fury about parking tickets – followed in his wake.

And then, once I was back on the shore, my belongings exactly where I had left them, I made myself do it. Listen to the music my dad left behind on his music stand, 'Rumores de la caleta', even though I wasn't sure I wanted to any more. As I sat alone on the beach, as the sun dried my skin, I listened.

I met them on a plaza where they were breakfasting. It had been a twenty-minute walk from the beach, and I was already sweating through my dress. Ulía roused herself to greet me from the shade under the table.

'Lola. José. I have some bad news.' They looked at me. 'I think we came to the wrong city.' La Caleta is in Málaga, five hours away.

'What?' said Lola. 'But everyone knows La Caleta is in Cádiz!'

I'd discovered on the beach that the Wikipedia entry for 'Rumores de la caleta' had been edited since I'd last looked. (I know, I know. Research commandment number 1: Never Rely on Wikipedia Alone.) Before, it had indicated that despite the piece's genre, the *malagueña*, being a 'sensual and emotional courting dance from Málaga', the beach was actually in Cádiz. But now it suggested that the music was named after somewhere in Málaga after all. I checked: there is indeed a La Caleta in Málaga. It's an area, rather than a specific beach. So which was it named for: Cádiz, or Málaga?

José had already pulled out his phone and started to do his own research, loading up Spanish-language articles.

'You're right, I think. It's not Cádiz's La Caleta.'

He sent me the links to some articles in Málaga's local press. 'It looks like Albéniz was in Málaga around that time. So it would make sense that he'd write about Málaga. Also, to be honest, it just sounds much more like Málaga. You'll understand if you ever go.' He kept reading, the end of his tea forgotten. 'OK, yep – he also got an honorary professorship at the conservatory in Málaga in 1882. So he clearly had links there.'

I ordered a croissant and more of this tomato-on-bread thing I was developing a liking for, while Ulía, done with greeting me, lavished her hand licking and leg nudging on the people at the next-door table. I felt a bit useless as I relied on the goodwill and Spanish abilities of my friends.

We briefly entertained, and discarded, the possibility that I would spend the last twenty-four hours of my visit taking a return five-hour high-speed train to Málaga, via Seville. The service was virtually fully booked, and also that was ridiculous.

Ulía, satisfied by the affections of the next-door table, was now staring at my croissant. I had been identified as the weakest link, the lowest-status member of our new pack of four.

There are seven pieces in Albéniz's *Recuerdos de viaje*. The first is titled 'En el mar (Barcarola)' ('At sea (Barcarolle)'), then comes 'Leyenda (Barcarola)' ('Legend'), setting up a sense of the region's folklore. The third is 'Alborada', which means the first light before daybreak. Next there's a series of three pieces that refer to specific places: 'en la Alhambra', 'Puerta de tierra (Bolero)', and our friend, 'Rumores de la caleta (Malagueña)', the penultimate number. The journey concludes with 'En la playa' ('At the beach'). Light and texture and mysticism play together in the titles and the music as Albéniz teaches us to dance.

'I think this is where the confusion comes from,' said José. 'Puerta de Tierra, the monument the next piece in the selection's named after, is definitely here in Cádiz.' So it would be easy to assume that the reference to La Caleta would also be to Cádiz.

'And', he said, looking up with delight from Google Maps, and gesturing in the opposite direction to the one I'd come from, 'it's about a ten-minute walk that way.'

We were off to rescue my grief research visit with a new site.

'Did you just tell me that La Caleta was in Cádiz so we could go to this lovely place?' I asked Lola, as we lounged on the beach again later that evening.

She smiled. 'I think it's for the best that you came to Cádiz. Cádiz is much nicer than Málaga.' She brushed some sand from the back of her ankle. 'Albéniz really should have written it about Cádiz.'

This beach kept drawing us back. Drawing us to the edges, the horizon. A hint at sunset, and the clean smell of salt.

We were on the beach like teenagers with nowhere to go but everything ahead, lying on our towels in our swimwear in a gesture at swimming, except we knew we'd never quite manage to get in the water. We'd left the dog at the holiday flat. And we were talking about everything. Big things, bleak things. The kinds of things that don't make a whole lot of sense to people who haven't experienced a really big death.

I couldn't believe I had made this real. That I was really here. That I had got on a plane, enlisted my friends, and finally: here I was. Here we all were.

The sun began to set behind the sea line. The sky was clear and red-orange above silhouetted beach-goers, all of us pausing on the pocked sand to witness this everyday miracle.

Sitting there, totally relaxed, talking things both nonsense and deep with beers in our hands at La Caleta, I came to understand something. That I didn't need to go to the exact beach. That my inner researcher didn't need to feel ashamed; historical accuracy, dutiful adherence to Albéniz's story, was not the thing that mattered. Chasing a pure experience. Coming to a particular beach. Who cared. Cádiz or Málaga. Málaga or Cádiz.

The point was that I was here with my friends. That they were here for this adventure, game for anything. That this was the new world we were forging together.

What mattered was that we were connecting about death and the life that comes after it, the incredible fact that you keep going in this gravity-less wilderness beyond, when the person who occupied so much space in your sense of the world disappears, all at once. The impossibility of that, the shock that you have to continue in this world that no longer makes any sense at all, that at times you'd rather not be in, that had once been secured, made of tethers and ropes, a web wrapped around you at the limits of where you were ready to stray, or the other way around, the web ready for you to fall against, but I hadn't known that it was there, that it was supporting me. Neither had Lola. And all those cables released, all at once, free-fall, and the question was: if that reality wasn't forever, then, what's it all for?

Every memory, as Lola put it, needing to be revised, revisited, recomputed and reassessed in the light of this vital new fact, a fact so big and confronting that it will be months, years before you can begin to believe it.

Without them, how does the world look different?

When it happened, we hadn't been ready. Neither of us. We didn't feel we had arrived in our lives yet. It wasn't time for this first phase – a phase we hadn't known was the first, a phase that at the time had seemed multiple and variegated – to end.

It had been like looking in a mirror and seeing that everything you thought you were is just a collection of lines and curves and shading now the meaning and purpose that held it all together is gone.

But the reflection in the mirror didn't look like that any more. There were other people in it, too. Lola. J.

And a bouncy black dog or two.

Knowing Lola was going through it as well was helping me put myself together in the afterwards, and to recognise and enjoy the vast possibilities for living here.

José left us briefly to collect Ulía, and then we all took a walk together through an entrance archway and down the short pier towards a former prison fortress, letting Ulía off the lead to sniff along the low wall. Evening sun in our eyes, glitter on the sea and the sand still packed thick with bodies. Most of the tourists were Spanish. English voices were rare; their owners stood out a mile. Boys were leaping into the sea from the heights of the pier. You could feel the testosterone throbbing through the air. José told me his sister was a neurosurgeon. 'You talk to her for ten minutes, you'll never do anything like that again,' he said. 'Second most common reason for needing brain surgery, after car accidents.' Regular gaps in the wall gave access to the rocks on each side of the pier, and Ulía wanted to clamber down. Here, further out, the sea was much emptier of swimmers than right by the beach. Ulía – supposedly a water dog – was still learning to appreciate the sea. They were trying exposure therapy. I went straight in, and Ulía bounded in the shallows, tried to leap waves as they got to her. It was cold, fresh. I swam out into the water – it was shallow – and there's a photo of me standing far out, back to the shore, the city of Cádiz and its palm trees on the skyline, a similar vista to that nineteenth-century drawing I'd seen. It still looked absolutely nothing like a little silver cup. Lola and José paddled in the shallows with the dog.

While I dried myself perched on the rocks, dampened and darkened by my body, Lola tried out some flamenco moves, twirling in calf-high water, arms raised, wiggling her bum, pulling very serious faces, while Ulía barked at her in the water, and then came out and shook herself all over my dry clothes. 'This is it! I'm a proper flamenco dancer!' We'd done a YouTube flamenco tutorial back at the flat that afternoon, where I'd learned the four basic steps between hysterical giggling fits. I still couldn't stop laughing as I sat on those rocks. Lola's underwhelming attempts at flamenco, the bastion of Andalusian culture. The kind of laughter where you have to pause to catch your breath.

How to make your own traditions.

I took a photo of that moment, and she's glorious, posed mischievous in the sea.

Chapter 16

MEMORIES OF A JOURNEY

Seville's cathedral is enormous. Possibly the largest place of worship in Europe. I was overawed by the tiniest fraction. I hadn't been ready for this sort of magnitude.

It made Sherborne Abbey look like a toy.

There wasn't anywhere I could stand to get a visual overview, because it's on a different scale to us. You can't get far enough away from it to see more than a part, and so always have the impression of being dwarfed. You're always walking, turning around it, turning it in your mind's eye at the same time, trying to understand what this monstrous thing *is*. The cathedral was a pale stone, and the sun was coming from behind it so it was hard to make out the shadowed details. It towered, imprinted against a diaphanous blue sky. Its shapes are part Gothic, part Arabic or North African. Unusually for a church, it has minarets. I was looking at an entrance, one of maybe ten, maybe multiple hundreds, since there's this sense of infinity to it, always more beyond the eye line. A surreal white gargoyle clutched its face as if objecting to the idea that water might spurt forth.

We had driven back to Seville from Cádiz early that afternoon. It was much, much hotter back in the city than on the coast, another day that week with a severe weather warning, and once we'd arrived, passing through the building's inner courtyards filled with potted plants in vibrant greens, sun blitzing our eyes, we'd slept until it was time to go out again, dark flat, blinds down, overwhelmed air conditioner puffing anaemically just under the ceiling. We were giving in to this brutal climate. There was no sense in fighting. Lola and I had a dinner booking at 9.30 p.m. in the city centre, the same restaurant Lola had visited on her last birthday. I had taken a pre-emptive cooling shower to lessen the impact of the weather on my clothes, and I'd put on a yellow linen dress and a perfume I don't normally wear. It smelled like roses, too strong in this air. My sunglasses were still on my head as we left.

'Only tourists wear sunglasses in Seville,' Lola informed me too late. 'It's how you spot them.'

We planned to do a perfunctory circuit of some of the major landmarks in the city centre before dinner so I could check at least some tourist sites off my list. I was quite happy enough ensconced in the narrow streets of Lola's neighbourhood, Triana, on the south side of the river, but then I imagined people asking on my return whether I'd liked Seville's cathedral, and having to reply, 'No, I didn't bother going.' It seemed it was worth going out an hour early to avoid a possible minor humiliation. But a lethargy had set in that wasn't just about the heat, and the limited hours in which you could leave the darkened flat. After the disappointment of my premeditated activities in Cádiz – realising I'd travelled to the wrong beach – I no longer trusted the parts of my visit that I'd mapped out in London and imagined would be about grief. I was no longer sure what my being in Seville was for, other than spending time with my friends, and today, any connection with Albéniz's music, even his 'Sevilla', written about this very city, felt remote. Sightseeing seemed banal and redundant: I could just as easily hang out with Lola without leaving the flat.

But, of course, I was hungry. It was 8.30 p.m. by the time leaving the apartment was even faintly bearable. The air was still overloaded with the heat of the day. We crossed the wide bridge that connected Lola's neighbourhood with the centre of the city. The sun was low, and once in the old town, no sunlight reached the street, giving everything an enchanted half-light quality, buildings with ethereal glowing edges. The anticipation of the midnight world of cigarette smoke, dance and secrets that came next. Calm before a storm. Heat still rose from the streets, and then, as we turned a corner, the plaza opened up, a building ahead so huge, so majestic, you couldn't get an overview. The cathedral.

We paused under an orange tree where there was a stone bench. That one had been long resolved: yes, Seville is indeed famous for its orange trees. It's just that in July the oranges were still green; harder to spot. Apparently I needed to return in November for the full Seville Orange Experience. I turned slowly, taking it all in. There was a tall fountain that would dominate the plaza, were it not for the cathedral. I could see the reflection of the water on the underside of the fountain's stonework. It cascaded, the sole visible movement on this smooth pillar of stone, of permanence. And what I could hear was the water's rush, an ostinato below the vibration of evening voices: Spanish, German, English, American. French teenagers with black bags strapped across their chests. The insistent chattering of birds; snorts of the horses attached to their carriages, waiting in the wings; the threshold of the night, when everything starts again. Looking up, swallows whirled against the evening sky. Standing still, I saw the choreography, the rhythm to this square. Moments of quiet, moments of movement as people crossed through. Trainers paused, weight on the heels as photos were taken; sandals passed by: locals with other business here.

I had not intended to linger. And so I wasn't ready for it when it happened. Not even a bit. I came here wanting to see Seville, the city my dad wanted to visit, but I'd got so preoccupied with my shame at managing to go to the wrong La Caleta that I'd lost sight of *this*, this enacting of a holiday that never was, how this might feel.

The splendour of it all, the thick evening heat, the sense that we would definitely have been here together. If we had come, we would have walked this square. Suddenly that drop came.

We would have been here.

We would have been *here*.

We would have pondered this wall together.

We would have developed a set of elaborate in-jokes about the cathedral's information board, testing each other on facts we couldn't possibly know. In-jokes about the perceived lack of oranges. *Seville: a city without oranges.*

The moment became overlaid with the feeling of every holiday I'd ever had with my dad. When my parents had visited me in Washington, DC, and that armed guard had accosted my dad for taking off his shoes in a museum. Visiting towns in Tuscany, for my Italian cousins' weddings. A feeling of him next to me, and a feeling of how I would relate to my environment with him there. What I'd say about it.

Everywhere else I'd been so far has been Lola's territory. About my relationship with her. This was mine and my dad's even if we'd never come here together. It was going to be ours. It was the aching immediacy of that parallel reality brought to life in front of me. The parallel lines we had taken.

They say that grief is like a ninja that comes out of nowhere. I didn't know that I'd be undone by the centre of tourism. I thought it would be the solitude of a quiet beach by the sea. Something about the sanitised pathways of tourism, prepackaged, the guidebooks, a vision of a city that's only for those on the outside meant I'd never have guessed this was what would release me, release my understanding of my father, and the loss of him. But of course: this, these spectacular sites, are why we would have been here, and this, seeing them, is what we would have done together. And then we would have ventured further into the city: an impression of blocks of orange, green, blue and white, passed these sky-high turreted walls, rich saffron, patchy in places, the scent of the vines and the white-flowered, purple-flowered foliage that spilled into the streets.

It's as if the moment were tuned to a frequency the world rarely hit these days, increment by increment, so I would crack, and out would course feelings I had sealed in. I was wound so tightly only tears could release the pressure. Briefly, I felt desperately alone. And then no longer alone, because I was here with someone who truly understood. Missing someone, a hole beside me, but also held, a new frequency emerging that supported me like delicate new strings, gradually strengthening, tightly drawn towards people like Lola. She gave me a hug, and her hair pressed against my face. How strange it was, I thought, that we were in this random place together, of all the places, all the things either of us could do. How strange that Lola was here. All at once it felt a bit like fate, and like coincidence, and like something we'd created together in our future.

As we walked on, glad to have a direction (the restaurant), both facing forward so I wouldn't have to show her my face, I levelled my voice. I tried to explain that I think that sometimes to be so sad is a feeling that's truly nice. A feeling I appreciate. Because I don't let myself go there often. Because it tells you that he was here and he mattered.

I was allowing myself to feel the loss. I was no longer numbed. Being here, with Lola, it let me feel it, talk about it.

Across the street there was a bench. I could imagine him, sitting there, wearing the terrible sandals he would doubtless have bought in Cádiz. Or a brand-new hat. Or something he had bought from someone who sells things from a blanket laid out on Seville's pedestrian thoroughfares. Maybe a fan: I'm sure that would have struck him as a good idea. A lot of people were selling beautiful, colourful fans. Maybe he would have got one for me, completely misjudging the kind of thing I would like, but I would have used it anyway.

And maybe he'd be absorbed in a book, waiting for everyone else to catch up, or he'd just be gazing out, lost in thought, tugging at his beard.

I suddenly knew that this would have been a wonderful holiday. This city is full of Dad things. It's so hot, and he loved heat. It's so green, and it's so different from the pastured and toxic ideals of Middle England. It's material evidence of centuries of struggle between Europe and North Africa. Evidence that Europe isn't the edge of the world, and nor is it bound by discrete borders of water in the way we tend to believe. It's porous; things, cultures get through. And that was everything Dad liked. He liked to be taken away from what we know, thrown into unfamiliarity in all dimensions, heat, smell, sound, body, language. All of it. The feel of the air, the character of the light.

Of course Dad and I would have gone to the flamenco, I realised. That was exactly the kind of thing Dad encouraged us to do when we were away. Go out. See things. Music especially. Experience things. Jazz mandolin in New York. Let's get stoned together at a coffee shop in Amsterdam. Now I bitterly regretted that I had been too uptight for that. My one chance to do drugs with my father.

Instead, I just wanted to drink actual coffee. We always imagine there will be more opportunities.

Walking alongside one another, Lola and I, attention landing on the walls, the ornate black wrought iron lamps, barred windows, things to notice, things to disrupt the surface of your attention, to mention and to keep you talking, and to overlay on your sadness so that maybe no one will notice as we burrowed deeper into the medieval city, ever tighter corners, lower archways, milkier stone, towards the restaurant. We were in oscillation between her grief and mine. She made space, I made space. In flow, in flux, in the belly of a city that contained multitudes.

'It's so strange that we both imagined being in Seville with our fathers,' said Lola. She told me that when he was dying, she had video-called her father from Seville to show him her future there with her job. 'My daughter, the professor,' he marvelled. 'You know,' he would tell people, 'she's going to be a professor.'

And here we were, without them. This holiday was still wonderful, even without my dad. It was simply a very different one.

The heat was freshly brewed again the following morning. It was my last. We awoke to strains of Romantic music. Someone in the building was listening to Wagner's *Tristan und Isolde*. It reminded me of what Nietzsche famously said (well, famously if you are a musicologist) about how Wagner was too dense, too pungent, too decayed: music of the decadent, dank and foggy north of Europe. In Nietzsche's essay 'The Case of Wagner', he contrasted Wagner's suffocating music with Bizet (who wrote the opera *Carmen*) and lightness and the south, as I mentioned before. (Nietzsche had previously idolised Wagner, but they had fallen out in a sequence of events that included Wagner accusing Nietzsche of masturbation.) Clearly I'd internalised those ideas to some extent, in spite of my best intentions, because when I heard the 'Liebestod' that morning, I felt the music's confrontation with this heat, how it curdled a 41-degree day. *This music does not belong in Spain*, I thought. It is too heavy, too sick. Here I am being Nietzsche.

Next the neighbour played *Carmina Burana* by Carl Orff, a work, by the way, that was fêted by the Nazis. That's no reflection on the neighbour: people tend not to know, and anyway it doesn't stop *Carmina Burana* from being a complete banger. But it's worth remembering that good music has nothing at all to do with ethics.

We ate a breakfast of defrosted banana bread before the taxi arrived downstairs. A choked, pressing sort of sadness at the thought of leaving Lola at her flat.

We faced each other, preparing the way for the goodbye. 'My headline would be: "one person can change everything",' said Lola. 'I think you're the only person in the world who can understand. Who has the empathetic potential for this. Who has had this experience.' I felt the same. You need someone who understands it all. All of it. I would miss her so much.

I had thought the trip would be more about the beach, and Cádiz, and listening to Albéniz's music, and the feelings it would elicit. But it turned out it was about hanging out with her, about connecting with someone else who has been through it, who knew the rage, who also had a deep relationship with their father and for whom losing him had been losing herself, too.

This music brought me here. And my dad brought me here. And these few days had been strange magic.

Because I struggle to tell people how much they matter to me, instead I said: 'I should move to Cádiz, where we will share an apartment by the sea.'

'No. You'll stay in London and come here for your holidays. Writing retreats. And I'll come to visit you in London.' Lola is very sensible, and also: perhaps she took my coded declaration of love a little literally.

She paused. 'I thought it was the heat that was the problem here, but it's not having anyone to experience the heat with. I've been reminded how important it is to have a friend.'

The pair of us, facing one another, and the academic fathers we wanted to impress no longer stand so close behind. And our two black grief dogs. Hers: 16 kilograms; mine: 5 kilograms.

On the baking street, I greeted the driver with 'Qué calor' like I was a local. We put my things in the back of the taxi.

Blinding sunlight reflected off the metal, the windows. Reggae came from inside the vehicle, volume increasing as I opened the boot.

I waved through the rear window as we turned the corner, and we pulled away.

In the car to the airport, I looked up Lola's father online, and the tears came. He looked so present, alive, young. He was sixty-six. Pharrell Williams's 'Happy' played in the background. Then Lewis Capaldi, 'Wish You the Best'.

As I looked out the window at the dual lanes of traffic, palm trees no longer noteworthy, I remembered that she was pregnant, and I felt a warm and tingly sadness rise knowing that when we next saw each other, things will be different again. Knowing we'd had a moment already lost. Knowing – having to accept – that this is what life is. Change.

You can get a full view of Seville's cathedral after all, but you have to wait until the flight out. As we ascended, it became visible, truly gargantuan against the rest of the city. I could spot it for its proximity to the rust-coloured tubular skyscraper, from which I traced a line along the river and could see the bridges we walked across last night.

I could see where Lola lives from up here.

On the flight here, my seat had been surrounded by a party of schoolchildren, high on sugar and anticipation, and they had lost their shit as we took off.

'Woah! We're going up!'

'I feel like we're going to die here!'

'You can't say that out loud, man!'

'I can't stop thinking about it, though.'

Remarkably, the exact same children were sitting in the row in front of me on this flight home too. Same seats, same order. Same boy with a hearing aid. Clearly, we had the same itinerary. But this direction they were virtually silent. The girl who had been so thrilled by the prospect of crashing as we landed in Seville was asleep.

We were all exhausted after our time in Seville.

And yet my mind was busy, flying too, full of protecting walls, of dancing. Of being on the edge, on the periphery, knowing things that other people don't, knowing the bigness of the world, knowing what's beyond, because you've been there, and others haven't, and that being OK. Because someone else, now, was there with me too. The seats at my terrible party had begun to fill; I supposed I could put the cheese sticks in the oven.

The world felt open. Full of potential. If I wanted something, I'd realised, I just needed to work out who to talk to to get it. Someone could be persuaded. Prices could be haggled over. Everything was an agreement. Nothing was just given out by a world that bequeathed prizes upon the worthy who had shown their merit. You had to fight, or at the very least, ask. Working within an institution, though, lulled you into a sense of security. It allowed you to believe that the world was fair, that if you were smart, worked hard enough and waited your turn, some kind of paternalistic figure would finally reward you for your efforts. And it tricked you into believing that when that reward came, that you had earned it.

My fury was how it turned out this grief of mine expressed itself. And I could feel it beginning to change, to loosen. Because this belief that you'd be rewarded for playing someone else's game, I saw now, was complete rubbish. Your worth will not come, bestowed from on high by The Great Man, his parental masculinity obscured within The Great Institution. Neither will this figure bestow permission on you to do the scary things you secretly want to do. They will not come and tell you that you are now ready, that you are entitled to be the thing you want to be, to take the risks. If you want something, you need to do it. You cannot wait for permission, for entitlement, for it will never come.

And what remained: what were my own memories of a journey? I was left with a little magnet of La Caleta, a stylised drawing I bought in a bookshop when I was first browsing books on Cádiz for grown-ups. When I got back to London, I put it on my fridge. After negotiation with J, who prefers a sparse fridge aesthetic.

What I think I will always remember is this, though. Arriving back at Lola's flat after dinner. We've left the subterranean restaurant built into excavated North African eighth-century cellar vaults, into a city that was still vibrating alert at midnight, with bats flitting through the air around the cathedral, air languid and smelling faintly of horse manure, a night that could go on for ever. It's 1 a.m., it's still relentlessly hot. We've walked along the riverside, past couples who've escaped the clubs and bars for late-night trysts, and now we are in her office, full with her father's two desks, his rug. Maybe we are opening the windows, getting the air to refresh throughout the flat during the night: I'm not sure. She is showing me a photo – I've spotted it on her desk, and I ask about it. It's the photo of her father and her together that he used to keep on his own work desk. They are relaxing on the grass somewhere. Totally at ease, he is wearing sneakers. He looks young. It's the kind of transparent plastic frame you can get for under a euro from a corner shop, the kind Lola says her dad always had. They look very similar with their dark hair and eyes, and they clearly adore one another.

It's a double-sided frame, and on its back, there's a Post-it note, contained flat behind the plastic. 'It fell out of his books when I went to his faculty after he died to give the talk in his memory.' It was the closest thing they had to a funeral. It reads: *back in ten minutes. Javier*. 'It was as if my father was talking to me.'

Nothing is enough for this, except for the fact that Lola knows I've been there too. I'm lost. 'I'm so sorry,' I say. It's too much. 'I think I'm going to cry.'

'Oh no, you'll make me cry too!' Our eyes are watering.

As we both sniff, she roots around at length in a desk drawer – 'Don't worry, I haven't lost it!' – and she produces his Montblanc fountain pen. She pocketed it right after he died, barely thinking about it, knowing it was the thing she wanted and the thing she did not want to have to discuss. She was never allowed to touch it growing up because her father said she would ruin the gold-tipped nib that had adapted precisely to his touch. She shows me the ink. She doesn't know how to fill it, but also knows she could easily find out. And she says that when she holds it, it doesn't feel quite right, she can tell it's for someone else. I try to make normal sounds, give normal responses, but I'm all cut up inside, seeing all these things that matter so much to her. Hearing her story, experiencing the objects that make him real.

'What was the music you played?' I ask Lola to remind me. It was Genesis's 'The Carpet Crawlers'. Over and over, to make the suffering as acute as she could, to take her to, and past, the edge.

I'll remember all of that. And, of course, I'll remember doing 'underwhelming flamenco' in a sea that's both an end and a beginning, with a dog conjured into being by loss prancing nervously in the waves. Living in the beyond.

And Lola now has a baby girl. I posted them a Jellycat puppy who wouldn't have been out of place in Cádiz's bookshop.

Here are some new memories of a journey.

I wrote that letter to my dad in the end. But it's only for him and for me.

Coda

JOHN/RAVI COLTRANE, 'GIANT STEPS' IN NEW YORK

The waitress has taken away our credit card, half-visible, sticking neatly out of the leather pocket containing our check.

'We played some John Coltrane in the first set,' Ravi Coltrane murmurs into the mic, 'so we'll play that shit again.' A beat, leaving the whole audience guessing, or hoping. 'Giant Steps.' It's a mic-drop moment. And he sweeps away, turning his back on us to catch the eyes of the rest of the quintet, knowing already the reception this icon, this standard, will get. The audience whoops.

Knowing the reception his father will get, as he brings his father's music to life.

It's the final number of his quintet's late-night set at the Village Vanguard, the oldest still-running jazz club in New York, the centre of the jazz scene. It opened in 1935, when the Empire State Building, my second-favourite building in the world after its neighbour the Chrysler Building, was practically brand new. And this must be an ambivalent note on which to end for a son defined by his father's fame. 'Giant Steps', sure, but also: giant shoes. I feel crowded in this compact space by shadow presences, by the mixed simmering intensity of love, legacy, rejection and escape. John Coltrane, one of the storming voices of the twentieth-century, one of the distinctive jazz voices hustling from my family's record player.

John Coltrane's fucking son. Right in front of us, a few cramped tables away. *Playing Coltrane.* My dad would have absolutely loved this.

I glance sideways at J and signal my excitement by pulling a face.

Coltrane, the opening credits to my father's funeral, on that recording of 'Freddie Freeloader' we played as people entered the chapel and found seats facing the coffin. The mood of a really sad jazz club. I think back to that moment in 'Freddie Freeloader' when Coltrane comes blazing in after Davis closes his solo. Something new has arrived; you sense him winch in the tension spun across the weft of the track. One more notch. Maybe two. And suddenly what you thought you knew already is a different landscape. He was the absolute fucking business.

They were all right here, in this cellar, once upon a time. All those men immortalised on that album I can't hear without travelling to my dad's funeral. Davis. Coltrane. Cannonball Adderley. To remind us, there are other icons: framed posters and photos of such twentieth-century giants covering the dark green walls. As a space it's both intimate and depersonalised, like it's both the real thing, and a Disneyland representing the ur-jazz club; signalling its own knowledge of its canonical status. You're simultaneously thrown between being a part of that history – you're there, after all – and being an unwelcome visitor, a tourist in someone else's story. In not New York, but the idea of New York, the idea of jazz. As new history is created on top of old, and the old feels like the Real. When Ravi Coltane's played here before, internet copy has described the Village Vanguard as 'haunted by the ghosts of his parents'. John Coltrane died when Ravi was two. Coltrane senior's poster is the length of the whole wall.

The players are arranged in front of a red curtain. We're packed into a tapered formation that begins at the stage, hemmed in around tiny round tables to hold the one-drink minimum we're required to buy. The couple beside us drink negronis. The dispersal of drinks and bills, collection and return of credit cards is a fine-tuned machine vibrating in the background of the set. It's dark out here, and up there Ravi Coltrane wears a shirt and jacket that look to be purple, but maybe that's a trick of the solder-bright light. He has a pocket square and these cherry-high cheeks. There's an opaqueness to his face, but great talent means you're left craving the idea that he might look into your soul.

We'd had to queue. Respectfully waiting to be admitted down into the cellar. Under the name lit up in pink neon, the door of the Village Vanguard has this distinctive New York awning, a taut canvas polytunnel reaching out into the street, scarcely wider than the door to the club. A large man stands outside it. Make no mistake, here be jazz.

My feet are touching the coat of the man in front, and Coltrane adjusts his reed, looking down at it through his glasses. He begins, alone, crackling and fizzing into the saxophone with something that sounds like echoes of a displaced theme, a displaced time: 'Giant Steps', the same, but different, using what might be an electronic loop-back effect, haunting itself. This motif develops around and around into an extended introduction. If you listen hard enough, you can hear the clack-keys of the saxophone move under Coltrane's fingers, his breath beyond the musical tone, the physical extras needed to make music. I love this. I love when we hear the person and the instrument, I love how they can't be erased. Sometimes, on recordings you hear traces of people breathing or humming. This motif cycles round for a while, maybe the drummer catches it, finds a way in and joins him in the cross-beat cacophony, until finally it coalesces in a moment of pure satisfaction, where they land right on the groove the audience knows so well.

'Giant Steps'. The first track on the eponymous album, *Giant Steps*, released 1960, recorded 1959, two weeks after Coltrane finished the recording sessions for Miles Davis's *Kind of Blue*. People say that Coltrane had been trialling the chart's changes – that is, its core chord sequence – at jam sessions since at least the year before, and may have composed it as early as 1957: its pace, its complexity and its frenetic energy meant it needed time to breathe. Dad would have been ten when they released it. Not long before he headed into his teens, a decade old when he was twenty, part of recent mythology. The album's at the heart of the twentieth-century canon, a rival to *Kind of Blue*, because it's Coltrane at his peak, with more ideas than there would ever be time for, and because of the title track's audacious underpinning chord sequence. Normally a chord sequence holds you down: in 'Giant Steps', the sense of where the ground is spins dizzying like a Rubik's Cube in the hands of an under-stimulated teen. Giant steps – hence the title – between chords with few notes in common with each other, Coltrane unassailable as he erupts into the radically compacted opening solo, his tone both urgent and dark, his precision absolute, as you hasten to keep up with him. 'Sheets of sound', as one critic put it, dense and vertical. Pay attention, or Coltrane will leave you behind.

I once read – well, actually, taught to undergraduates – an academic article from 2010 about what the authors called 'deadness'. It was hot off the press in terms of academic theory, and it centred around the 1991 Grammy Award-winning recording of 'Unforgettable', what the authors describe as a 'posthumous duet' between Natalie Cole and her father, Nat King Cole, who by that point had been dead for thirty years. 'Deadness' explored the revivification of figures from the past and how recording technology offers the opportunity for musicians of the present to collaborate with the dead; their ability (as the article made clear) to make money (or, as the authors put it, generate capital) from beyond the grave. At one point, the authors introduce the term 'rhizophonia'. That's not a criticism of the article; I enjoyed it. But it gives a sense of the sort of people who wrote it: the sorts of men I would have fancied in my early twenties. Natalie Cole had experimented even earlier, in the early 1980s, with singing that song live with her father's track. Nat King Cole would sing the first line, and then she would respond to his voice with the second. She reflected: 'The audiences were so moved that I backed away from doing it more than a few times. Singing that song stopped the show. It completely changed the mood and left me with nowhere to go as a performer.'

This, however: Ravi Coltrane performing his father's music, seems a more elegant recreation of a relationship, of a voice, analogue, both ephemeral and enduring. No one's being fixed in place. Music's already got that complexity of time contained within it, in how it expands the now as you listen, in how it gathers up the past and infuses it into the present moment: here, in how it reanimates the man who wrote it through his son.

Piano, double bass, kit form a tripod from left to right, with Coltrane at the centre, and the trumpet player, with his square glasses and Afro, to the right by the kit. Space is at a premium, even on stage. The inside of the piano lid is a mirror, so polished is the black varnish. A Steinway grand. The space is softened angles – a red velvet backdrop – wedge shapes that flip and refract our attention on to those performers and their relationships; so does the sound, sending us through distorted layers of time. Now, last week, then. The early sixties, when Coltrane senior played this, here. But mostly: a heightened sense of now. Someone's foot taps behind me and through my tailbone, keeping feverish pace.

He's a big guy, the piano player, but he's oh-so-light on the keys.

They solo in turn. Trumpet first. The trumpet player holds his trumpet at his stomach, bell down, ready. He adjusts his glasses, licks his lips before putting the mouthpiece to his face, that all too familiar movement, simple, elegant precision from waist to face that takes me back to a thousand rehearsal rooms, hundreds of concerts. Some players bed in as the trumpet arrives, all muscles tensed as if they were getting ready for a heavy lift at the gym.

The spotlight off him for a moment, Coltrane wriggles his fingers, limbering them up. He stands, eyes closed, listening, tilts his head. And then turns away from the audience to adjust and prepare his reed.

And the bassist. His bass is that kind of beautiful multi-tone textured wood that has history and depth, and you fall in love with the wood and the craftsmanship and its uniqueness. I've fallen for individual instruments – it's a dark-sweet, possessive love, *mine,* one that contains its own nostalgia, one that contains the possibility of loss and betrayal – and the fierce relationship between the person and that unique object, as they choose one another for their mutual tone, and become devoted to one another. His solo starts to work right across the space of the beat, treating it as a fluid spectrum, which is really, really hard. We watch the bassist's hands flying over the neck of the instrument. Where even is the beat? Shifting his positioning gradually back and forth so he lands on one end of it, slides by degrees right through, then lands on the other. He's got total control of time, every microsecond is his, he knows exactly where he is. He sticks out his tongue in delight, makes a face at the pianist. (*I love him*, I think.) It's a kind of virtuosity that makes you want to get so close to someone you could actually be them. He thrusts out his chin, back and forth, this syncopated chicken motion of joy under the lights.

'Play that shit again.' How much is contained in those four words; how Coltrane acknowledges a debt, affection, an ambivalence and our parents as tragically inescapable, all at once. And as he stakes his claim to a father he never really knew, but a father who's public property. How delicately he personalises that relationship that's his alone. I almost don't know whether I should look.

That shit is never going to stop playing, is the thing. I suppose the trick is to know what to do with it.

And then we've paid for our rock-and-roll tonic waters; it's over. The house lights come up and, awkward in the aftermath, J and I remove our jackets from the backs of our chairs. We've forgotten how to move, and there's a pressure between us to *say something* about it all. But what can you say that doesn't sound banal when you've witnessed something like that? I wonder how long the quintet will stick around in the club, where they will go next, have they eaten? The mundane stuff of life comes back in. We are exhausted and pace back to the apartment where a bed awaits.

We're here, it's a moment together, and then it's gone. Back up the stairs, and from the entrance we disperse into the New York late-October evening, unseasonably warm, all going our separate ways.

This is my dad's music. I've never been more aware of that than I am right now. Sure, it's mine, too, of course. There's a familiarity not just in the harmonies, but in the physicality of these men as they move with their instruments, adjust reeds, lean the bass from side to side, that comes from years of rehearsal.

But really, it's my dad's music. He loved it, and I don't really know why, but I'd guess because it wasn't stuffy, wasn't establishment, because it stood for a way out.

I love it, too, but I love it most because I love him. There's enough of a Pavlovian element that it gives me pause. I don't know what to do with that, exactly, and probably I never will, but who knows. Time will keep marching on, and things will keep changing, because that's what things do, and some things will stay the same.

We who made up that audience are a dandelion clock, blown away from one another into the night. The funeral was on my mind again as we left, past late-night bars with people still stirring the leafy West Village streets, crossed an expansive avenue with a view south of the One World Trade Center, standing alone, ruby and sapphire in the night. John Coltrane's incredible solo on 'Freddie Freeloader'. The steps up to people's front doors are decorated with cobwebs and pumpkins and skeletons this time of year: it's Halloween once more. Mexican Day of the Dead influences are all over New York. Mexicans put out the food people liked as a tribute. For my dad, it would be strong Cheddar, and kippers. Late October, when that membrane between the world of the living and the dead, the past and the present, is supposedly thin. I thought back to my mum, reading *Four Quartets*, T.S. Eliot, and I knew what this had been about all along. How she'd read a whole poem about music, about love, about place, about desires and desires frustrated, about how all are woven together, and in my numb avoidance I hadn't even known that was what I was listening to.

Sometimes the closest places are the hardest to look. And it took being in New York, place, history, future, to realise it. *Just playing all that shit again, somewhere new.*

It's all about time, trying to hold on to it as it slips through our fingers, and away into the somewhere else.

And now, pacing home up Fifth Avenue, J beside me, the Empire State Building a bright blue lodestar ahead.
It was time.

NOTES AND FURTHER READING

This is a book that's informed by a decade and a half spent absorbing the key research and debates within music studies. If you're interested in learning more about some of the themes raised and some contemporary ways of thinking about music, I'd recommend the following:

- David Hesmondhalgh's *Why Music Matters* (John Wiley & Sons, 2013).
- Tia DeNora's *Music in Everyday Life* (Cambridge University Press, 2000).
- Peter Szendy's *Listen: A History of Our Ears*, trans. Charlotte Mandell (Fordham University Press, 2008).

I mention specific sources throughout the manuscript, which I acknowledge below. In listing them, I also wanted to give a sense of the academic discussions that have shaped how I think about the music I write about – but be warned that having enjoyed this book is absolutely no guarantee that you will enjoy reading any of the things I mention.

In the **Prelude: In Cádiz** and **Chapter One: A Music Stand** I touch on a lot of general themes within current music research – first and foremost, the fact that we don't yet know why music triggers emotions. Annoying. What we do know, however, is that there are at least eight mechanisms by which music might arouse emotion, and that they also interact with one another. These include things like the brainstem reflex (e.g. a startle response to sudden loud music), episodic memory (if music triggers a memory that comes with a particular feeling), visual imagery (e.g. you might feel relaxed if particular music evokes a landscape in your mind) and, taken together, they are known by the acronym BREKVEMA, combining the first letters of each of the mechanisms. At the time of writing, the BREKVEMA framework is probably the most comprehensive, widely accepted contemporary model of how music gives rise to emotions. You can read more about it in Patrik N. Juslin's *Musical Emotions Explained: Unlocking the Secrets of Musical Affect* (Oxford University Press, 2019). He also explains what we know about music's ability to provoke tears.

Some researchers are starting to wonder whether the emotions we experience while listening to music are actually different to the emotions we experience otherwise, which I think is a fascinating idea.

Other topics I gesture at include how listening to music tends to bring up specific memories from our pasts (for instance, Kelly Jakubowski researches this, and you might take a look at Kelly Jakubowski and Anita Ghosh, 'Music-Evoked Autobiographical Memories in Everyday Life', *Psychology of Music*, 49: 3 (2021), 649–66. A related idea is that listening to music is an embodied experience, and that it plays out in the motor areas of our brains that register movement. See Arnie Cox, *Music and Embodied Cognition: Listening, Moving, Thinking, Feeling* (Indiana University Press, 2016). As Elizabeth Margulis puts it in *On Repeat: How Music Plays the Mind* (Oxford University Press, 2014):

Across repeated listenings, the particular sonic and temporal trajectory of the piece [of music] grips and regrips motor circuitry, solidifying a kind of motor routine that makes the music increasingly feel like a familiar way of moving, rather than merely a familiar series of sounds. The more this happens, the more the music seems to dissolve boundaries, occupy your subjectivity, and connect your inner sensibilities with the outer world: important parts of the pleasure of repeated listening.

I wholeheartedly recommend Elizabeth Margulis's book, a compelling and very readable exploration of the impact of repetition on our experience of how we hear, comprehend and recall music – including answering questions like: do we enjoy music more the more we hear it? (Yes, up to a point of saturation, when enjoyment then drops off), or, as discussed in **Chapter Two: Tunes for Ten Fingers**, to what extent can we condense our memory of a piece of music into a single moment, the way we might recall a painting or a photo as a composite impression? (Not very well). The second chapter also features Denise Riley's *Time Lived, Without Its Flow* (Picador, 2018), a beautiful meditation on her experience of time after the sudden death of her son. The Emily Dickinson poem is found in *The Complete Poems of Emily Dickinson* (Little Brown, 1924; Bartleby.com, 2000). The German philosopher G.F.W. Hegel talks about music securing us into time in one of his lectures, published as G.W.F. Hegel, *Aesthetics: Lectures on Fine Art, Vol. 2,* trans. T.M. Knox, 2 vols (Clarendon Press, 1975), 2, 908, and is mentioned in Riley, *Time Lived*, 72.

While writing **Chapter Three: Kinds of Blue**, I referred to several books about Miles Davis, including Eric Nisenson's *The Making of Kind of Blue: Miles Davis and His Masterpiece* (St Martin's Griffin, 2000); not to be confused with Ashley Kahn, *Kind of Blue: The Making of the Miles Davis*

Masterpiece (Da Capo Press, 2007). Davis being Bob Dylan's 'definition of cool' comes from Kahn's book. My godfather highly recommends Davis's autobiography: Miles Davis with Quincy Trope, *Miles: The Autobiography* (Picador, 1990).

My edition of T.S. Eliot's *Four Quartets* was first published in 2001; the original was first published in 1943, T.S. Eliot, *Four Quartets* (Faber & Faber, 2001). George Williamson wrote the explainer that began to unlock *Four Quartets* for me: *A Reader's Guide to T.S. Eliot: A Poem-by-Poem Analysis* (Thames and Hudson, 1971 (1955)); but more importantly Michelle Taylor gave me what was effectively a personal lecture on Eliot and the *Four Quartets* from her home in Atlanta, Georgia. You can read her writing on T.S. Eliot and Emily Hale in *The New Yorker* magazine: Michelle Taylor, 'The Secret History of T.S. Eliot's Muse', 5 December 2020, https://www.newyorker.com/books/page-turner/the-secret-history-of-t-s-eliots-muse. Eliot's comments about 'difficult' poets can be found in 'The Metaphysical Poets', in Frank Kermode ed., *Selected Prose of T. S. Eliot* (Faber & Faber, 1975) 59–67, 65, and originally published in the *Times Literary Supplement*, 20 October 1921.

Since the Eliot and Hale letters were disembargoed in 2020, they have all been made freely available online, and can be read here: https://tseliot.com/the-eliot-hale-letters.

In the discussion of journal articles about how and why people choose the music they do for funerals, I responded in particular to: Sue Adamson and Margaret Holloway, '"A Sound Track of Your Life": Music in Contemporary UK Funerals', *OMEGA – Journal of Death and Dying*, 65: 1 (2012), 33–54. The quotation about memories steeling us 'against the terror of the forgettable self' at funerals comes from Elizabeth Hallam and Jenny Hockey, *Death, Memory and Material Culture* (Berg, 2001), 4; and was cited in Adamson and Holloway's article.

Sally Berkovic is the author of *Death Duties: The Chevra Kaddish Burial Society: What Being Around the Dead Taught Me about Life* (Fishburn Books, 2022), and she generously talked me through Orthodox Jewish grief rituals. To read more about the Kaddish, Leon Wieseltier's *Kaddish* (Picador, 2000) comes recommended by rabbis (or at least by the one I spoke to).

Jill's book, quoted in **Chapter Four: Oblivion, with Nadia Boulanger**, is published as Jillian C. Rogers, *Resonant Recoveries: French Music and Trauma between the Wars* (Oxford University Press, 2021). She's also written an article which I drew on extensively in this chapter: Jillian C. Rogers, 'Living Intimately with Loss: Embodied Memory in Nadia Boulanger's Post-1918 Work of Mourning', *Music & Letters*, 104: 2 (2023), 229–70. The pamphlet 'How to Speak with the Dead' Jill mentioned is B. Thomson, *Comment parler avec les morts: Procédés pratiques* (Hector and Henri Durville, 1919), and there are more details on this in her above-mentioned article.

Because scholars only started taking the Boulanger sisters seriously relatively recently, the range of English biographies is patchy, but for a book about Nadia's life, Jill told me she rates Jérôme Spycket's *Nadia Boulanger*, trans. M.M. Shriver (Pendragon Press, 1992). On the more academic side, there's Jeanice Brooks's fantastic edited collection *Nadia Boulanger and Her World* (University of Chicago Press, 2020). There's even less in English on Lili, but Leonie Rosenstiel's *The Life and Works of Lili Boulanger* (Fairleigh Dickinson University Press, 1978) is a good general introduction.

Lola writes about the experience of time in music in Lola San Martín Arbide, 'Music and Nostalgia', in *The Routledge Handbook of Nostalgia*, eds Tobias Becker and Dylan Trigg (Routledge, 2025), 96–107. Her observation that music cannot create a past tense borrows from work by the musicologist Carolyn Abbate in *Unsung Voices: Opera and Musical Narrative in the Nineteenth Century* (Princeton University Press, 1991), 54.

Lola's observation is explored in more depth in Kristina Knowles's chapter 'Music as Time, Music as Timeless', in *The Oxford Handbook of Time in Music*, eds Mark Doffman, Emily Payne and Toby Young (Oxford University Press, 2022), 57–76, in which Knowles introduces various conceptual positions on time in music, especially two opposed ideas: 1) 'music as an art form that exists only in and through the unfolding of time', and 2) 'music as capable of evoking a static temporality', a sense of 'stasis or timelessness'. Michelle Phillips works extensively on the psychology of music and time, and has shown some factors that affect our perception of time while listening to music. For an introduction to her work, take a look at Michelle Phillips and Matthew Sergeant eds, *Music and Time: Psychology, Philosophy, Practice* (Boydell Press, 2022).

In **Chapter Five: The Right Instrument for Your Child**, the David Foster Wallace quotation is from a commencement speech he gave in 2005 to graduating students at Kenyon College, USA, subsequently published as a short book, *This is Water: Some Thoughts, Delivered on a Significant Occasion, about Living a Compassionate Life* (Little, Brown and Company, 2009).

Atarah Ben-Tovim and Douglas Boyd's *The Right Instrument for Your Child* was reprinted by Orion in a revised and updated version in 2012; I haven't taken a look at the new version, but reading the original edition (Gollancz, 1985) when I was growing up inspired me a lot, controversial take on the oboe notwithstanding.

If you'd like to read more about how the early twentieth-century eugenics movement tried to co-opt ideas of musical talent, and you're in the mood to tackle some academic writing, Alexander Cowan's current scholarly work can be found in a book I co-edited with Emily I. Dolan and Arman Schwartz, *Sonic Circulations: Music, Modernism, and the Politics of Knowledge* (University of Pennsylvania Press, 2025), as well as in *The Science-Music Borderlands: Reckoning with the Past and Imagining the Future*, eds Elizabeth H. Margulis, Psyche Loui, Deirdre Loughridge (The MIT Press, 2023).

You can read the Stanford Encyclopedia of Philosophy entry for Gilles Deleuze here: https://plato.stanford.edu/entries/deleuze/.

In **Chapter Six: 'Elegy for Mippy II' and Other Dogs (Mine)**, the Leonard Bernstein biography that I'm assured is the standard go-to volume ('all the rest of us are just fluffing around the edges, really' as an American twentieth-century music specialist told me) is Humphrey Burton, *Leonard Bernstein* (Faber & Faber, 1994). More information about the excellent (according to me) and one star (according to the *Guardian*) exhibition of dog portraiture at the Wallace Collection is available in the exhibition catalogue: Xavier Bray, *Faithful and Fearless: Portraits of Dogs* (D. Giles Ltd, 2021).

The dual process model of grief, mentioned in **Chapter Seven: Silence**, was first outlined in: Margaret Stroebe and Henke Schut, 'The Dual Process Model of Coping with Bereavement: Rationale and Description', *Death Studies*, 23: 3 (1999), 197–224.

Janieke's own research on present-day funeral culture in the Netherlands includes Bruin-Mollenhorst, 'The Musical Eulogy and Other Functions of Funeral Music', *OMEGA – Journal of Death and Dying*, 82: 1 (2020), 25–41 and Bruin-Mollenhorst, 'Funeral Music Between Heaven and Earth', in *Music and Death: Interdisciplinary Readings and Perspectives*, eds Marie Josephine Bennet and David Gracon (Emerald Publishing Limited, 2019), 7–18.

Some of the research Janieke sent me in advance of our conversation – and which I found infuriating – includes: Sue Adamson and Margaret Holloway, '"A Sound Track of Your Life"; Glenys Caswell, 'Beyond Words: Some Uses of Music in the Funeral Setting', *OMEGA – Journal of Death and Dying*, 64: 4 (2011), 319–34; Lauren Patrick DiMaio and Alexa Economos, 'Exploring the Role of Music in Grief', *Bereavement Care*, 36: 2 (2017), 65–74; Jane W. Davidson and Sandra Garrido, 'The Modern Funeral and Music for Celebration: Part I', in *Music and Mourning*, eds Davidson and Garrido (Routledge, 2016), 9–17; Marianne Viper, David Thyrén and Eva Bojner Horwitz, 'Music as Consolation – The Importance of Music at Farewells and Mourning', *OMEGA – Journal of Death and Dying*, 85: 1 (2022), 1–23.

The idea of the 'sacred conservatory' comes from Alexander Stein, 'Music, Mourning and Consolation', *Journal of the American Psychoanalytic Association*, 52: 3 (2004), 783–811, 794; found in Clare C. O'Callaghan et al., 'Sound Continuing Bonds with the Deceased: The Relevance of Music, Including Preloss Music Therapy, for Eight Bereaved Caregivers', *Death Studies*, 37: 2 (2013), 101–25, 118–19.

The studies of dementia patients I mention took place in the early 2000s and were led by Lola L. Cuddy. See Lola L. Cuddy and Jacalyn Duffin, 'Music, Memory, and Alzheimer's Disease: Is Music Recognition Spared in Dementia, and How Can It Be Assessed?', *Medical Hypotheses*, 64: 2 (2005), 229–35. This research was groundbreaking not only for what it tells us about memory, but because it was only then, as Michelle Phillips explained to me, that we first understood how significant a role music may play for people living with dementia, and how perhaps musical memory may remain when other aspects of memory are lost. Whereas visual stimuli are mainly processed in the occipital lobe at the back of our brains, music seems to be deeply enmeshed throughout: complex musical tasks engage many processes in, and parts of, the brain.

It's a fast-moving area, though, and new research continues to reveal more about music's effect on the brain with every new publication.

Mike Goodrick's *The Advancing Guitarist: Applying Guitar Concepts and Technique* (Third Earth Productions, 1987) was the surprisingly philosophical guitar technique book my dad used, appearing in **Chapter Eight: Rumores de la caleta**. That book review I read after I listened to 'Rumores de la caleta' at my mum's house was by Carol A. Hess, '*Isaac Albéniz: Portrait of a Romantic* by Walter Aaron Clark (review)', *Notes*, 56: 4 (2000), 946–8. The books I consulted at the British Library were Walter Aaron Clark, *Isaac Albéniz: A Guide to Research* (Garland, 1998), 32, and Clark, *Isaac Albéniz: Portrait of a Romantic* (Oxford University Press, 1999). The newspaper articles I cited from *La correspondencia musical* are found in Clark's *A Guide to Research* on page 82. I also looked at Albéniz's own *Impresiones y diarios de viaje* ('Impressions and diaries of travel'), published by the Fondàcion Isaac Albéniz in 1990. Friedrich Nietzsche compared Richard Wagner to Georges Bizet in a 1888 essay titled *Der Fall Wagner*, found in multiple translations, but you might look at the most recent, *The Wagner Case: A Musician's Problem*, trans. Tim Newcomb (Livraria Press, 2024).

In **Chapter Eleven: Bells**, much discussion of the bells at Sherborne Abbey draws on a book chapter by Dolly MacKinnon, '"The Ceremony of Tolling the Bell at the Time of Death": Bell-ringing and Mourning in England c.1500–c.1700', in: *Music and Mourning*, 31–3; the observation by Samuel Pepys comes from Clare Gittings, *Death, Burial and the Individual in Early Modern Britain*

(Croom Helm, 1984), 135; and the 1725 publication on the habits, opinions and ceremonies of the common people (and the quotation with the excitingly placed capital letters) is Henry Bourne, *Antiquities Vulgares; or, the Antiquities of the Common people* (J. White, 1725), 2. Both are found in MacKinnon's chapter. I also referred to chapter 12, 'Funerals and Mourning Rituals', in *Music, Nostalgia and Memory: Historical and Psychological Perspectives*, eds Garrido and Davidson (Palgrave Macmillan, 2019), 241–63.

Some of the historical details about Sherborne Abbey came from Huw Ridgeway, *Sherborne Abbey* (Scala Arts and Heritage Publishers Ltd, 2014), which you can buy in the abbey's gift shop, and perhaps even other places too.

A good chunk of the discussion of the history of funeral music in **Chapter Twelve: Dies Irae and Hardcore Death Dances** refers to various chapters in Wolfgang Marx ed., *Music and Death: Funeral Music, Memory, and Re-evaluating Life* (The Boydell Press, 2023), especially the chapter written by Marx, 'Types of Mercy and Non-liturgical Dramaturgy: The Musical Requiem as a Concert Piece', 53–68, which deals in depth with Mozart's Requiem; Miriam Wendling's 'Construction and Instruction: Medieval and Early Modern Masses for the Dead', 11–33; and the chapter by Nicole Grimes, 'Manifestations of Death in the Music of Johannes Brahms', 93–109. On Brahms's *German Requiem*, I also read Robin A. Leaver, 'Brahms's Opus 45 and German Protestant Funeral Music', *The Journal of Musicology*, 19: 4 (2002), 616–40. My discussion of cremation and its impact on funeral music draws on Brian Parsons' article 'Identifying Key Changes: The Progress of Cremation and Its Influence on Music at Funerals in England, 1874–2010', *Mortality*, 17: 2 (2012), 130–44.

I learned about music for eighteenth- and nineteenth-century English funerals from Vic Gammon, 'Singing and

Popular Funeral Practices in the Eighteenth and Nineteenth Centuries', *Folk Music Journal*, 5: 4 (1988), 412–47.

In **Chapter Thirteen: Gustav Mahler, Alma Schindler and Songs for Lost Dreams**, I referred extensively to Cate Haste's *Passionate Spirit: The Life of Alma Mahler* (Bloomsbury, 2019), which I recommend highly to a general reader interested in Alma's life. She works with archival materials including Alma's diaries, some of which are published here: Antony Beaumont ed. and trans., *Alma Mahler-Werfel, Diaries 1898–1902* (Cornell University Press, 1998), as well as with Alma's and Gustav's letters: Alma Mahler, *Gustav Mahler: Memories and Letters*, ed. Donald Mitchell (University of Washington Press, 1975); Henry-Louis de La Grange and Günther Weiss eds, *Gustav Mahler: Letters to His Wife*, trans. Antony Beaumont (Cornell University Press, 2004).

For much of the twentieth century, many historians and musicologists vilified Alma, painting her as a difficult woman and an obstacle to studying the person who really mattered – her husband. More recent academic research on Alma Mahler has therefore had to deal with rehabilitating her, and studies have titles such as 'Redeeming Alma', or Oliver Hines's *Malevolent Muse: The Life of Alma Mahler*, trans. Donald Arthur (Northeastern University Press, 2015), which problematises the remorselessly negative characterisation of Alma. An excellent article by Nancy Newman reevaluates the sexual politics of Alma and Gustav's relationship: '#AlmaToo: The Art of Being Believed', *Journal of the American Musicological Society*, 75: 1 (2022), 39–79. Rachel Scott of the University of Memphis has written a 2021 doctoral dissertation on Alma's music, and I hope scholars continue to engage with Alma as an artist.

This chapter was influenced by books about Gustav Mahler's *Kindertotenlieder* and his life around that time, including: Donald Mitchell, *Gustav Mahler, Songs and*

Symphonies of Life and Death (Faber & Faber, 1985); Henry-Louis de La Grange, *Gustav Mahler, Volume 3, Vienna: Triumph and Disillusion (1904–1907)* (Oxford University Press, 1999); Peter Russell, *Light in Battle with Darkness: Mahler's* Kindertotenlieder (Peter Lang, 1991); Edward F. Kravitt, 'Mahler's Dirges for His Death: February 24, 1901', *The Musical Quarterly*, 64: 3 (1978), 329–35; Peter Revers, trans. Irene Zedlacher, '"… the heart-wrenching sound of farewell": Mahler, Rückert, and the *Kindertotenlieder*', in *Mahler and His World*, ed. Karen Painter (Princeton University Press, 2002), 173–83.

I think I was the first person ever to open the British Library's copy of Hartmut Bobzin, Ralf Georg Czapla, York-Gothart Mix and Thomas Pittrof eds, *"euer Leben fort zu dichten". Friedrich Rückerts "Kindertotenlieder" im literatur- und kulturgeschichtlichen Kontext* (Ergon Verlag, 2016).

The *New York Times* reported on Adams' alleged sexual misconduct in: Joe Coscarelli and Melena Ryzik, 'Ryan Adams Dangled Success. Women Say They Paid a Price', *New York Times*, 13 February 2019, https://www.nytimes.com/2019/02/13/arts/music/ryan-adams-women-sex.html.

A lot of **Chapter Fourteen: Playing Chopin (Badly)** was written with reference to work by the scholar Jeffrey Kallberg, in particular his article 'Chopin's March, Chopin's Death', *19th-Century Music*, 25: 1 (2001), 3–26. The idea that in the funeral march, Chopin was mourning not a person, but Poland, is his. See also: Ewelina Boczkowska, 'Chopin's Ghosts', *19th-Century Music*, 35: 3 (2012), 204–23. Wilhelm von Lenz was writing in the *Neue Berliner Musikzeitung*: 'Übersichtliche Beurteilung der Pianoforte-Kompositionen von Chopin', 26 (1872), 289, as cited in Jean-Jacques Eigeldinger, *Chopin: Pianist and Teacher* (Cambridge University Press, 1988), 86 (trans. slightly modified), and found in Kallberg, 'Chopin's March'.

Chopin's remarks about Marquis the dog are from a letter from Chopin to his family in Warsaw, dated 11 October 1846, and found in Frédéric Chopin, *Chopin's Letters*, trans. Ethel Lillian Voynich (A.A. Knopf, 1931), 305–13, 307 (trans. slightly updated). I originally discovered this letter on the blog of the classical pianist Jack Gibbons: http://jackgibbons.blogspot.com/2020/04/la-valse-au-petit-chien-composers-and.html.

In Cádiz (**Chapter Fifteen: Open Strings and Underwhelming Flamenco**) I bought a wonderful book called *Cádiz: Descubre la ciudad con la guía turística infantil* by Iván Cano Rueda (maybe Carmen is Iván's real life little sister?), published by DeFabula in 2011. It has great pictures, and great puzzles. At no point did I get hold of an actual guidebook to Seville.

I read about John Coltrane's 'Giant Steps', played by Ravi Coltrane at the performance described in the **Coda: John/Ravi Coltrane, 'Giant Steps' in New York** in Steve Sullivan's *Encyclopedia of Great Popular Song Recordings* (Scarecrow Press, 2013). For further reading on John Coltrane, try: Ben Ratliff's *Coltrane: The Story of a Sound* (Faber & Faber, 2020) or – if you want more detail and music analysis – Lewis Porter's *John Coltrane: His Life and Music* (University of Michigan Press, 1998). Val Wilmer's *As Serious As Your Life: Black Music and the Free Jazz Revolution, 1957–1977* (Serpent's Tail, 2018) – a book originally published in 1977 – gives some of his cultural context, as does reading contemporary reviews of the 1960s jazz scene, for instance these by *The New Yorker*'s jazz critic: Whitney Balliett, *Collected Works: A Journal of Jazz 1954–2001* (St Martin's Griffin, 2002).

The article on 'deadness' discussed in some undergraduate seminars I taught is by Jason Stanyek and Benjamin Piekut: 'Deadness: Technologies of the Intermundane', *TDR/The Drama Review*, 54: 1 (2010), 14–38.

MUSIC FOR SOMEONE ELSE'S LOSS

Never look on the bright side. You don't need to. There's nothing good about it. Don't even feel tempted if the bereaved person is doing so. I remember saying things like: 'I suppose I've been spared a deteriorating illness twenty years in the future?' I didn't feel these things. I was numb, and trying to make sense of everything. No one really cares about being spared things twenty years in the future – if we worked that way, more would be done to tackle climate change. Just agree that it's truly terrible, and say how sorry you are, and that you're thinking of them.

Send a card. Don't sweat the details too much. Especially not the picture. Just say how sorry you are. If you knew them well, write things you remember about the person who has died. If you have photos of the person who has died, brilliant. Send them. Everyone will want to have them and everyone will want to see them. Likewise, music you associate with the person who has died. Everyone wants to know about the memories you shared with them, and music summons moments together incredibly well. People who've experienced a death want to make the person who's died three-dimensional, want to dwell in the details; they want to learn about facets of the person they never knew, see them completely in the round. Tell them about the music you shared together, the nights out, the gigs, festivals, concerts; the nights in, red wine and secrets heavy in the mouth, music they taught you about for the first time.

Oh, and if you send flowers, send the kind that come with a vase as well. No one ever has enough vases for all the flowers that arrive.

And do send flowers. Send scented candles. Bath bubbles. Fancy moisturiser. Their favourite crisps. Make a big fuss of people who've experienced a death. Text them to check in, making clear that you don't expect a reply. They need to know people are thinking of them, that people know they've experienced the unimaginable. Leave food on their doorstep, unasked. Or send a gift subscription to one of those meal kit companies. Don't say 'Let me know if there's anything I can do.' Say 'How can I help?' and give concrete suggestions. Hell, say: 'I'm going to come by and do your laundry/walk your dog this week, unless you wrestle me to the ground.'

You can still text them about normal things, too, by the way. They still like reading funny articles.

Show up, don't stay away. I mean this literally: show up at their door. Make sure the bereaved person doesn't find themselves telling you the story of the death for the first time three months down the line. That will create distance in your friendship. If you can't visit, call. If they don't pick up, don't be put off. Try again another time. Make sure you hear that story in the first few weeks. If you don't know what to say, tell them that you don't know what to say, that you've never experienced anything like this, but you're here for them.

If you're trying to decide whether or not you know someone well enough to send your condolences, you should send your condolences. You won't be encroaching on something private. They won't think *Why did* she *send condolences? We barely know her!* They will appreciate other people acknowledging that this is about the most monumentally shit thing that someone can go through, that a wrecking ball just hit their family. Just tell them you're sorry it's so shit.

If you can, a few months later, check in again and say you're thinking of them, and remembering the person they lost, and you know it's still really shit. There's a special place in heaven with a champagne reception that definitely features Turkish delight for people who remember the first anniversary of the death, and send a message, or even better, another card. It makes what happened still real, still a thing that matters.

Don't stress if you don't get it all right. Maybe you were afraid of encroaching at the beginning, and you didn't know what to say. That's OK. But tell them. Be honest about it, even if it's hard to admit. They also know what it's like to be a person who's never experienced a bereavement; they'll get it. Show up, listen to your friend, talk about the person who died, and be honest.

While I've got you, make a will. It's not that hard. It might save someone you love a lot of heartache. And – I know this runs counter to security recommendations – but do tell someone important all your computer passwords, and maybe at least one piece of music you'd like at your funeral. And make sure they're actually taking it in. Dad told me his phone's passcode and I didn't really pay attention, thinking this wasn't information I needed yet, and I'd get more chances to hear it. I don't remember if he ever mentioned music he'd want at his funeral. Even if he did, it's the kind of conversation I would have wanted to screen out.

ACKNOWLEDGEMENTS

They are playing 'Iris' by the Goo Goo Dolls in the café as I write this. You can do a lot worse than wistful nineties rock when you're writing about gratitude.

There are a lot of people to thank. Ben Dunn, agent *extraordinaire*, for his confidence in me and my writing. I've had the enormous fortune of being edited by the wise and thoughtful Hannah MacDonald. It's been an amazing experience: thank you to all at September Publishing and Duckworth Books, especially Charlotte Cole, Amie Jones, Matt Casbourne, Rob Wilding, Josie Cassaglia, Clare Hubbard, Claire Maxwell, and thanks to Holly Ovenden for the brilliant cover.

I'm grateful for the generosity of everyone I interviewed, as well as those who shared their expertise and their experiences more informally: Sally Berkovic, José Brownrigg-Gleeson Martínez, Helen Carvell, Matthew Chan, Phillip Clark, Nick Coleman, Alex Cowan, Matt Davis, Janieke Bruin-Mollenhorst, Christopher Edwards, Nathan Godleman and all at the South London Liberal Synagogue, Nicole Grimes, Katy Hamilton, Matthew Head, Bobbi Isaac, Jenny Olivia Johnson, Mark McCloskey, Douglas MacGregor (no relation), Hugh Morris, Chloe Miller-Smith, Emily Payne, Michelle Phillips, Tim Phillips (bell captain at Sherborne Abbey), Jillian C. Rogers, Lola San Martín Arbide, Christabel Stirling, Michelle Taylor, Thomas Ware and Maria Witek. Apologies if I've missed anyone, and any errors or omissions are of course my own.

Many people shared their stories of grief and music with me during this process, some on social media. Hearing and reading them has been one of the great privileges of writing this book.

Thanks to the incredible community of writers, readers and friends who commented on drafts at different stages: Cherline Bazille, Helen Carvell, Grace Edgar, Gaia Fenn, Nell Frizzell, Tobias Jones, Charmian Mansell, Caitlin Schmid, Toby Sharpe, Sarah Thickett, Jackie Thompson, Flora Willson, as well as new friends made at an Arvon narrative non-fiction writing course.

My lovely colleagues in the Department of Music at King's College London explored some of this material with me at a research workshop: Susan Daniels, Emma Dillon, Kathy Fry, Elisabeth Giselbrecht, Marco Ladd, Sophie Redfern, Ditlev Rindom, Katherine Butler Schofield, Martin Stokes and Gavin Williams. Thanks all for the encouragement, and the incisive perspectives and suggestions for further reading. And likewise, thanks go to all my other wonderful musicology colleagues, mentors and friends living all over the world who've opened my ears, my mind and my heart over the last fifteen years. Apologies to music theorists. You're actually really cool, and you don't all wear bow ties. I'm just jealous.

Mark Addison, Lucy Booth, Heather Holden-Brown, Samantha George, Oskar Jensen, Sarah Thickett and Emma Whipday are just some of the people who helped me to realise I could really do this. Thanks to all those incredible organisations that put out material for free to help writers work out how to craft query letters and book proposals, including, but not limited to, Jericho Writers.

Thanks to Tim Coombes for the drawings for the proposal, and to Mia Pistorius for putting up with my bleakness in New York. To all my friends with dead parents: you are the best, and thanks for listening. Conversations with Olivia Butler first sparked the idea for a book about what it meant to listen to music after my dad died.

Jeremy Sams kindly provided the translation of the lyrics to Mahler's *Kindertotenlieder*. Thanks to the T.S. Eliot estate and Faber & Faber Ltd for permission to print lines from *Four Quartets* (including this book's title) and *The Love Song of Alfred J. Prufrock*. Thank you to the copyright holders, Atarah Ben-Tovim and Douglas Boyd, as well as Watson, Little Ltd as the licensing agents, for permission to reproduce material from the 1985 edition of *The Right Instrument for Your Child*.

I was privileged to get to discuss music, grief and my dad on BBC Radio 3 and 4 while I was working on this book: thanks to the producers and presenters of *Freethinking*, *Record Review* and *Soul Music*. Thanks also to Kate Holland.

To my music teachers through the years, particularly Paul Colman, Rosalyn Davies, Rose Nolan, Helen Porter, Jacqueline Trenchard, Karen Wimhurst and all at the Dorset Music Service and Dorset Rural Music School: thank you for making me a musician. Nigel Carver, all-round music legend, you are greatly missed.

Finally, thanks to Oliver Bennett and Karen Jones, to my family for letting me put them in a book, to Datch for being so very fluffy; to my mum Heather for always supporting and encouraging my love of music; and to Jakob for all the rest.

Dad: I miss you. Obviously.